"I have always believed
that opera is a planet
where the muses
work together,
join hands, and
celebrate all the arts."

— Franco Zeffirelli
director & designer

the Art of Making Opera
two seasons with San Diego Opera

the Art of Making Opera
two seasons with San Diego Opera

a personal view
photographs and notes of
ML Hart

SAN DIEGO OPERA
We Make Music Worth Seeing.

The Art of Making Opera
two seasons with San Diego Opera

a personal view
photographs & notes of ML Hart

First edition 1998.

ISBN: 0-9661995-8-8

Library of Congress Catalog Card Number: 97-62536

Published by San Diego Opera

Post Office Box 988   San Diego, CA 92112-0988 USA

Book and jacket design by ML Hart

Printed in Los Angeles, California by
Applied Graphics Technologies

Find us on the web at
mlhart.com
www.sdopera.com

To anyone who's ever cherished the notion of the artist struggling to create great works in a garret – alone – I'll just say: forget it. All artists are interconnected and we work with a huge support group. The people I have met, been inspired by, and made friends with in the course of this project are the best part of an astounding two years. I've always laughed at awards-ceremony honorees who thank everyone from their kindergarten teacher on up... but now faced with this impossible task myself, I solemnly promise never to laugh again. And to single any two or five people out is to ignore ten others who make it all worthwhile, easier or simply more enjoyable... but I'll risk it.

First, and most obviously, my thanks go to the whole company of artists, crews, and the production and administrative staff at San Diego Opera. Without your interest and support, to say nothing of the over-the-top assistance freely given, this project never would have been realized. I am grateful for the way everyone involved in rehearsals and performances was willing to allow me to be there and be a part of the work. Almost by definition cameras can be rather intrusive, but no one objected to my documenting the process of their work; in fact, the continuing enthusiasm has been one of my great joys in connection with this project. I could quite literally list every single person in the Company here... but my particular thanks go to my friends, Stephanie Saad Thompson whose assistance goes far beyond cooperation into collaboration; and Todd Schultz, my exuberant cheerleader.

I appreciate the cooperation of several opera companies and designers in granting permission to use images in this book of the sets and costumes seen in San Diego Opera's productions during the 1996 and 1997 seasons. I would also like to thank the composers, librettists, and their publishing companies for permission to quote selections from their work. Thanks too, to David Gregson for updating his *Brief History of San Diego Opera* and allowing us to use it here...

... and my special thanks to Maestro Richard Bonynge for contributing the Foreword. Not only has he been a significant participant in San Diego Opera's history, but several of his recordings from the 1960s and 1970s helped me learn what opera was all about. It was (and is) a pleasure to be able to work with him – I'm delighted that he's on the marquee.

And I know I'll stumble and fail miserably when it comes to finding the words to express my thanks to Ian Campbell. For taking a risk and giving me the chance to do the work, for extraordinary support in helping to get the book to print, for both the listening and the talking... thank you, thank you, for sharing the vision.

Others... Thanks to Richard Bram for making a photograph that prompted me to start down this path; to Nona Powers for some first steps; and a world of thanks to Donna Salk who helped me find the path to begin with. Thanks to Erich Parce for his patience through two *months* of back-to-back roles; and to Mary Yankee Peters for an inexhaustible supply of patience through two *years*.

My heartfelt thanks go to friends and colleagues who have listened, inspired, encouraged, and shared their particular insights: Linda Brovsky, David Chambers, Sandra Davis, Jim de Blasis, the FAB Group on AOL, Myron Fink, Adria Firestone, Marianne Flettner, Vivica Genaux, Jerry Hadley, Barbara Hart, Ken Howard, Chris Jones, Karen Keltner, Rick Leech, Leon Major, John Malashock, Anne Miriello, Don Moreland, Edoardo Müller, Lana Pennington, John David Peters & the best stage crew in the known universe, the SDO Ensemble, Kathleen Smith, James Warren, Kim Wetherell... and special thanks to Diane Winterton.

Now, to get to the book you're holding... this part of the process has been far more of a collaboration than the image-making, and I have been extremely fortunate to work with a talented group of artisans. Those from The Photo Factory in San Diego who helped turn my work into finished prints, and the group at Applied Graphics Technologies in Los Angeles and Foster City who translated it into book form, all have my deepest thanks.

Thanks to others on my team, who have given me so much: Rusty Adams, Deb Jones, and Robin Reese; John Magee at Acorn Press in San Diego for technical advice; John Menier at UCSD-TV for help in reviewing videotapes; and a stellar cast of characters at the Opera and elsewhere for assistance with proofreading and making sure the words are right. Mistakes, though, are mine and not theirs.

Finally – the book would never have happened in this way without the initial interest and continuing encouragement from Robert Godwin, whose generosity includes his professional expertise and guidance as well as our friendship... I am often overwhelmed and always grateful. And for my chief problem-solver, Pamela Forney, who took on the most difficult problem by becoming my editor... there are no words, my friend – I owe you everything.

I'm lucky to have been able to share the journey with each of you...

... and with Michael, who recognized the potential a very long time ago.

Thank you all – we are truly not alone.

Martha Hart
December 1997

Prologue

Martha Hart has been fascinated by opera since childhood. She studied theatre design and has a passion for history and sociology. She brings knowledge and enthusiasm to her book about the San Diego Opera.

Martha has followed the backstage (and onstage) doings of the company for two entire seasons, and documented in extraordinary living photos the thought, preparation and hard work necessary to produce the final performance which the public sees on stage. No one was spared, not the singers, musical staff, wardrobe, stagehands or orchestra.

At no time was one aware of the presence of a photographer, and the natural quality of the photographs proves this.

This book not only captures a history of the wonderful working company which is San Diego but gives an insight into the joys and problems of opera companies everywhere.

It has been produced with much thought, much care and much love.

Richard Bonynge

Table of Contents

PROLOGUE   foreword by Richard Bonynge   ix

NOTES   introduction by ML Hart   1

IT BEGINS WITH THE MUSIC
the orchestra & conductors   5

Curtain up ... *Turandot*   14

BRINGING IT TO LIFE
the directors   19

Curtain up .... *Tosca*   30

NUTS & BOLTS
design work & backstage preparations   33

Curtain up .... *Aïda*   44

THE WORLD PREMIERE
The Conquistador   49

Curtain up .... *The Conquistador*   68

MUSICAL TAPESTRY
the chorus   75

Curtain up ... *The Elixir of Love*   85

15 SECONDS OF GLORY
supers & dance   87

Curtain up .... *Cinderella & The Italian Girl in Algiers*   94

RUNNING THE SHOW
          stage management & tech crews   **99**

      Curtain up .... *La Traviata*   **110**

TAKING THE LEAD
          the principal singers   **113**

      Curtain up .... *Carmen*   **138**

IN THE SPOTLIGHT — ONE SINGER, TWO ROLES
          baritone Erich Parce   **143**

      Curtain up .... *The Passion of Jonathan Wade*   **153**

THE BUSINESS OF ART
          administration   **157**
REACHING OUT
          the education & outreach program   **165**
THE REASON FOR IT ALL
          the audience   **173**

EPILOGUE   *afterword by Ian D. Campbell*   **176**
Nights of Glory: A History of San Diego Opera *by David Gregson*   **178**
San Diego Opera Chronology 1965 - 1997
          Performances   **201**
          Operas   **211**
          Composers   **212**
          Artists   **213**
San Diego Opera: the Company 1995-96 & 1996-97   **218**

It's a tempting thought just to let the book speak for itself. I work in a visual medium and make no claim to being a writer – the words tumble out in the wrong order in an attempt to keep up with my thoughts. So I'll use someone else's words to start. Alfred Stieglitz, the photographer-artist in the early-20th century, said: "If an artist could explain his work in words, he would not have to create it." This is less about finding the right words and more about the process of creating art. And that's what this book is really about.

All artists go through a similar process, no matter what medium we use. All the explorations, attempts, failures, and adjustments teach us something about what we're trying to say or how we're saying it; the unexpected discoveries, surprises, and triumphs only add to the process. Any creation, whether it's a painting, a poem, a photograph or a song, exists at a particular moment. Its meaning and impact change from one moment to the next, depending on who is looking at it, hearing it, or experiencing it. This is part of what art is about. The artist creates the work, the audience responds to it – there are no wrong moves here. Artists may be driven to create for any number of reasons: a desire to communicate, a need to earn money, a deep-seated conviction... they may not even know what the reasons are. None of this is important (though it might be interesting) to the person looking at the work.

All this theoretical discussion is fine... but what does it have to do with this book? There's nothing here about the techniques of singing or making music; there's even less about the techniques of photography. It's not intended to be solely a history or a celebration of San Diego Opera – it is about opera; it is about art and the artist. Talent may dictate that one becomes an artist instead of a plumber or an accountant, but in all other respects, artists work at their jobs the same as anyone else. Anne Truitt notes in her *Daybook* that we're different from the plumber – not special – because we spin our work out of ourselves, discover its laws, and then present ourselves turned inside out to the public gaze. What's important are the reactions of both the artist who presents this work and the audience which experiences it.

I find that all artists are searching for a way to express a truth that is important to them. In that search we are by turn motivated, enthusiastic, questioning, passionate, doubtful, afraid, and confident. We generally know when it's right, even if we're not always sure what *it* is. And part of that knowledge is learning to trust the process; there's nothing abstract about this. The process is what it's about; the resulting photographs or performance mark where we were at a particular time. It's hard to visualize, but these pages attempt to give a look – a very subjective look – at the entire process. From opera to this Company to individual artists, it's all the same story.

Throughout the process of shooting, I worked from a general outline of how to tell these stories with vague ideas of how to capture on film this not-very-visual process. Whether it was an emphasis on a particular singer or any other aspect of the opera, I started with specific plans. Some days I knew when I was seeing well; that next day's contact sheets would not be a surprise. But most days weren't that clear. Not at all. My intellect battled with my emotions. I'd tell myself that I *should* be looking for this specific idea, or I *ought* to be pursuing that particular aspect... when what was happening in front of me was really something quite different. On those days, the results of the shooting were disappointing and discouraging; I wondered, am I going to be able to do this? am I going about it the right way?

Clearly, I was not going about it the right way. Maybe I was thinking too much... this isn't paint-by-numbers. When I stopped to watch and listen, when I stopped trying to control the project, I was able to see – really *see* – what was taking place in front of me. What the artists were actually doing in rehearsal or in the shop or in the pit was a more interesting story than any I was trying to impose from the outside. I was interested, intrigued, and inspired by what I saw and I found a way to let that story be told. My job seemed to be to show up, keep film in the camera, and figure it out at a later time... and with this kind of freedom, it all started to come alive for me. It was as if The Opera Project had a voice of its own.

In fact, the project seemed to have its own energy from the very beginning. While working at a desk job and aching to spend more time on my photography, I dreamed this project up. If money were not an issue, I thought, and with my background and interests, what would be an ideal *something* at this time in my life? Daydreams turned into notes on a pad and, listening to instinct, I wrote a proposal and sent it to San Diego Opera. It never occurred to me they would respond; it was simply an exercise. In an unrelated move, I gave notice at my job with no idea of what was next. Two days after that I got a call – the Opera wanted to talk. In hindsight, it looks like some kind of artistic inspiration. At the time it merely seemed like a wonderful coincidence, imperfectly understood, overshadowed with concerns about money and the scope of the project.

It was to be one season plus the world-premiere opera in the second season. It ended up needing far more of my attention and time to capture it all. "All" is a relative term here, because in many ways, I felt I was only starting to fully understand the project about five weeks before it ended. This is something you hear from other artists, too. You have to *do* the work in order to learn *how* to do the work. An actor who plays in a long-running show learns more and more about his role as the run goes on. The first time a violinist attempts a new piece is exactly that: a first attempt. The second and tenth and fortieth time allow the musician to discover more about the work and about her own relationship to the work. Same thing with a sculptor or a novelist or a photographer. Before the first season actually began, I wrote: "This project is changing me; already I'm having trouble imagining my life without rehearsal schedules..." My involvement with the project continued (and continues) to transform my life in ways I could never have known or seen.

I learned about the project as it went along, changed, evolved. During the two years of shooting I intended to use the thoughts in my journal as the text for this book. It became more of a pressure-release valve for me, filled with complaints about exhaustion, worries about money, and bleak expressions of doubt about my ability to do the work at all, let alone do it justice. It is tedious, reading it over. What I did use from the journal: notes from casual conversations and formal interviews, my impressions of what happened in rehearsals, and what others felt about their work. Some days in rehearsal I spent more time watching and listening than shooting.

People often ask if I had an interest in opera before this project. Yes, the human voice is my favorite instrument, whether it's singing jazz or opera. My background, training, and several years' work are in theatrical design, but I had been confined in the business world (worse: law!) for 15 years. In many ways, stepping into the theatre again was like coming home. While working with the Opera, I have relished the one night in each performance series when I again become a member of the audience. For one night, I could watch and listen, enjoying the glory of the voice and the emotional impact of the work, without being concerned about light or film or cameras until the next morning's rehearsal.

The photography part of the project began with the Cecilia Bartoli recital. It ended on closing night of *Turandot*, a night I finally made an image I'd had in mind from the very first weeks, almost two years before. A month later, the book part of it began in earnest, and I was immersed in printing, publishing, budgets, writing, and editing. Selecting the images was sometimes like deciding which child you love best; several of my personal favorites did not make the cut.

Other people's reactions to the photographs have been intriguing – conductor Karen Keltner told me she was surprised to see what some of the productions looked like because when she's in the pit, the only thing she sees on stage are eyes and mouths. Others may have a more emotional reaction based on how they remember the day. They may like (or dislike) a particular image because of who is in the photograph and not necessarily what is depicted. In any case, what they see is different from what I see. Every reader, every viewer, every member of the audience brings their own perceptions and experience – everyone sees it or feels it in a slightly different way. There are no wrong answers. Whatever the question, the right answer is that it's all part of the process.

And while the process part fascinates me, technique cannot be completely ignored. For those who need to know about the photography: I use older cameras, Minolta SRT 101s – all metal, all manual, no auto-anything. No flash, no filters, no auto-winder, no decisions made for me. The format is 35mm because it's portable and relatively unobtrusive. The only posed images you'll see in this book are those that are obviously posed – some portraits in the Administrative offices and a couple of backstage shots. Nothing else was staged or set up at any time. I found ways to get into position... everyone knew I was there, but they often forgot about me. (The nicest thing I heard from people looking at the contact sheets was wondering how I'd gotten a particular shot, they hadn't been aware of me... though in many cases I was only about five feet away.) Because I often work in low- or variable-light situations, my film is high-speed (3200) which can sometimes be grainy; it's a look I happen to like. On a daily basis I use three different lenses, all fast (2.8): 50mm, 135mm, and 300mm on a monopod, with occasional use of a 3.5 35mm lens. I rarely stop down below f 5.6, preferring to shoot almost exclusively at f 2.8, for the look as much as the light.

All these technical things are just tools. They help me do my work; they don't affect it. None of them dictate how I see; that's in my mind and in my heart.

It's an understatement to say it's been an extraordinary experience. I don't know what the next part will be. I'll just have to wait and see... and trust. For that's mostly what I've learned from all this, to trust, especially when I'm unsure. Never mind the darkness of that uncertainty – I just keep working away at it and know that it will become clear later. That's also trusting the process of creating. It happened with this long-range photography project, it happens in rehearsals, it happens in planning opera seasons four years in advance... it will happen every night when an audience sits in the dark and becomes a part of the experience themselves. The details differ – the process is the same.

This book, then, is a way to show what we go through in this process we all share. This book is about what we felt and learned and achieved in two years; it's about what I saw.

Once again I'll borrow words from another, the writer, Henry James:

"We work in the dark
We do what we can – we give what we have.
Our doubt is our passion and passion is our task.
The rest is the madness of art."

it Begins with the Music

the orchestra & conductors

It begins here.
The music is the starting point...

... but it's more than just the music.
More than the voice.
And it's not just the drama, or the costumes,
or the any one thing by itself.

Each can be magnificent.
If that's the case, then they have
something different to say.

If it's not everything together,
it just isn't opera.

below left: *On the podium so all can see him,*
conductor Edoardo Müller guides his orchestra during
the Tosca Sitzprobe.

below right: *Eavesdropping on The Powers That Be. In*
rehearsal for a concert, Plácido Domingo (tenor/
conductor/artistic director) with Edoardo Müller
(conductor) and Ian Campbell (general director/tenor).

opposite, upper right: *Michelangelo Veltri in the pit*
during dress rehearsal for Aïda. The illumination from
the music stand lamps is enough to reveal the
conductor's hands and eyes, his wishes and commands.

6

left: *Karen Keltner, Resident Conductor and Music Administrator for San Diego Opera.*

It's not just about being in front of the orchestra... When she is, her passion for the work takes over and the paperwork piled up on her desk for administrative tasks is long forgotten.

Like all opera conductors, she loves the human voice and loves to work with singers. The other part of her task is shaping the sound of the orchestra. Karen simultaneously leads and controls the orchestra as they become one, as the one becomes an integral component of the opera.

"The way I make music, how I conduct ... it's not only with the stick, but with the eyes. I need to be in constant eye contact with the members of the orchestra. Communication is happening *all the time*... I know when they need guidance or are playing with complete confidence."

The orchestra is the clearest example of individual pieces being brought together to create something new. Each section brings its own sound to make the whole greater than the sum of the parts. The faces and hands, artists and instruments, contribute their unique sounds within each section. They all create the one sound the audience hears.

right:
Dorothy Zeavin, principal viola

far right:
Richard Levine, cello

8

Damian Bursill-Hall, principal flute

Concertmaster Karen Dirks tunes the orchestra

Arlen Fast, second bassoon

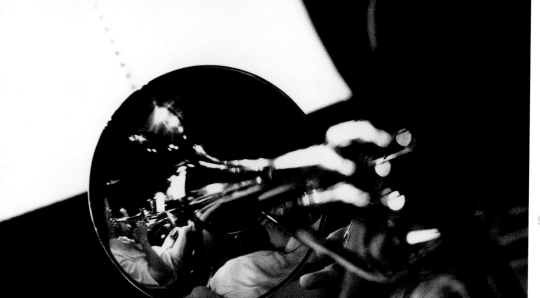

opposite page, clockwise from top:
Hernan Constantino, violin

James Hoffman, principal percussion

Edmund Stein, violin

this page:
The xylophone, part of the extensive percussion section for the world-premiere opera, The Conquistador.

Charles Ellis-McLeod, principal clarinet

Alex Palamidis, violin

"A conductor's
instrument IS
the orchestra."

– Karen Keltner

11

above left: *Karen Keltner leads tenor Richard Leech during a rehearsal of* Carmen. *Like most conductors, Karen sings most of the time in rehearsal. Some conductors sing all the time; every note, every phrase, every part. Some of them even sound pretty good...*

above right: *During the three-week rehearsal period for* The Italian Girl in Algiers, *time to work on musical (rather than staging) aspects of the opera is found only in moments sandwiched between everything else. Bass John Del Carlo (Mustafà) and mezzo-soprano Vivica Genaux (Isabella) take a moment to clarify musical details with conductor Karen Keltner (center).*

right: Carmen, *Act IV – Adria Firestone and Richard Leech*
Singers are always watching the conductor – though rarely this obviously – by way of television monitors in the wings, in the front part of the auditorium, and in the orchestra pit. Singers who are good actors, as these two are, rely primarily on their peripheral vision. This way they stay in visual contact with the conductor rather than looking straight on – directors love this! An experienced opera director will set up duets, trios, and group scenes so that principal singers can easily stay in eye contact.

Singers also rely on their own sense of rhythm. If the conductor has set a tempo in the rehearsal period and they're working together, singers can go for many bars without direct contact. Some singers have great musical instinct – they can feel the phrase, they know where they are, they're in the music. Others need more constant contact with the conductor. When adding complicated action on stage – running down stairs, fighting with swords, dancing (all of which were a part of Carmen*) – the music becomes just one more element to coordinate, and singers will rely more on the conductor.*

However, Italian Girl *had another problem... In the coloratura duet between Mustafà and Lindoro, the singers were on bicycles, riding around in circles, in and out of the wings. Karen Keltner says "It takes a total act of faith to just wave your arms and expect someone riding a bicycle to actually sing, what with disappearing offstage... and trusting that when it's the right time, one or more singing artists will again appear on their bicycles!"*

Does the conductor follow where the singer wants to go, or do the singers follow the conductor?

Maestro Edoardo Müller answers that question by posing one of his own: "When you make love with your wife," he says, "who's in charge? who takes the lead? It constantly changes, it's balanced."

Like everything else in opera, it's a collaboration. Maestro Richard Bonynge says you can't let the singers entirely control the pace – the conductor must lead, not merely guide. Yet the conductor must be sensitive to a singer's needs for "space" to breathe and to express the dramatic intent of the scene or phrase, while staying within the boundaries of the composer's dynamic markings and the conductor's interpretation of them.

right: *Richard Bonynge – curtain call for conductor and orchestra, Carmen.*

The ice princess, Turandot (Jane Eaglen), laments th[...] of her ancestors as her father, the Emperor Altoum [...] Fischer), watches in the background. The title chara[...] stage for a relatively short amount of time – but eve[...] minute is intense.

below: Act I – Calaf, a prince in exile (Richard Marg[...] defies all counsel and signals his desire to answer Tu[...] three riddles and win the hand of the princess. Dazz[...] her beauty, the Unknown Prince refuses to listen to [...] entreaties of his father, Liù, or the Imperial trinity of [...] Pang, and Pong.

David Hockney's spectacular set of monolithic, force[...] perspective architectural-block pieces dominated the [...] The huge gong in Act I looked wonderfully imperial [...] had the most glorious *gong-ing* sound I've ever hea[...] act, from Liù's *"Signore, ascolta"* through the clima[...] chords that bring down the curtain on Act I, has alw[...] been for me the most perfect eight minutes in all op[...]

opposite, left center: Act I – The executioner (Gayl[...] Kuamoo) presents the instrument of execution, infla[...] bloodlust of the crowd. They will be satisfied, as the [...] of Persia pays the price for failing the riddle test.

opposite, lower left: Act I – Calaf (Richard Margis[...] recognized by the devoted slave girl Liù (Ai-Lan Zh[...]

opposite, right: Act III – Timur, the exiled king (Kev[...] Langan), is heartbroken when he learns that Liù has [...] herself rather than be forced to reveal the name of [...] Unknown Prince.

TURANDOT
by Giacomo Puccini

opposite:
above – Ping (Stephen Powell)
below – Pong (Joseph Hu)
center – Pang (Beau Palmer)

All three artists performed these roles for the first time in their careers. They were dramatically, athletically, and vocally immersed in it from day one of rehearsal – director Lotfi Mansouri had them running in circles, jumping off platforms, and wielding oversized fans, all with exaggerated gestures and facial expressions. The exhaustive rehearsals paid off. The artists turned in a trio of performances that were strong individually and as a unit. They were far more than just stage decoration, as sometimes seen in productions of *Turandot*.

The costumes designed by Ian Falconer were as architectural and structured as was the set. Heavy in both line and weight, they created stylized silhouettes for the characters. For example, Timur's cloak weighed more than 30 pounds; and the tunics for Ping, Pang, and Pong were made of padded layers of wool, which was a bit like wearing a very thick quilt. Underneath all that, Pang (Beau Palmer) had to wear a "fat suit," additional padding to make him appear round and plump.

right: Act III – Grand Chancellor Ping (Stephen Powell) demands that Liù (Ai-Lan Zhu) reveal the name of the Unknown Prince... while Turandot (Jane Eaglen) watches, uncomprehending that this girl would sacrifice her life in the name of love.

Bringing it to Life

the directors

Now the real work of rehearsal begins…
below: Tosca *rehearsal: Director Bliss Hebert works out details with the conductor (hidden) while assistant director Scott Fields looks on; pianist Michael Parker and (at far left) bass-baritone David Downing (Angelotti) wait to resume.*

left: Turandot *rehearsal with chorus and supernumeraries.* Turandot *is a mob-scene opera, with the chorus functioning as a separate character; the individual characteristics of each member are unimportant to the work. Director Lotfi Mansouri wants them to gleefully anticipate the Prince of Persia's execution in Act I. Mansouri, with arms raised, demonstrates.*

The director is responsible for realizing the visual and dramatic impact of the opera. Rehearsals are the key. Here, with the director and conductor, the music and action are integrated, characters developed, and the blocking dictates who shows up on stage (and where and when).

In opera, there never seems to be enough time. The director is constantly under pressure to contend with the larger-than-life groups of characters and to make the most of what time there is.

"When you have two weeks, there's basically no process. When you have two weeks to work with the singers, you come in here, Ah! make an adjustment, and you do it. But if you have four weeks, it's a whole different story. Because then you can take each scene, what it means, what you want, how you get it, and then it emerges from that. But in two weeks if you did that, you wouldn't get through the show."

– Leon Major, director

While what Leon says is true, most directors do find a way to get to the heart of the opera in about two weeks. It comes down to the contributions of the singers, director, and conductor, and their skill and experience in working towards the common goal of the production onstage.

I believe directors become directors, at least in part, because they want to play all the roles… and most of them do exactly that.

Jim de Blasis, with the Carmen quintet in Act II (Beau Palmer, Adria Firestone, Sarah Blaze, Stephen Powell, Sylvia Wen), sang and strutted his way through every minute, every scene in the opera. Jim is intelligent, analytical, and extremely articulate. He lets none of those things get in the way of going directly to the emotional heart of the work.

While Jim enjoys the acting, its serious purpose is to quickly show – rather than slowly tell the singers the director's intent. Faced with only two weeks of one-on-one rehearsal before dress rehearsal week begins, anything that can help save time is a plus.

"Always I tell the singers, don't trust the stage director.... Ask *why*. Make the director explain why he's asking what he does."

– *Wolfgang Weber, director*

right: *Tenor Joseph Hu (Gastone in* La Traviata*) listens to director Wolfgang Weber explain the relationships among the principal characters at Violetta's party. He detailed each character's position in Parisian society and their reasons, both stated and underlying, for being where they were. None of this changes what they sing... but it does affect how they carry themselves, their interaction with other characters, and the visible way in which they react to what others are singing. These things help communicate the feeling of the opera. This kind of detail may help the audience believe in the setting or the time period of the story (as in Traviata); or it may help them feel more empathetic towards a particular character. This is all part of searching for the truth of the work.*

They want to play all the parts... director Bliss Hebert plays Tosca.

right: *Bliss works with baritone Duane McDevitt on Tosca's Act II confrontation with Scarpia. Duane, a member of the San Diego Opera Ensemble (part of the Education & Outreach program), was Scarpia during the two weeks of work in the rehearsal hall. The real Scarpia did not join the company until dress rehearsal week and although that's a common practice in some opera companies, it's unusual at San Diego Opera. Regardless of how many times a singer has performed his or her role, there is something new to learn. In the three weeks a singer spends working with colleagues, more layers and nuances of character are added. Having Duane present in rehearsals allowed the other singers to complete their own character reactions and blocking, rather than trying to work to an empty space or with a non-singing assistant director standing in.*

As a young singer, Duane had an opportunity to work with the director, conductor, and colleagues in a major role, one he is not yet ready to sing on stage. Being able to work with it in the rehearsal hall, though, was an extraordinary confidence boost to his career.

below: *Bliss shows Nelly Miricioiu (the real Tosca) a way to physicalize her mental agitation after killing Scarpia.*

opposite page, top left: Carmen – *Director Jim de Blasis and assistant director Knighten Smit arrange people onstage for a tableau curtain call.*

opposite, top right: Tosca – *a between-rehearsals meeting with director Bliss Hebert, at right, Amber Gunn who was in charge of supertitles, and assistant director Scott Fields.*

bottom: Cinderella, *piano tech rehearsal. The cast in street clothes (women in rehearsal skirts) work through some of the technical aspects of being on stage. These include negotiating stairs, opening and closing doors, and precise timing of entrances. In later rehearsals, they'll add costumes, makeup, and the orchestra. The production team watches from a work table in the house (at lower right hand corner). The director and designers, in walkie-talkie contact with the stage manager, make notes, adjust lighting, and solve problems.*

Directors may sometimes play all the parts, but what they do most of the time is watch. During the rehearsal-hall process they watch to see what the overall pictures look like – is this telling the story? who are the characters and how are they relating to one another? would it be more clear by making this change or that one? is this logical within the story line? if they act one way here and react another way there, how does that affect the action later in the opera? does it all work with the music?

The answers to most of these questions have already been worked out – or at least anticipated – long before rehearsals began. But sometimes the work looks different live than it did on paper. It's also a time for the singers and conductor to get to know how the other works. The conductor learns what the singers need in the way of guidance and support at various places in the opera. After the first week of rehearsal, you can see the trust being established – singer to singer and singer to conductor. The work is collaborative, too, with each singer bringing individual ideas to the process. As they all work through rehearsal together – singers, conductor, director – changes are made and details adopted to give this production a life of its own. And when they trust each other, it creates an atmosphere of freedom that allows a performance to take off and rise above pleasant or merely competent, and become something truly exciting.

above: Carmen – *Director Jim de Blasis watches as mezzo-soprano Adria Firestone (Carmen) and tenor Richard Leech (Don José) work through the first part of the Act I Seguidilla.*

Sharon Ott   Leon Major

Lotfi Mansouri
          Linda Brovsky

"We're all magpies, directors most of all – we see a singer do something in rehearsal and think 'I can use that' or we catch a singer playing with a prop while they're waiting to go on, and think 'Aha, that's going to show up in the staging…'"

– Linda Brovsky, director

far left: The Passion of Jonathan Wade. *Assistant director Scott Fields and director/composer Carlisle Floyd watch. Photographs of the set for each of the different scenes are taped to the wall behind them for reference.*

left: La Traviata *Director Wolfgang Weber and assistant director Garnett Bruce watch…*

25

right: *Director John Cox studies the score for* The Elixir of Love.

below, left: *Director – and composer – Carlisle Floyd identified strongly with his* Jonathan Wade *characters. Whenever Nicey was singing, he had a serene smile on his face; watching a scene with Enoch Pratt is quite a different story.*

below center: *Director Leon Major gets to be the Italian Girl, with bass John Del Carlo towering above him (and everyone else in the cast).*

below right: *Director Dejan Miladinovic listens...*

opposite page: *Jim de Blasis watches... and listens... during* Carmen Sitzprobe *as the singers and orchestra work through the opera for the first time together. This is a rehearsal for the music, so no action is going on – the singers sit or stand in a row on stage. Tech and dress rehearsals have begun by now, and the director's former undivided attention to blocking and characterization is given over to coordination of all the onstage elements – sets, lights, orchestra, costumes, and makeup – that bring the opera fully to life. The rest of it isn't abandoned, of course... the assistant director will give daily notes to the singers to remind them about timing of entrances or details of blocking. Adjustments are constantly being made as the singers find out what they can do onstage with the sets and props and how to handle the costumes as part of the ongoing development of their characters. In the rehearsal hall they've had skirts and capes and some furniture – but it looks and feels different up on stage.*

Aïda – *The Temple Scene.* The men's chorus of priests was instructed to line up across the front of the stage, kneel, and raise their offering bowls, all at particular places in the music.

With conductor Michelangelo Veltri leading the music, director Dejan Miladinovic and assistant director Chris Jones attempt to cue the raising of the bowls... but the execution was never right.

For the frenetic Act I finale in Italian Girl, the music is complicated, the blocking intricate and precisely timed to certain spots in the music – kneeling, standing, turning to look, stopping, moving, hands, eyes, feet – the singers worked over and over, again and again, to get it right. It took the better part of a full day. While all this is going on, they are continually maintaining their characters and the light comedy feeling of the scene... and, of course, the musical line, shading, and intensity.

Leon feels that a big part of comedy is about obsession. Mustafà is so intent on getting his Italian Girl, he doesn't ever see that Isabella and the others are mocking him. And that's what makes it funny – the audience is in on the joke.

Leon was delighted with his cast. They all entered into the spirit of the production and worked with each other beautifully, executing his most difficult requests with great enthusiasm. This dedication and energy in the rehearsal hall always translates to the stage.

below: *Director Leon Major works with John Del Carlo, Bruce Fowler, Vivica Genaux, Reinhard Dorn, Ava Baker Liss, and Anita De Simone (partially hidden) on the finale.*

They want to play all the parts ...
Turandot *director Lotfi Mansouri wanted exaggerated facial expressions from Ping, Pang, and Pong, the trio of ministers who both propel and comment on the action. Mansouri, who is the General Director of San Francisco Opera, had originally helped create this particular production, but had never directed it until now. He worked intensely with his singers, yet had an ease of communication and command that made him a favorite among principals, chorus, and supers. Lotfi demanded – and received – the highest level of commitment. Again, this showed up on stage; it's unlikely anyone in the audience will ever forget this* Turandot.

below: *Tenors Beau Palmer and Joseph Hu along with baritone Stephen Powell carry out the director's instructions to perfection.*

DDAK 5054 TMZ   23

▷ 22A   23

TOSCA   *by Giacomo Puccini*

ODAK 5054 TMZ 24 K

▷ 23A 24

31

Act III: Mario Cavaradossi (César Hernández) is just another pawn in Baron Scarpia's final game – the "mock" execution at dawn, atop the Castel Sant'Angelo.

Nuts & Bolts

design work & backstage preparations

The warehouse next to the railroad tracks may be plain on the outside, but inside... this is where magic is made.

I first walked in to the Scenic Studio a month before the season began. Construction on the Aïda set had just begun and I wanted to meet the crew and the designer. I wasn't prepared for the memories brought on by the smell of sawdust and paint... My college training was in theatrical design and I was looking forward to being back in the theatre itself; but this – the shop – smelled like home.

At first it seems like barely organized chaos, but it makes sense once you get a good look at it. The shop is 40,000 square feet and every square inch is utilized. There are places for trucks to unload and spots for trucks to be loaded. Building materials of wood and steel are stored vertically. The carpentry shop has huge work tables with power outlets everywhere. The prop room is filled with floor-to-ceiling shelves packed with chairs, books, candelabras, spears, guns, trays of food, table lamps, and little glimpses into other worlds. There's an industrial sewing machine sitting at one end of a very, very long table in the fabric area; here they work on drapes and upholstery for onstage items. They can also shorten, create, or mend legs and scrims. (Legs are the black fabric panels hanging at the sides of the stage. A scrim is essentially a piece of painted netting, usually the width and height of the stage. When a scrim is lit from the front, the audience sees what's painted on it; when lit from behind, it seems to vanish and the singers and scenery behind it can be clearly seen.)

Everything from the shop becomes magical on stage... and this is where the "magicians" make it happen.

San Diego Opera operates a year-round Scenic Studio, building sets and props for new productions for the Company and other opera companies. In today's world of rented productions, not every opera company has a scene shop; this one keeps a core crew employed during the seven months of the off season.

above: *The spray room at the Scenic Studio. Styrofoam sculpting is done here; for full-stage sized pieces, the main part of the shop is cleared and work takes place in a large open area.*

right: *Doug Resenbeck welds one of the framework sections for the huge mobile towers that dominate the new Aïda set.*

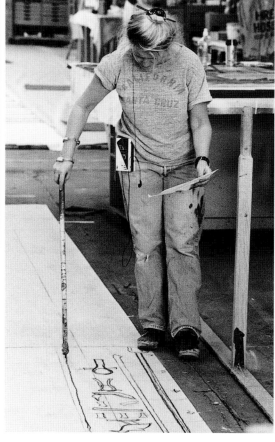

above: *Scene painter Tim Wallace adds details to a set for* Papagayo, *the puppet opera for children performed by the Education Department.*

right: *Following the designer's sketch (below), Scenic Artist Victoria Petrovich outlines hieroglyphic designs in charcoal for one of the* Aïda *set towers. These were then painted in shades of blues and greens, browns and reds, on a white background detailed with gold – a vibrant and alive contrast to the gray monolithic look of many productions of* Aïda. *The floor was made up of panels covered with gold leaf and then protected with a half dozen coats of polyurethane finish.*

above: *This tapestry in the Viceroy's palace (from the opera* The Conquistador*) appears to be a detailed example of the traditional scene painter's art... but it was actually created using a modern blend of technologies. Set and lighting designer Kent Dorsey worked with Charge Scenic Artist Debrah Kaye-Jolgren and Production Carpenter John David Peters from the Scenic Studio to find the best approach to turning this part of the design into reality. "Best" in this case is somewhere between an ideal result from the artistic point of view and the most practical result in terms of time and money, especially considering that there were no plans for* The Conquistador *to go anywhere else after the San Diego performances. The image here was digitally scanned and color corrected in the computer, using a standard image-manipulating program. The file was then electronically transferred to a company in Los Angeles specializing in large printouts, where a color ink jet printer reproduced it on seamless vinyl 20 feet wide and 25 feet high. The "tapestry" was shipped back to San Diego, prepared for hanging, and installed as part of the finished set design.*

On the down side, the scenic artists knew the tapestry would have appeared more realistic, had more depth, dimension, and greater texture if traditional scene painting techniques had been used. From the positive side, use of the modern techniques saved an estimated 60 percent in the cost of producing this set piece – and still gave the desired illusion onstage.

The Conquistador, *Act I. The Viceroy (Louis Otey, seated) with the Chief Inquisitor (John Duykers)*

right: *Set model for the Triumphal Scene,* Aïda. *The actual size of the model is a little less than three feet wide and slips into a presentation box that is a scaled representation of the stage. The tower pieces, the staircase units, and the floor sections were on cable-driven rails and slid further onstage or completely offstage for different scenes.*

above: *Pre-season meeting between Production Carpenter John David Peters and set designer Michael Yeargan to discuss the building of the* Aïda *set. This new* Aïda *co-production was between San Diego Opera and Dallas Opera, with San Diego constructing the sets. John David's position as Production Carpenter means he is not only head of the Scenic Studio but is also in charge of the sets when they are on stage – so potential difficulties that might come up later can be adjusted while the sets are being built, heading off major problems. Some concerns might be how scenery is flown in (the winged arches in the model, for example) or how much offstage room there might be (not much in this production, not by the time the towers were offstage and dozens of people – chorus, principals, supers, and dancers – were assembled in the wings waiting to go on).*

Since this set was new, motorized, big, and complex, it was anticipated that the stage crew would have the week of tech and dress rehearsals to practice scene changes and be able to work out any problems. This is why that final week is structured the way it is: piano tech rehearsal introduces the elements of the sets, props, and lighting. At piano dress, the costumes are included; at orchestra dress, wigs, makeup and – of course – the orchestra are the last components to be added to the mix. Final dress is a run-through of the whole thing, in front of a student audience.

Unfortunately with Aïda, *it didn't quite work out that way... During piano tech, the director and assistant director were up on stage with the singers, repositioning whole groups of people, changing entrances, and re-blocking entire scenes. That work was supposed to be finished. The results were confusion, frayed nerves, a few heated confrontations, and half an evening of wasted rehearsal time before it all got straightened out.*

above: *Costume Designer Allen Charles Klein instructs fitter Annette Seppanen on final adjustments for Colonel Wade's Union Army uniform, worn by Erich Parce in* The Passion of Jonathan Wade.

above: *Ron Vodicka, Assistant Lighting Designer. This stance is typical – the designer looking down, always down, at the stage floor, as a small area of light is shaped and focused. It is the blend of several factors: light from hundreds of individual lighting instruments – called lamps – at different intensities, with different colored gels, illuminating different parts of the set and stage.*

The Tosca set was painted in a dozen different shades of gray – all three acts were gray on gray on gray. It looked flat and boring under the low-power work lights while being set up, but the stage lights transformed gray paint on canvas into architectural details that seemed three-dimensional: archways appeared to be richly carved, walls seemed made of impenetrable stone. It's partly the genius of the set design, partly the skill of the scene painters, partly the intensity and color of the lighting design. The designer begins the creative process for the visual impact of the magical world the audience sees when the curtain rises.

right: *Master Electrician J. Eric Keel shows Don Clifton a lighting instrument that needs adjusting. All the tech crews work from charts, lists, and plans.*

39

ACT II FIREPLACE STATUE

far left: *Dave Easterling helps position one of the winged arches from the Triumphal Scene of* Aïda. *By attaching it to a pipe, or rail, the arch can be flown in – lowered from the stage house into the stage area during the performance.*

left: *In Act II of Jean-Pierre Ponnelle's stunningly imposing set for* Tosca, *the fireplace mantel at the Palazzo Farnese is supported by two near-life sized statues. This one is still strapped into his shipping crate for the journey from the San Francisco Opera Scene Shop, arms permanently upraised... I liked to imagine he would be grateful for his release.*

right: *Rick Adams and William Reilly Jr. maneuver the stage left vertical support for the light bridge into place. The light bridge sits directly upstage of the proscenium arch, out of view of the audience; attached to the horizontal catwalk that spans the stage are lighting instruments and small follow spots. Two vertical supports with ladders provide crew access to operate the spotlights or make adjustments to the lamps.*

right, top to bottom:
lamps, secured to the pipe and ready to be raised into place

Fred Nace

the stage during load-in – the light bridge spans the entire width of the stage floor

John Walchuk

below: *Production Carpenter John David Peters is the man in charge of the stage during load-in. The equipment needed for the entire season has been installed; now the Tosca set is assembled onstage. Crew members match columns to the archway being flown in to create the Act I interior of the Church of Sant'Andrea della Valle.*

far left: *Dale Burgess attaches a lamp to one of the lighting pipes.*

left: B*arry Bunker touches up a corner of the Tosca set before final dress rehearsal, painting over a scuff mark.*

below: *The stage crew is in the orchestra pit, installing a supporting rope net underneath the pit scrim, a black screen-like material that prevents the light of the music stand lamps from spilling up towards the stage. The support net is necessary to catch people who stray too close to the edge of the stage – not a problem during performances, but guests backstage had been known to mistake scrim for floor and fall through it into the pit.*

opposite: *The view from the loading bridge, 50 feet above the stage floor and about two-thirds of the way up the stagehouse. To get there, you climb up (and up!) a steel ladder bolted against the wall... not an outing for the faint of heart.*

Season load-in is the first thing that happens on stage – a completely bare stage. A single light bulb on a stand downstage right pierces the darkness. Early morning, before the crew, stage managers, singers, or anyone but the stage-door security guard arrives, the stage floor is black, newly painted; an hour later, it's already gray with footprints.

Since the opera company does not own the theatre, they bring in everything to be used during the season. Trucks roll up to the loading dock and discharge tools, lamps, desks, portable work-station booths, costume racks, computers, coffee machines, music stands, boxes of shoes and boots, sewing machines, the supertitle screen... "and there's even more."

The load-in operation is smooth, the experience showing; there's little wasted time or motion. They know what they're doing, know how to work together, and have the means to do it – dollys, tool belts, cherry pickers, boxes filled with extension cords, gaffer's tape, staplers, glue guns – whatever they need. The transformation of the bare stage is a fascinating process to watch; it looks something like assembling a jigsaw puzzle on roller skates. Many of the crew have been with the Opera for years. The teamwork that is so evident in all other areas of the company is maybe even more visible here. And in less than two days, everything has been installed and the first set for the season is being moved into place, ready to face the music.

AIDA
by Giuseppe Verdi

above: The Triumphal Scene. On a dazzling white and gold stage filled with light, the victorious Radames (Lando Bartolini) is carried forward. Amneris (Stefania Kaluza) is seated at right, with the slave-princess Aïda (Michèle Crider) standing behind her.

opposite, left: The High Priest (Hao Jiang Tian) accepts Radames' sword in surrender.

opposite, center: Princess Amneris (Stefania Kaluza) pleads in vain for Radames' life. All eight principal singers were making company debuts; Michèle Crider and Stefania Kaluza were also making United States debuts in this production.

opposite, upper right: The Temple Scene dance

following pages: Amonasro, the King of Ethiopia (Mark Rucker), and his daughter, Aïda (Michèle Crider), in the Nile Scene. Verdi's most emotional, and often most beautiful, music is found in duets between the father and daughter characters in many of his operas – think of *Rigoletto, Traviata, Luisa Miller* – this is perhaps the finest.

the World Premiere

The Conquistador

The Conquistador, by Myron Fink and Donald Moreland, was given world-class, world-premiere treatment by San Diego Opera. It was intense, demanding, often exhausting – and everyone involved in the experience was touched and sometimes transformed by it. The writing began approximately ten years earlier, with the Company stepping in as producer about three years before opening night. Tenor Jerry Hadley, who created the title role, was intensely involved with the composer and librettist throughout that period, and the three of them adapted and re-worked segments of the opera for both musical and dramatic purposes.

The rest of the singers were engaged (and all were first choices for the roles: no one said no); the conductor and director became involved early on, with the designers joining in – long before rehearsals began in February 1997. The community outreach programs started early too, with excerpts from the opera being incorporated into vocal presentations and special performances offering music along with lectures, panel discussions, and art exhibits. The process of assembling this one opera, start to finish, embodied the creative process. It was all part of what happened before the curtain went up on March 1, 1997.

right: Karen Keltner, San Diego Opera's Resident Conductor and Music Administrator, was the conductor for The Conquistador. She describes the score as being a very 20th-century piece – it has lyricism along with some heavily percussive and rhythmic sections that depict what's happening in the story, rather than being solely an accompaniment to the vocal line. And it's a difficult score to conduct. A key element for Karen, someone who infuses all of her mind and body into her conducting, was to figure out what it means and how to show that to an orchestra and singers... how to physically conduct it. "I don't just hear it in my head," she says. For her, the physicality is strong even though that's not necessarily something anyone would see; it's there. It's what helps her communicate with and lead the singers and orchestra. With new music, it's something she has to learn how to do, quite literally, for the first time. She finds a way to make it a part of herself, creating muscle memory for the job of conducting. It becomes less difficult as it becomes more physicalized, the music becoming more and more an integral part of her.

opposite page, top: Because the work was unfamiliar, the first half hour or so of each rehearsal segment was allotted to concentrating on the music alone, with the staging element added later in each session.

opposite page, bottom: Donald Moreland and Myron Fink. The librettist and composer attended every rehearsal. They were available for consultation and questions and were fully involved in watching the director, conductor, and singers add their own colors and interpretations to the work.

The Conquistador *is based on the true story of Don Luis de Carvajal, a prominent 16th-century soldier and governor of the Northern Frontier of New Spain (today's Mexico/U.S. border, just a few miles from San Diego). Like many others of that society, he was of Jewish ancestry but, because of the political climate of religious intolerance, had been sent away from his family and raised as a Catholic. In the opera, Carvajal's growing power and advocacy of Indian rights earns him the bitter enmity of the Spanish colonists, and his romantic alliance with the Viceroy's niece turns the court against him. Don Luis' family attempts to convert him back to the faith of his ancestors, but fearing for his reputation, he breaks all ties with them. They are denounced to the Inquisition and arrested. Don Luis, imprisoned and awaiting permanent exile, struggles to reconcile his dual identity – a Jew by birth and a Catholic by faith.*

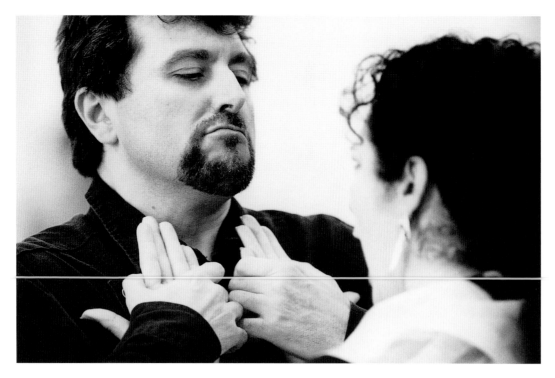

Even though much of the work of The Conquistador *had been going on for three years, there were many questions that didn't come up until the rehearsals actually began. The questions and the answers that come from the dialogue are the elements of collaboration that give a strong finished product. When the singers, conductor, and director work together, each one's style blending with the others, the results are beyond what each group or each individual is capable of producing alone. And when they explore together, the result is far beyond what each might have imagined.*

The first few days of rehearsal were stop-and-go... mostly stop-and-talk. There were entire sessions where interruptions happened every 20 or 30 seconds, questions were raised, and debates raged over everything. Everything. Music, tempo, coloring, shading, length of notes, pitch, breathing, pacing, words, character motivation, blocking. The director and conductor had input, the singers had concerns and questions, the composer and librettist were consulted... half a minute later, there would be something else and it would start again. They finally got past the phase of stopping every minute, but the rehearsals continued to be intense – filled with discussion, experimentation, triumphs, failures, consultations, refinements, changes – I don't think there was a single day we didn't go home emotionally and physically drained. There was the constant awareness of how short the time was and how much there was to do – but overriding that was the need to get it right. Each artist individually – and all the artists collectively – needed to trust the process of working it out, coming to terms with the music, getting to understand the characters and the story. Even though the onstage result was not easily arrived at, it was all worth the struggle. Everyone drove themselves to the edge on this one, never giving anything less than full effort and total commitment.

Tenor Jerry Hadley (Don Luis) and mezzo-soprano Adria Firestone (Doña Francisca) in discussion with director Sharon Ott.

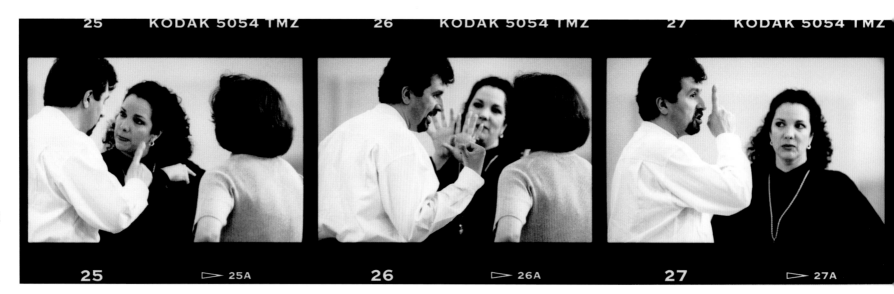

When asked where the idea of The Conquistador *came from, Myron Fink good-naturedly told this story at least a couple hundred times in the three years leading up to opening night:*

"I was teaching at Hunter College and had classes that were an hour apart; I shared office space with 14 other people, so what do you do in between classes when there's no place to go? You go to the library. I was wandering through the stacks one day and a book caught my eye – the title was The Martyr. *Well, I'm always looking for operatic subjects and that sounded pretty dramatic. When I opened the book and saw the subtitle:* The Story of a Secret Jew and the Mexican Inquisition, *I was astonished. I'd never heard of the Mexican Inquisition. Of course I grew up with stories of Jews fleeing Russia and through Europe... but escape routes to New Mexico? Jews fleeing through Texas??*

"There was nothing unusual about the book, oh the color of it was garish, but nothing else really. Understand though, that when Ian Campbell tells this story... There was a Shaft of Light striking the book, and the Heavens opened up and Voices started to Speak to me... but let me tell you, it didn't happen that way!"

Chorus Master Martin Wright with pianist Kristin Roach leads the Palace Scene with Louis Otey (the Viceroy, in light shirt next to the piano) and the merchants, soldiers, and landowners from the men's chorus. Staging for this scene would follow immediately after this ten-minute musical rehearsal.

Kristin was a significant member of the rehearsal team, since the piano score was very difficult. Not only is it impossible to play all the instrumental colors and sonorities that you get from the orchestra, but the music was new to everyone, so the singers relied on Kristin to give pitches while she continued to maintain the rhythm and flow of the scene.

One afternoon when Karen Keltner (above) was off because she had a performance of Italian Girl *to conduct later in the evening, Kristin ended up conducting with Myron playing. At the end of the session, Myron looked at her in amazement and said "I can't believe I did that to you... that's hard!"*

53

top left: *Baritone Louis Otey (the Viceroy): "You find yourself wondering what Verdi had in mind with a particular phrase... here you can just turn around and ask the composer, he's right here. It's a big difference."*

above: *Baritone Stephen Powell (Felipe Núñez): "It's a very exciting time, working on a new piece with the composer. There's an energy that's like nothing else. It's priceless."*

left: *Tenor Jerry Hadley was intrigued when Ian Campbell first called to ask if he would be interested in looking at this new opera. He has a passionate interest in history and already knew the somewhat obscure story of Don Luis de Carvajal. He knew too, that the Company would put together the production team and singers necessary to bring this work to life without the interference of backstage politics or other distractions – everyone's focus would be the same.*

Although Jerry has worked with composers in performance and on recordings of their works, he says there haven't been as many opportunities as he would like to do new works. The challenge of creating a character in a work that has no history, that has never been done before, is compelling.

First he read the libretto, and only later was sent the vocal score... but he was already hooked. Jerry loves the appeal that music has. "Intellect alone is not enough for music to have a life, to touch people, because it reaches you on an emotional level."

left: *Bass Kenneth Cox works on his music in the role of Sahagún, loyal friend to Don Luis.*

below left: *Director Sharon Ott watches...*

bottom: *Rehearsal time is often spent waiting for instruction. Director, assistant director, stage manager, assistant stage managers, prop master, and fight coordinator work out the complicated Northern Frontier scene. Principals, chorus, and supers wait with banners and swords.*

below: *Myron Fink and Donald Moreland at rehearsal. "There's an energy, the excitement of hearing it come to life – what works, what you thought would work, what doesn't – you just don't really know until you're there."*

right: *Mezzo-sopranos Adria Firestone (Doña Francisca) and Vivica Genaux (Isabel) are mother and daughter in the opera; in this scene, Francisca comforts Isabel following a violent confrontation with Don Luis. It's unusual to have two mezzos singing together; their duets were moments of the most haunting melodies. During their non-rehearsal time, Adria and Vivica frequently worked together, finding their way to the heart of the music. For Vivica, a singer at the early stages of her career, it was fascinating to watch and learn from singers with more experience. She saw how others got through the emotionally draining rehearsals, especially with music that is very difficult to sing.*

below: *Soprano Elizabeth Hynes plays Doña Elena, a noblewoman in love with Don Luis. In the prison cell scene, she tells Luis that she has been ordered to sail from New Spain, leaving him to face his fate alone. Tenor Jerry Hadley is in the background.*

Elizabeth found The Conquistador *to be a journey of discovery. "There was a lot of pressure, but it was a wonderful working atmosphere. You always hope for good relationships, but this was very special. We all want to work towards one goal, to create a wonderful performance... and you generally get that. The myth of squabbling colleagues is something I've never run into." Most interesting for her was joining the other singers and seeing the qualities they brought to the work together, after each had been working on their roles by themselves.*

Adria came up with the phrase "a delicious chromatic madness" to describe Myron Fink's music. "The percussive aspects of the work are so expressive," she adds, "the instrumentation is a backdrop for the words and often with very little accompaniment. The music expresses the emotions."

Vivica, who sings quite a few modern works along with Rossini and Handel, notes that the music is written for the voice, which isn't always the case – there's a different consideration, a need to be concerned with the placement of vowels or the sequence of consonants. And the closeness of the harmonies means the singers must be in the center of a note with great accuracy, or the effect is ruined. All the different colors of the voices create a rich texture.

For Adria, the uncharted territory of The Conquistador *was stimulating. "It's an important work. The honesty of the words is echoed in the music, and it touched us all deeply."*

Nearly everyone involved made the comment at some point that when they first read the libretto they thought it was a play rather than an opera. To make sure the dramatic aspects of the work were emphasized, renowned theatre director Sharon Ott was engaged. This was her first opera and wonderfully intense stage pictures started to appear.

Sharon's accustomed to having as much as four or six weeks of rehearsal time, rather than the two and a half weeks she had here. She also needed to contend with the singing. Although she has often utilized extensive musical elements in her directing, the physical demands of operatic singing are different. Further into the rehearsal

period, Sharon relied more and more on her team: assistant director, stage manager, choreographer/movement coach, and fight coordinator. She learned quickly how many people she had to collaborate with – that's how many were available as well as how many she must work with: coordinating costume fittings with wardrobe and stage manager, not going overtime in rehearsals, blocking people so they can always see Karen, placing certain voices together in the chorus, taking advantage of the singers who move well on stage and hiding others who don't... She learned a lot in a short time. On the Monday of the second week, she told us: "I talked to some friends over the weekend. They said, 'What do you mean you staged 290 pages in a week?! Are they out of their minds??'" Juggling all this and more, Sharon's ability to stay relatively calm in rehearsal was a great asset. After this, directing a "regular" opera, something simple like Aïda maybe, should seem tame.

The cast was filled with strong actors, not just singers, and they all relished working with a stage director who was focused on the dramatic impact of the work. Even with the stylization of the lighting and staging, Sharon ensured that the characters' interaction, motivation, and movement were based on real emotions.

above: Adria Firestone and Jerry Hadley work out a sequence of pushing and shoving under the guidance of Fight Coordinator Jamie Newcomb. Adria felt that Luis sees Francisca as a reminder of his past, of a heritage he denies. It's about basic human conflict. Before rehearsals began, Jerry expected these brutal scenes between Don Luis and his sister to be the toughest to rehearse. He found that since Adria "lives and breathes theatricality" and is such a warm person, they both felt safe in working through these harsh scenes filled with ugly emotions.

" I don't dislike the character any more; I've come to respect him. In fact, I don't even think of him in the third person any more. After having gone through the process in rehearsal of digging things up, now we can step back and let the music and words flow through us without layering any other dramatic or musical agenda on top of it.

"One of the things that's been most interesting is watching how my colleagues, as the other characters, react to what I'm saying to them. That helps me discover things about myself and about Don Luis."

– Jerry Hadley

Jerry Hadley in his first costume fitting – as the costume designer works with the fitter to adjust the doublet, Jerry faces Don Luis in the mirror, beginning to assume more of the look as seen in the sketch at right.

below: Assistant Stage Manager Kim Wetherell posts copies of Deborah Dryden's costume designs on the rehearsal hall wall – a constant reference for the singers, supers, and dancers as they take on the movement and posture characteristic of another age.

Jerry says he doesn't "become" a character – he can only be himself. He's very intellectual and literate, so he does a lot of research in order to play a historical person like Don Luis de Carvajal. But after a certain point, all that information has to be pushed aside. What he's left with, what any singer has, is only what the composer and librettist have given him.

He found it intriguing to portray a character who is in a profound state of denial about who he is. This is also a character who cannot allow the facade to crack for a single moment – and yet Jerry had to find ways to show the audience that Don Luis' facade exists. The only way to do that is to show it slipping or show the effort required to keep it in place.

58

right: *Sharon Ott in rehearsal.*

below right: *Dance rehearsal, Academy Scene – as always, a handful of people are watching what goes on. Supers Ben Randle, Marcus Chavarria, and Charles Kempf, with dancer Peter Kalivas, are the "conquerors" in the pantomime dance. It's easier here, before the bulky costumes and set are added in.*

below: *Composer Myron Fink lives in San Diego, so he and conductor Karen Keltner had opportunities to work together on the score during the three years leading up to the production. Once rehearsals began, the consultations were held daily.*

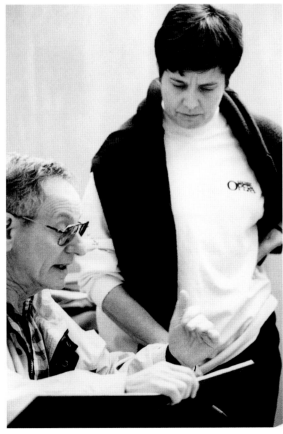

left: *Bass-baritone David Downing is the priest, Gaspar, one of Don Luis' nephews in his service, all of whom would ultimately desert him.*
"And when, in confession, he spoke his heart, I covered my ears..."

below: *Baritone Louis Otey is the Viceroy, suggesting to tenor John Duykers as the Chief Inquisitor, a way they might eliminate the "problem" of Don Luis.*
"There is *always* hard evidence..." *he says.*

The work in the rehearsal hall was sometimes – often – slow, with the seemingly endless discussions and questions. But by the end of the first week, visible progress was being made, with the story starting to take shape. The scenes taking rough form in front of us are splendid, absolutely bone-chilling. I watch and listen, and the hair on my arms and across the back of my neck stands straight up.

And as everyone else is questioning and exploring and searching in rehearsal, I find that I am, too. Am I an observer? a recorder? or in Stephen Sondheim's words, "a part of the event"? What is the best way to show, in the visual medium of photography, the emotional and intellectual battle going on? can I show this and not be involved in it myself? I am certainly as moved, as drained at the end of the long days as anyone else – the experience has affected me profoundly. It has changed me.

Whatever the answers to my other questions, I know I'm not alone in thinking that opening night will be one of those times you're grateful just to be a part of it. This result – and most of all this process of exploring, reaching, learning – is why we do what we do.

Film and stage actor/director Kenneth Branagh says "Actors are the most courageous people I know." He's right; it takes courage to open yourself up completely and remove the protective barriers we live with in order to find the truth of another person and be willing to show that to an audience... or perhaps more accurately, the character reveals his truth through the actor rather than the actor demonstrating to the audience what the character feels. The role of Don Luis dominates the opera, demanding – and receiving – an enormous commitment of emotion and energy on Jerry Hadley's part.

Myron Fink: "Jerry was Ian's first choice for the role, one I instantly concurred with because Jerry is a marvelous acting singer."

Karen Keltner: "Jerry works an opera like an actor works a play – it's been a wonderful relationship, with Jerry being very involved. We both like to find things out in different ways, from different angles."

Don Moreland: "It's been fulfilling to watch Jerry exploring the role, how he connects Don Luis with his own life, his inner self, to give him a reality beyond merely standing and singing something beautiful or powerful."

Adria Firestone: "Jerry was willing to risk everything, every day... willing to make mistakes in trying something first one way, then another. I have the highest respect for him."

Don Luis' family plays a central role in the story. In rehearsal at left are the nephews in a playful moment: Alvaro (Beau Palmer), Gaspar (David Downing) and Baltasar (James Scott Sikon)... and the women, more seriously: Francisca, Don Luis' sister (Adria Firestone, center) and two of her daughters, Catalina (Diane Winterton, left) and Isabel (Vivica Genaux).

One of the most powerful scenes in the opera is the confrontation at Tampico, the family home. Doña Isabel, Don Luis' favorite niece, had promised her dying grandmother she would be the one to return him to the faith of his Jewish ancestors. One night while Don Luis is praying, Isabel asks him why he neglects his soul and Luis learns, perhaps for the first time, of his heritage and his family's ongoing secret practice of Judaism. This knowledge and Isabel's seeming betrayal infuriate him. In his rage, he strikes Isabel, knocking her down, then pulls her up by the hair (below) and hurls her to the ground where she rolls down two steps (marked on the floor by tape lines and an arrow).

Not only do the actors have to do all this safely so no one gets hurt, it has to appear real – and they have to project the emotion of it all. The singers must also stay with the music and sing some intense and difficult passages throughout. Remember too that Isabel will be wearing a 17th-century farthingale (represented by the rehearsal skirt). With director Sharon Ott's guidelines, Fight Coordinator Jamie Newcomb plotted out the scene and worked with Vivica Genaux and Jerry Hadley to create it – first walking and talking through it, then in slow motion, then at full speed with words only, and finally with the singing.

Vivica enjoyed working with colleagues different from those she usually meets in the world of Rossini. She found the nature of the work intensely dramatic, and the character of Isabel, almost an ingenue role, suited her well. Isabel's strength lies in her innocence, her faith, and her belief that she alone can be the one to reach Don Luis.

Jerry finds "There is a tremendous ambiguity in Luis, who knows of his heritage but is not accepting of it because of the threat to his own position in society. This man, who has the entire world at his feet through the court of King Philip, only comes to a sense of clarity when he has nothing left and must finally face himself."

"It's an incredible feeling to have everyone working at the same level, in the same direction. You're risking everything in the rehearsal process… the rehearsal hall is the place to do that; then when you move to the stage, you step away from the character – you can't *do* that on stage every night, you'd go crazy. The rehearsal process has been emotionally wrenching. There are no direct parallels between myself and Don Luis, but it has been cathartic with some issues, human conflicts that we all share.

"Elena says 'we are not what we think we are' which is so true for performers who often try to hide behind a facade. But the process is actually that of divesting yourself of the facade. The more you can become... the more willing you are to be naked, figuratively, in front of your audience, the more likely it is that you'll actually reach them. You also find that simplicity and directness become very powerful. It's been a gift to go through this process."

– Jerry Hadley

63

Librettist Donald Moreland and composer Myron Fink have known each other for some 40 years, collaborating on three other operas before The Conquistador. Myron says that Don's libretto gives him a lot of choices and colors for the music, ranging from moments that are soaring and lyrical to those of agony and despair. The language is clean, but can expand poetically, or go the other direction, becoming hard and martial.

Don writes in a way that leaves plenty of space for the music to do its work, as well as for the singer-actors and the director to do theirs. A singer himself, writing lines for the human voice is, to him, "a delight." He knows what fits well for the singers' instruments, where the emphasis needs to be placed so a line can be sung, where open vowel sounds need to be. And he knows what can be musicalized in a scene and where the music needs to step in and take over from the words. Don likes to throw out the adjectives and the descriptive words, leaving that to be expressed by the music.

On the surface, his words seem basic, very simple. But once heard in context, I was staggered by their power. He said it was a conscious decision not to use overly poetic or "operatic" language – he chooses words which are immediately understandable by the audience, and yet: "It's hard to write this simply."

The libretto is constructed in a cinematic way, with times and locations flowing back and forth from one moment, one scene to the next. The story can be confusing with its many characters and settings; the scenes are condensed, going right to the core without a lot of time spent on background or narrative. Yet the audience never failed to "get it," never failed to be moved. It made it all worthwhile.

left: Don, with Myron in the background, watching rehearsal. "What's wonderful about this as everyone adds to it, it ceases to be yours, it becomes something more. It has a life of its own."

"What was so amazing was the collaboration – everyone working together. It made our brains come alive. This time of heightened concentration, of stretching – it was a wonderful opportunity – this is fertile ground to be working in. We all added something, we reached a goal that without the contributions of the others, we couldn't have achieved alone...

"I find more than anything I've done, that on officially off time, everything reminds me of something about the opera, I hear it all the time, I'm obsessed with it. The interaction with Myron is the best part – I know when we're finished with this, there will be a void."

– Karen Keltner

It was obvious to everyone from the first day of rehearsal that the entire cast had the personality that was right for the work. And they shared a common esprit in working towards the same end.

right: *Myron Fink and Jerry Hadley*

Myron Fink: "We found there are qualities in the characters that are only now being brought out with the contributions from the singers – sometimes Don and I didn't even know we'd written them that way."

Jerry Hadley: "There is a collective desire for the piece to be truthful, with no manipulative devices, no exotic musicality or dramatic conventions for their own sake, but to get through to the integrity of the work."

right: Sitzprobe *is the first time the singers work with the orchestra, the first time the orchestra adds in the factor of the singers. It's the final phase before going into full dress rehearsal, and takes place about four days before opening night. Before then, the orchestra will have had two sessions, or readings, with the conductor. Like the singers, they first learn the work on their own.*

Because this music was new, a third reading was scheduled and principal singers were invited to participate, resulting in a unique collaboration. Several discussions were held with Karen, Jerry, and individual members of the orchestra about tempo, shading, or volume; Kerry O'Brien worked directly with the percussionist on the marimba for her Ghost Aria. The orchestra rarely gets face-to-face interaction with the singers; this was a chance for them to see how all of them worked together. The singers were equally pleased and sometimes astonished to hear how the music fit in with what they'd been doing; it made an enormous difference. "When you get bodies singing and instruments playing," says Karen Keltner, "it starts to live."

The realization of a new opera is an enormous task, presenting creative challenges to the administrators and staff of the Company as well as the artists. This production of The Conquistador, the most expensive San Diego Opera has ever put together, was huge: a cast of 84 including an unusually large number of principals plus a full chorus and children's chorus; 26 supernumeraries; 2 additional dancers; 1 fight coordinator; 1 choreographer/movement coach; 58 orchestra members; 68 members of the running crew; 800 pounds of dry ice; 30 swords; 160 live-flame candles and 4 battery-powered candles; 250 light cues; 480 lighting instruments; more than 400 costumes assembled from 7 different locations throughout the world; 64 local, national, and international press passes; and 98.9% of audience seats sold, an unusually high number for an unknown opera.

above: The World Premiere Photo Op!
Company photographer Ken Howard (on ladder) has just finished making the record shot of everyone at dress rehearsal – although only about two-thirds of them are visible onstage in this photograph.

top: *Because of the large cast, dressing room space was at a premium. Vivica Genaux shared a small room with Adria Firestone...* and *their hoop skirts...* and *the opening-night flowers...*

center: *"Ourselves the Uncharted"*
Three of the five men (though none of the women) responsible for bringing the work to the stage: General Director Ian D. Campbell, who decided to produce the opera after hearing the composer play the score in a piano reading and sing through all the parts ("croak through" the composer says); tenor Jerry Hadley, who was signed to create the leading role of Don Luis more than three years before opening night; and composer Myron Fink who wrote the music in nine months once he received the final draft of the libretto. Missing here are librettist Donald Moreland, who took nine years, off and on, to research the historical material and get the words right; and Maurice C. Kaplan, major underwriter and a driving force in the efforts to raise the money needed for the most ambitious project in the Company's history.

bottom: *March 1, 1997. Curtain call for the composer and librettist with the entire cast. The opening night crowd is sometimes perceived as a high-society group, more interested in being seen than in seeing what's on stage. But on this night they gave something to the performers that I have never witnessed – a genuine standing ovation. When Jerry Hadley stepped forward for his bow, the entire audience, in every section of the theatre, surged to their feet as if they were one body, unleashing a roar of sound, the kind you expect to hear more at a sporting event rather than in the opera house. They were returning in full measure what they had been given that evening by the cast on stage, and by everyone who participated in this work. It was an extraordinary journey of exploration and creation in the years and final weeks of preparation – and perhaps an even more fascinating journey of discovery each night of performance. The work demanded a commitment from audience as well as performers, and all who took the risk were richly rewarded for their efforts.*

68

THE CONQUISTADOR
by Myron Fink

"It was in Tampico
that what was done
could never be undone,
that what was said
should never
never
have been spoken.

"We could not help
ourselves.
The words were like
flames and
consumed
us.

"It was in Tampico
the bonds were
broken
and something lost
forever."

opposite, top left: The Viceroy's Palace. Merchants, landowners, and officers complain to the Viceroy (Louis Otey) that the conquistador, Don Luis, has become too powerful in New Spain, a law unto himself. The Viceroy is concerned for the threat this poses to his position. Much of the staging was done with the simplest and sparest of set pieces, using richly detailed costumes and dramatic lighting to define the scenes.

opposite, top right: The Viceroy, Don Alvaro Manrique de Zuñiga (Louis Otey). Louis is very tall with a baritone voice that is part velvet and part fire, and a natural ability to command the stage from the moment he appears. The role of the flamboyant Viceroy, with golden earring and floor-length swirling robes, suited him perfectly.

opposite, below: Don Luis de Carvajal (Jerry Hadley) and his nephew, Alvaro (Beau Palmer) confront one of their captives, the defiant Indian chief, Tamorros (Marcos Chavarria). In his soliloquy following this scene, Don Luis notes that the audience does not approve... *"You think me cruel, merciless. But how else does one build an empire except by force of a greater culture..."*

right: Father Bernardino de Sahagún (Kenneth Cox) serves as both narrator and integral character in the opera. Along with Don Luis himself, this Franciscan was a real person in 17th century New Spain, and his writings are still a major source of research for this period in history.

above: Don Luis (Jerry Hadley) argues with his sister Francisca (Adria Firestone) when she asks about the promised riches and society of the New World. He reminds her of the bargain they made in Spain when he agreed to bring her entire family across the ocean: *"...that here in the New World, you would receive the protection of my name in return for your loyalty to Christ."* The scenes at Tampico with Don Luis' family were crucial to building the layers of his character and setting up the conflict between his belief and his blood, "a single human being struggling to understand his fate and die perhaps with some shred of insight and dignity," says Donald Moreland.

opposite: The Sabbath Scene. The de Matos family holds a secret ceremony to pray for the dead and the living. Because of the danger of practicing their religion, secret Jews – separated from Rabbis and official rites – put together inaccurately recalled remnants of what was passed down from generation to generation. Since the characters have forgotten what should be, the Sabbath Service in the opera does not follow real-life practice. From left, Lee Jessica Froelich, James Scott Sikon, Vivica Genaux, Beau Palmer, Philip Larson, Adria Firestone, Diane Winterton, Mark Loewen, Scot Fagerland.

right: The Ghost of Doña Leonora (Kerry O'Brien). Don Luis dreams that the ghost of his mother appears to remind him of his Jewish blood and family ties. In one of the most extraordinarily unforgettable arias you will ever witness, the ghost's voice is almost completely exposed, accompanied from the pit only by marimba. She truly seems like a ghost, imploring: *"Do not deny me. Do not forsake me. We are one... forever,"* culminating in an ethereal floated high C.

below: The Nightmare Scene. While in prison, Don Luis (Jerry Hadley kneeling at right, covering his ears) conjures up visions of the different threads of his life, including all the characters from the opera – Indians, victims of the Inquisition, soldiers, Catholics, Jews – all in frenzied motion, chanting and singing, moving towards a crescendo that sends Don Luis over the edge into the final sequence of linked soliloquies that form the climax of the opera.

"Tell them my story does not end here.
Tell them I cursed my God, my very self...
that my enemies should triumph so!
Exiled forever to a living death.
Where can I go that shame will not precede me?
Better I had been burned as the Jew I am not
than to live as the Catholic I am.

... ...

"My name forgotten, my deeds undone.
As though I had never been!
Is this my reward? Extinction, oblivion?
Nothing, no one to remember me!
Hear me, Great Punisher, is this your mercy?
This your justice?
Who is so innocent that I alone am guilty?
Who accuses? Who condemns?"

... ...

"There is an abyss.
What am I? Who am I?
Depths we cannot fathom,
shoals we cannot see,
ourselves the uncharted,
the unknown!

"But am I less a Catholic because of my blood?
And they less human because they are Jews?
Do we not walk the same earth
and breathe the same air?
Are we not all made of the same clay?
Who then shall judge... but God alone?
There is none else worthy,
no one, none!

"O Christ, son of a Jew, save me from myself,
from the emptiness that fills me.
Teach me to be what in some unsayable way I am.
Help me to begin again... that, against all hope,
I may return to these shores
and not be forever unremembered."

Don Luis de Carvajal y de la Cueva
in prison awaiting exile after being
sentenced by the Inquisition

Far more than just a background for the principal singers, the chorus weaves in and out of the action at center stage, both vocally and dramatically. Sometimes prominent, sometimes more subdued, they are always there as support, shading, and texture. You may never notice the individual members of the chorus – and generally that's as it should be – but each of them has a story to tell about their work in the chorus, about their involvement with music, and how it all fits into their lives.

Chorus rehearsals are in the evenings and on weekends since most members have other jobs, too – school teacher, bank executive, private investigator, real estate broker, painter, accountant, massage therapist, church choir director, bartender, aerobics instructor, voice teacher.

Starting with 20 or 50 or 70 individuals and weaving their voices into one cohesive sound – a "core" sound – is the job of the Chorus Master. The skills needed for this job are varied: conducting, piano, language, vocal music. The challenges are different with every group of singers. The challenges vary with every production, too, because of the musical style of each opera and the requirements of the director or conductor.

The continuity of choristers from year to year helps create a distinctive sound for the San Diego Opera Chorus. There's a lot of competition to be selected for the chorus because of the high standard demanded and achieved.

During musical rehearsals, which begin approximately one month before the season starts, the Chorus Master shapes the different aspects of the voices and may work up several varieties of tempi or articulations (staccato, legato, etc.) so the conductor can later choose. By the time the chorus finishes musical rehearsals and begins staging work, the music must be ready.

left: *Alto Martha Whatley in musical rehearsal.*

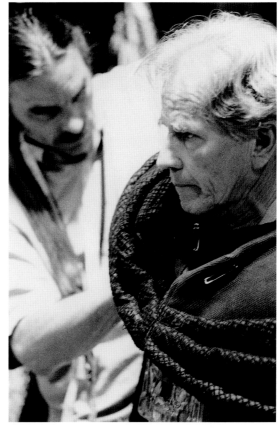

As a whole, the chorus is an important part of The Elixir of Love and director John Cox gave groups of people entire scenarios to play out, with family relationships and specific personality traits (simple-minded, jealous, bored). He also gave in-depth assistance with translation of text so that the individual choristers' reactions would seem real, as each moment unfolds in the story. The result was more than just characters – you saw people you thought you knew as you watched them onstage.

below: *Staging rehearsal for* Elixir. *Gianetta (Sylvia Wen, at right with hands outstretched) tells the village girls "in the strictest confidence" that Nemorino has inherited a fortune. From left, Ava Baker Liss, Martha Whatley (front, in profile), Patty Minton, Nicky Adams, Janet Goggins (standing in back), Debra McLaren (next to her), Andrea Mays, and on the other side of Gianetta, Anita Colet.*

above: *Costume fitting. Gerald Whitney gets a sleeve adjusted on his priest's robe for* Aïda *by fitter Greg Burke.*

above left: *Joe Grienenberger in musical rehearsal.*

77

Ava Baker Liss, mezzo-soprano
Originally from Baltimore, Maryland, Ava has been gaining performance experience while pursuing a career as a principal singer. She was a core member of the chorus for five years; the mezzo in the San Diego Opera Ensemble (part of the Education & Outreach program); an Artist-in-Residence for the Education Department presenting bilingual programs to Spanish- and English-speaking audiences; a cantorial soloist at Temple Beth Israel; and in 1997, made her mainstage debut in a principal role as the slightly goofball Zulma in Rossini's The Italian Girl in Algiers.

She has a wonderfully dramatic stage presence and can play comedy or tragedy, gypsy or noblewoman, with equal flair. "I just love to sing. That's all."

top left: Act III, La Traviata. The "Spanish" ladies in rehearsal. Ava is at center right with long dark hair and a dark shirt; with her is Priti Ghandi. Behind them, from left: Erin McOmber, Erica Rose and, partially visible, Megan Weston and Jane Bishop.

center left: Act II, The Elixir of Love. Nemorino (tenor Patrick Power) is sure this sudden attention from the girls is due to the wonderful elixir he's been drinking rather than his newly inherited fortune. Ava reaches out to touch his hand as the village girls celebrate.

lower left: Ava plays Carmen in The Magic is You!, a work performed for elementary school children by the Ensemble (with Walter DuMelle).

right: Act I, Aïda. Ava (standing) is one of the handmaidens attending the princess Amneris. Other maidens here are Susan Ali, Melody Smith, Janet Goggins, and Wendy Greene.

78

left: *Dorothy Randall wears many hats for San Diego Opera. At various times she is the rehearsal pianist, vocal coach, chorus master, or* banda *leader backstage.*

Banda *refers to any kind of music that is made somewhere other than the orchestra pit. This can be on stage or an offstage chorus (the revelers in Act IV of* La Traviata *or the cantata singers in Act II of* Tosca*); trumpets, gong, woodblock (all in* Turandot*); drums (Act II of* Tosca*); or any other type of instrument. The musicians cannot see the conductor in the pit, so the Chorus Master becomes their conductor, watching Maestro on the backstage television monitor, and slightly anticipating the beat so that the sound from the instruments or voices reaches the audience precisely when it needs to.*

The banda *is positioned where the sound will best be heard, or sometimes wherever there's room. The* Traviata *revelers were not actually in the wings, but all the way offstage out in the dressing room hallway with the stage door open... the sound was just too strong, otherwise. In* Turandot's *"Nessun dorma," the offstage chorus clustered just behind the set around the Chorus Master, who wore glow-in-the-dark gloves so the singers could see his hands in the backstage gloom.*

The Company celebrates birthdays in style. Dottie's was one of several during the season, greeted with birthday cake and a serenade... you've never heard anything as grand as the sound of 30 or 40 trained voices attacking the traditional song, "Happy Birthday To You," embellishing it with exotic harmonies and trills.

lower left: *Tenor David Schmidt makes notes during musical rehearsal.*

lower right: *Sometime-alto / sometime-soprano Patricia McAfee with alto Anita Colet next to her.*

Staging rehearsals:
above left, *Act III,* La Traviata. *Soprano Catherine Ireland enjoys the festivities as one of the "Spanish" ladies at Flora's party.*

above right: *Overture,* The Italian Girl in Algiers. *If you're one of the purists who insists that overtures be music only and not be contaminated with staging, you wouldn't have been laughing during this one – but you'd have been in the minority. Leon Major's production and Zack Brown's designs updated the setting to the 1920s. The chorus of eunuchs (from left, Greg Long, Mark Loewen and Danny Leal) appear on stage before any music begins, discover a wind-up victrola (part of the baggage from the shipwrecked Italian boat), and put on a record to "play" the overture. Unfortunately, it turns out to be the lively overture to* Carmen *(the production immediately preceding* Italian Girl*). Flustered at the "mistake," the men quickly replace the record with the "correct" one, and as the orchestra starts to play the languid opening of the* Italian Girl *overture, the eunuchs turn to glare at the conductor as if it were all her fault... I'm sure the purists were glaring into their programs, but the rest of the audience howled with laughter and often burst into applause – and it certainly set the tone for the show that followed.*

In staging rehearsals, the chorus must be able to move, to blend in, to ad lib background dialogue, to convey character as a group and often as individuals. The "park & bark" style is rare anymore – rows of choristers filing onstage, facing front and singing without showing emotion, and then marching off. Choristers have to act appropriately for the time period of the opera and for the social level of people they are portraying (often several different types in one opera). They may have to wield fans, forks, champagne glasses, handcuffs, muskets, candles, prayer books, flower petals, bowls, baskets or torches. They often have to dance, eat, climb, riot, interact with children, respond to the principal characters, restrain a principal character or tie him up, crawl on the floor, or jump for joy. And, of course, sing – correctly, in character, and always always always keeping an eye on the conductor.

Center: Soprano Deanna Barraza returns to the dressing room area upstairs after the opening scenes of The Elixir of Love*; others are making their way from the stage door. They'll await their next call for entrances, heard over the backstage intercom system.*

upper left: *Act I, The Elixir of Love. Jeff Shipman leads a group of field hands.*
upper right: *Lesley Torreson gets ready.*
lower right: *Act I, Carmen. Janet Goggins and Robert Roseberry are two of the townspeople in Seville being watched by Morales and the soldiers.*
lower left: *The neverending bridge game, played by the die-hards in every spare moment.*

right: *Soprano Megan Weston has found a few onstage friends from the children's chorus in Act IV of* Carmen.

far right: *Soprano Debra McLaren is a flower seller in one of the street scenes from* The Passion of Jonathan Wade.

left: *Act I,* Aïda. *Some of the men's chorus during "Guerra! Guerra!" with the King of Egypt (Andrew Wentzel) at far left and two supers in elaborate headdresses. In the foreground are cut-out soldiers on a huge three-dimensional war map that was flown in for the strategy consultation at the beginning of the opera. This set piece is stored at the Scenic Studio in a crate marked "Aida Game – action figures included – some assembly required."*

Joseph Sundstrom, tenor
Joe was an elementary school teacher for 27 years before retiring early to pursue something he'd always dreamed of – a full-time career in singing.

With San Diego Opera chorus for the past three years, he has also performed with other opera companies and choral groups in Southern California, often performing as a soloist and on tour, including eight years with the Roger Wagner Chorale. "That's where I learned about being a professional," he says, "it's about always being prepared."

Joe looks like your everyday next-door neighbor, the one you borrow the lawn mower from, which gives him the ability to adapt seamlessly onstage to almost any character. He knows that total commitment to his role, no matter how insignificant it may seem, helps give a layer of reality to the overall stage picture. He's a very effective actor onstage, without drawing attention away from the principal singers.

above left: *Act I, The Conquistador. Joe (center) and other "friends of Don Luis" (there was also a group called, simply, "enemies") with Rita Cantos Cartwright and Ken Labertew.*

above right: *Act I, The Italian Girl in Algiers. Joe stares at Zulma (Ava Baker Liss).*

lower right: *Act I, La Traviata. Joe as a party guest at Violetta's house, with Erin McOmber.*

For Chorus Master Martin Wright, the process is about choosing the right people. Leading San Diego Opera's chorus for 13 years, Martin would hear 200 auditions a year. Depending on the composition of the existing chorus and the needs of upcoming shows, he might select as many as 60 or 70 people at a time, sometimes only two or three. And he must find voices that work for the production. Perhaps he would choose a voice because it has volume, or high notes, or because it's good in the lower register. The individual voice alone, no matter how good it may be, is not enough; it must complement the others in the section.

Choristers have already learned the notes and text before rehearsals begin. Martin helps them refine style, phrasing, music, and the language. They need to become familiar with the words in Italian, French, German, Czech, or Russian and know what they're singing so they can express the emotions on stage. He helps them create a vocabulary of ingrained muscle memories – pronunciation, vowel colors, diction, and all the musical aspects, too. "If it's only notes and words, it's just data – not music," he says.

He accomplishes this by pushing, issuing challenges, giving examples – he is knowledgeable, funny, insulting, and encouraging. As if that isn't enough, now add all the union requirements (recall the film Meeting Venus...), illness, absences, overall happiness. Even though the chorus occasionally might be involved for only ten minutes during a three-hour rehearsal call, the chorus is a crucial component of the production. It's Martin's job to keep morale high, making sure they feel valued, no matter how much onstage time they have.

left: *Some of the 105-member* Aïda *chorus in the rehearsal hall.*

Martin Wright, during chorus rehearsals for Aïda *and* Cinderella: *"I've been rehearsing with the men, 84 of them, all those heavy* Aïda *sounds... Then last week we went into* Cinderella *rehearsals with only 16. They're both in Italian, but somehow it's a completely different language."*

top: *Martin Wright, Chorus Master*

Peter Allen calls *The Elixir of Love* "the happiest of all operas" and it's always been that way for me, too. The music and the charming characters bring smiles every time I hear it.

right: Act I – Doctor Dulcamara (Andrew Shore) offers a taste of his magical elixir to one of the children (Blair Hollingsworth, in Patricia McAfee's arms) who shows what she thinks of it – to Dulcamara's astonishment.

below, right: The dashing soldier, Sergeant Belcore (David Malis), has a winning smile for every occasion, from his first entrance to his curtain call.

below, left: Flirtatious, Adina (Deborah Riedel) informs Dulcamara (Andrew Shore) his elixir cannot possibly be more powerful than her own alluring glance in her effort to win back Nemorino... and of course she's right, and even Dulcamara knows it.

85

THE ELIXIR OF LOVE
by Gaetano Donizetti

15 seconds of Glory

supers & dance

Dance has long been one of the arts that "joins hands," in Franco Zeffirelli's words, to create opera. In the 19th century, the ballet was an important, often required, component of opera in Europe, more for social reasons than for any kind of artistry. But dance and movement are more elemental, more primitive than society's customs, and they hold a traditional place in the theatre, extending back dozens of centuries and crossing hundreds of cultures.

Dancers' work is the expression of emotion through their instrument – the body – a basic way of communicating. It is also a strong visual means of expression, ideal for a photographer.

left: *the men in the Triumphal Scene for* Aïda
above: *Peter Kalivas, featured dancer*
top of page: *Malashock Dance & Company core dancers, Tammy Dunsizer, Maj Xander, Gwen Ritchie, in the Temple Scene*

opposite page: *Choreographer John Malashock outlining the basic dance*
below: *daily rehearsal in the studio*

Although in modern opera productions the ballet is rarely performed, Aïda is one opera that generally retains it. A long-time admirer of Malashock Dance & Company, I was thrilled when I found out they would debut with San Diego Opera's 1996 production of Aïda. John Malashock's choreography is equally challenging and accessible, with a tremendous energy and emotionalism. The core of the Malashock company is usually five or six dancers; another ten joined the company for this project.

I spent mornings and afternoons at the dance studio during the week they were working out lifts for the entrance in the Triumphal Scene. While I photographed feet and hands and body lines, they invented several different variations of lifts so that three dancers moving together as a unit could form a kind of walking statue. Imagine a huge creative brainstorming session, but in physical terms instead of mental. No one in this company sits around and waits to be told what to do! Everyone by turns is collaborator, dancer, choreographer, teacher. Once the dancers moved from the studio onto the stage, they used videotape as a tool for analyzing the work. The next day, they would all sit on the floor around the video monitor watching the tape and then worked to make improvements and changes based on what they saw.

John wants audiences emotionally involved with the dances – anything but indifference. Liking the work or understanding his intent are less important than reacting in some way, any way, to it. "Suspend your desire to make perfect sense of each step. Just feel it."

right: Aïda – *Temple Scene*
This was the first rehearsal with everyone present – chorus, supers, principals, and dancers – and you wouldn't think that even one more person could be squeezed into the rehearsal hall. Many of the singers are visibly in awe of the body control and ease of movement the dancers exhibit, even though the execution of the choreography is still in rough form.

When the entire company runs all the way through the Temple Scene for the first time, it is the dancers' turn to be shaken by the power of the full chorus: "Immenso Fthà! Immenso Fthà!" turning their heads to look, as if they could see the sound itself, reverberating through the rehearsal hall. The next day at the dance studio, it was all they could talk about – the intensity, the emotion, and their fascination with the singers' breathing.

below left: The Conquistador – *Academy Scene*
Rehearsals for this huge production were held everywhere: swords in the basement, music in the hallway... dance rehearsals were in the upstairs lobby.

A pantomime-dance of the Conquest of the New World as if presented by native school children required creative solutions. First, no room in the budget for a corps of professional dancers; second, professional dancers were not the solution anyway. The dance needed to have a "charming folk naïvete" about it, according to librettist Donald Moreland. Choreographer John Malashock brought along two of his company dancers to perform the more complex parts of the dance, and held "movement auditions" from among the supernumerary pool to choose the rest of the dancers. Those selected needed to have some basic sense of rhythm and couldn't be too tall, since they were supposed to be children. Most had no dance experience beyond aerobics classes.

Rehearsals were held primarily with Peter Kalivas and Chris Morgan, the Malashock dancers, teaching each group of "conquerors" or "natives" the movements, in little bits at a time, repeating the sequences over and over again. Peter and Chris were constantly watching the other's group and talking with each other too, so no one was working in isolation. The dancers had to carry little wooden swords and shields, wear huge full-face masks, and negotiate a flight of stairs up and half a flight down for their entrance. These supers got a chance to do far more than just stand upstage... and they loved the challenge.

The supernumeraries – or supers – are non-singing, usually non-speaking roles in an opera. Sometimes called walk-ons, supers fill in part of the crowd in the background, giving color and texture to a scene. Supers might play guards, soldiers, butlers, harem girls, priests, or townspeople. They have a rehearsal schedule just like everyone else, and have to carry out the director's instructions onstage.

Super work is a hobby for most, essentially volunteer work, as the stipend just barely covers parking costs. But it often becomes an addictive hobby as they find themselves acquiring a taste for it. They'll tell you the rush of standing on stage, just to be there and see the audience applauding and exuberant... it's worth the long hours of rehearsals.

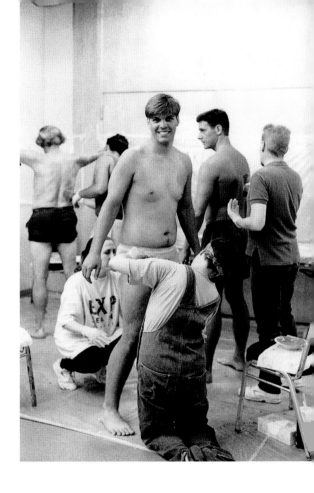

above: *Supers for Aïda submit to the nightly ritual of having body paint applied by the makeup crew. Jeremy Hersch, smiling, is one of the Pharoh Guards.*

left, top: *Turandot director Lotfi Mansouri shows one of the princess' handmaidens (Karen Conole) where the Prince of Persia will be standing when Turandot ignores his pleas for mercy.*

left, bottom: *Super John Zeglin (a Pharoh Guard in Aïda) tries on part of his costume, clearly to his liking. Wardrobe assistant Annie Armatis is helping... well, laughing, too. Everyone was.*

91

above: The Italian Girl in Algiers. *Mustafà (John Del Carlo) gets a first look at the Italian Girl, to the dismay of his harem. Clockwise from upper right are supers Hallie Denhart, Cynthia Hawkins, Melanie Rynne, Jennifer Sapienza, Veronica Fusaro, and Sharon Muyco.*

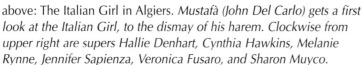

top: *Charles Kempf, a Nile Scene guard in* Aïda. *Supers in a big show like* Turandot *or* Aïda *are often only in the background, but the production wouldn't have the same feel – and the audience would feel cheated of the spectacle – if they weren't there.*

center: *Kelly Clark, a valet in* Cinderella. *"In this show we were able to act, relate to the principals. Linda [director] knew what she wanted, she demanded a lot of us. There was a lot of grumbling backstage, but all that fun stuff, it really reached the audience."*

bottom: *Kenneth Caesar, one of Mustafà's guards in* The Italian Girl in Algiers. *The supers, characters in their own right in Leon Major's production, received a lot of attention from the director.*

The quintessential super role: spear-carrier.

top: Turandot director Lotfi Mansouri and assistant director Garnett Bruce instruct super Steven Jensen on the proper angle for spear-carrying. Other super priests in this scene, holding bowls, wait to join the Act I procession.

Kelly Clark, landscape designer, super with San Diego Opera for 17 operas: "I like doing the smaller shows, where you get a chance to be more of a character, be more involved... One of the first shows I was in was La Bohème, and I got to be the one at the end of the café scene who swept up the broken dishes, right downstage, and looked directly at the audience... that was fun. The most emotional show I was in was Dialogue of the Carmelites."

center: Aïda, the Radames Guards. Assistant director Chris Jones (far left) joins in the fun, filling in for one of the supers.

Hallie Denhart, school teacher, 15 operas with San Diego Opera: Hallie first brought her daughters to a casting call for supers; after sitting through rehearsals as "just a mom," she was determined to do it herself. Now she arranges family vacations and commitments at school around the opera season. "After a day of teaching school, it's like living another life. It's a dream world where you get to meet beautiful people and hear great music."

bottom: Supers in Aïda, the Triumphal Scene.

Bob Borntrager, contracts administrator, super for more than 25 operas over 15 seasons: "I love the music, and I like doing something completely different. I go from my job of numbers and contracts to total relaxation." His favorite operas to be in... Carmen, Tosca, Dialogues of the Carmelites.

Charles Kempf, student, super for 6 operas: "You're able to get away to a make-believe world, away from real life for a while. In opera, you've got it all – acting, singing, drama, dance – opera is everything!"

CINDERELLA
by Gioachino Rossini

opposite, left: Alidoro (Kevin Langan), in a role somewhat akin to the Fairy Godmother, consoles Cinderella and promises she can attend the ball.

opposite, right: Cinderella (Margaret Lattimore) lifts her veil and reveals her face to those at the ball. Dandini, the Prince's valet (Erich Parce), disguised as the Prince while the Prince is disguised as him, is as astonished as the rest of them to see that their glamorous Mystery Guest bears an uncanny resemblance to Cinderella.

above: All movements of the Dancing Tables sequence were timed to the music in a riotously complicated scene – from left, Cinderella (Margaret Lattimore), The Prince, Don Ramiro (Bradley Williams), one of the "sisty uglers" Tisbe (Carter Scott), Dandini (Erich Parce), and the other step-sister, Clorinda (Evelyn de la Rosa), holding the flounder... all await the next steps in a typically silly Rossini ensemble.

"Let us not forget that Delight must be the basis and aim of Musical Art."

– Gioachino Rossini

THE ITALIAN GIRL IN ALGIERS
by Gioachino Rossini

opposite left: Mustafà, The Bey of Algiers (John Del Carlo). John is a splendid buffo specialist, and uses his 6'5" height to great comic advantage.

opposite right: The Italian Girl, Isabella (Vivica Genaux).

this page, above: Isabella (Vivica Genaux) is shipwrecked on the shores of Algiers while in search of her boyfriend, who has been kidnapped by the Bey of... yes, Algiers. Her travelling companion and erstwhile fiancé is Taddeo (Reinhard Dorn), but it's just a good cover story as far as Isabella is concerned. As in all Rossini comedies, the women are clever, spunky, and run circles around the men who are usually ridiculous, inept, pathetic, or all of the above. Reinhard brought an endearing quality to his portrayal of Taddeo along with strong acting and vocal skills, making the scenes between these two a pleasure to watch.

below: One of several times in this charmingly silly opera when *all* the characters are confused... From left, Lindoro (Bruce Fowler), Mustafà (John Del Carlo), Isabella (Vivica Genaux) and Taddeo (Reinhard Dorn). In the background, even super guard David Putigano is confused.

97

Running the Show

stage management & tech crews

Once everyone has arrived in town and just before the first rehearsal of each show, a meeting of the production team is held. Details that have been discussed during the previous year by letter, phone, and fax are finalized. Representatives from all branches of the production, design, and technical teams attend: stage managers, director and assistant director, conductor, chorus master, props, costumes, makeup, stage crew head, lighting, scene design, and others (choreographer, for instance). This is where all the elements are coordinated so that by the time the union members – singers, chorus, stage crew, and orchestra – are added into the equation, time is used efficiently and rehearsals run like clockwork.

above: *Stage Manager Mary Yankee Peters directs Bob Sharp and Jon Salyer as they measure and tape the rehearsal room floor for the next production. The floor plan for each act is outlined in a different color of tape, so the singers can see where walls, doorways, fountains, and fireplaces are located. Stairs are the most interesting, because nearly everyone ignores them in rehearsal – it's hard to pretend you're actually walking up or down stairs on a flat floor, you just note where they are. But once onstage and faced with the real staircase, it can be a different story. If a singer finds it takes longer to get up or down the stairs due to bulky costumes, entrances may have to be re-cued, as happened in* The Conquistador. *The biggest stair surprise, though, was in Act II of* Carmen. *The stairs were very steep, and no one walked up and down. Carmen, Lillas Pastia, Zuniga, smugglers, chorus, Don José, Escamillo... they all ran. This is why they have technical rehearsals, every bit as important as the singing or staging rehearsals.*

Prior to each new set of rehearsals, just before tech rehearsals, and every time any piano gets moved, it gets retuned.
left: *Lee Hintz tunes the piano*

100

top: *There are two Assistant Stage Managers throughout the season, one for stage left, one for stage right. ASM Kathleen Smith corrals the super kids during a rehearsal for* The Elixir of Love. *The assistants are responsible for making sure everyone is in place for entrances and for giving the singers and supers their cues to go onstage. They also do a little bit of everything (a lot of things!) to help keep rehearsals running smoothly – phone calls, distributing the next day's schedule, making coffee, assisting with rehearsal props and costumes, standing in for anyone missing... a dozen different tasks.*

below: *Bruce McCoy, Property Master works on charts – every prop is logged with its location and notations as to which character uses it. Attending rehearsals and making sure substitute props (furniture, swords, candles, to name a few) are available is only one of the tasks for the Property Master.*

above: *Propman Ned Krumrey consults with tenor Jerry Hadley about manacles for* The Conquistador. *Two singers had to be able to fasten them quickly and quietly onto Jerry's wrists over a shirt and doublet at the end of Act II; Jerry wore them through all of Act III. There were two different needs, and Ned came up with two solutions, constructing two pairs – one set worked quickly and easily and was a little bit bigger in circumference, and the other set was more comfortable to wear. Writer Brian Aldiss says that part of the definition of creativity is finding a solution to a problem... the prop crew members are among the most creative people in the theatre, always providing solutions by way of innovation, making one thing seem to be something else.*

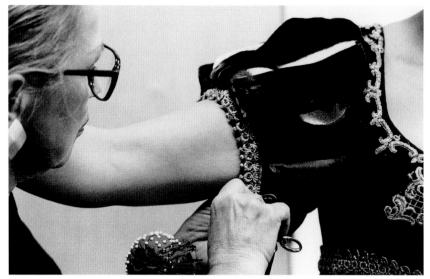

below:

Terry Baliel, the Company's Wig & Makeup Designer, works with the costume designer, the director, and sometimes in consultation with a principal singer, to craft the look for the faces of each production. Wigs are then made up historically accurate or stylized, as needed.

Rarely does an artist appear on stage without a wig, in part because modern hair seldom has the required look for the period in which the opera is set, and partly because a wig, even if it simply echoes the singer's own hair, is fuller and will "read" better from the balcony seats... it's not like film work, where everything is seen in closeup. A wig also saves the singer's hair from the wear and tear of hair spray and the hot lights onstage.

Here, Terry hand ties a wig for Scarpia in Tosca, looping sections of hair onto a base of netting, a few strands at a time. Once the hair is placed on the netting, it can be trimmed and styled for the look required.

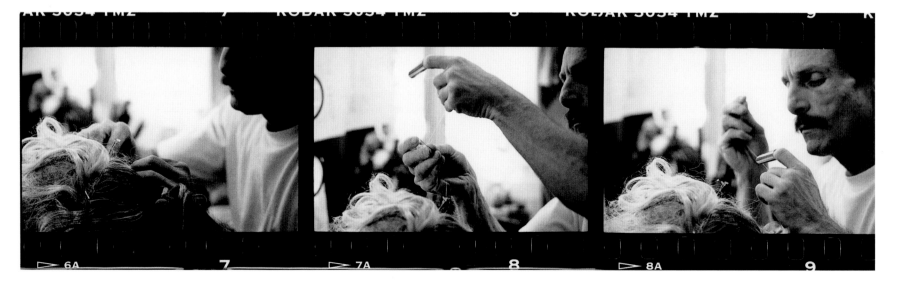

A section of the makeup storage cabinet drawers outside... and inside.

The wardrobe department is busy before the singers arrive in town. Height, body measurements, shoe size, and other statistics are kept on file for all chorus members and supers; for the principals, an up-to-date set of measurements is usually faxed from an opera house where the singer has recently appeared. Costumes are rented from other opera companies or from a rental house; fittings begin as soon as everything is unpacked and inventoried.

Detailed notes are made about alterations needed as the costumes are fitted to the singers. The notes are attached to each costume, with new stitching lines or hemlines marked with oversized safety pins, and it then gets sent to the stitchers. Charts are kept for each act and each scene as to which costume pieces each singer or actor must be wearing at that time: do they wear a hat or overcoat when they make their entrance? do they keep them on the whole time, or does a costume piece turn into a prop (something worn versus something left on stage – for instance, think of Baron Douphol in Act III of La Traviata who challenges Alfredo to a duel by flinging a glove in his face).

Once the costumes have been completed to the designer's specifications and fit or modified – or new ones built for a particular singer – they then become the responsibility of the running crew for the show. The dressers, one assigned to each principal singer and one to each group of chorus and supers, help with fastenings, make sure that the costume is being worn properly, and collect costumes for storage or laundry at the end of each performance.

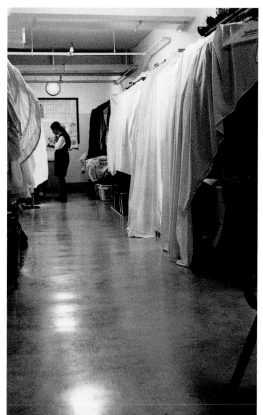

opposite page, top: Fitter Anne Miriello works on the sleeve of Tosca's Act II gown during a preliminary fitting.

center: Stitcher Ellen Adams makes adjustments to a skirt for La Traviata.

this page, right: The upstairs dressing room hallway, costume racks in shrouds.

103

above: *Donna Couchman, waiting. Between flurries of frantic activity, this is what dressers do – along with mending (as Larry Evans is doing, below right), pressing, making tea, defending against too many autograph- and snapshot-seekers in between acts, and generally providing support for the singers while making sure they look perfect.*

below: *Sue Noll sets out the next costume change for Sheryl Woods in* The Passion of Jonathan Wade.

The wardrobe crew is made up of fitters, sewers and dressers for the singers – sometimes playing all three roles in a single day, working on the next show during the day and running the current show at night.

Additional crew are called in to work on the bigger shows, but most of the core crew have been doing this work for many years, watching singers come and go, succeed or fade away; many have been working with the Company for more than 14 years, so they span two administrations...

... and the best stories can be found among the wardrobe people (this is true in any theatre). They have the best opening night food, too, as everyone from the cast to the prop crew to the General Director can be found in the wardrobe room on opening nights, sampling the buffet.

Principal singers have their makeup applied by senior
members of the makeup crew. Makeup calls, the time a singer
has to be in the chair, are generally spaced about 20 minutes
apart. On a show with a large number of principals, this work
can easily start two or three hours before curtain. The singers
have their makeup and wigs in place before getting into
costume.

above left: *Makeup Artist Sandra Davis begins the
transformation of Alan Fischer into the ancient Emperor
Altoum in Turandot. After more makeup, he will have a long
white wig and moustaches added, plus a set of very long
fingernails, painted gold... it's a fun role to play.*

above right: *Makeup Designer Terry Baliel applies David
Downing's makeup, turning him into the escaped prisoner,
Angelotti, in Tosca. During the Act I intermission, David was
then re-made into Sciarrone, one of Scarpia's men in black.*

The Passion of Jonathan Wade
Just before Act I, stage left. Umbrellas wait in the wings for the chorus to pick them up for the opening scene.

Gumby, the backstage mascot of the stage crew, has made an appearance in more productions than anyone else. Sometimes slipped in a chorister's pocket, often lounging in a bowl of fruit on a table, he is beloved by guest artists, well cared for by the crew, and never misses a cue. Sometimes he plays a leading role, sometimes he's a super, always turning in his usual (quietly) dynamic performance. (For those who have never met him, Gumby is a little toy figure, bright green in color, with flexible arms and legs.) Wardrobe wizard Emily Christopher has designed and made his costumes for years.

right: *Assistant Director Scott Fields, tenor Beau Palmer, and Prop Master Ned Krumrey provide coaching and spotlights for Gumby's portrait. He was a wounded Confederate soldier in* The Passion of Jonathan Wade.

above: *The scene change for Act II of* La Traviata *is almost complete as the side walls are moved into place to form a room in Violetta's home.*

left: *Propman Milt King is backstage to light torches for the riot scene in* The Passion of Jonathan Wade. *Any time open flame is used on stage, the Stage Manager must get approval from the Fire Department. A few days before technical rehearsals begin, she meets with the Fire Marshal to demonstrate each instance of flame that will appear. This generally involves candles or torches. Items such as campfires or sacrificial bowls that flare up are usually handled with lighting effects rather than fire. Singers who carry fire must have their costumes flame-proofed. Double and triple safeguards are always in place, along with fire extinguishers in several locations backstage.*

107

Supertitles, the English translation of what's being sung, are projected on a screen above the stage. The choice of the words themselves is almost as crucial as the timing of their appearance – a dramatic moment can be interrupted or a comic bit spoiled by careless intrusion of the titles.

Chris Mahan directs the supertitles from a booth at the very back and top of the house. He works from a precisely marked score and cue sheet, prepared after attending several run-through rehearsals and in consultation with the director. This is designed to help things run smoothly... until a singer forgets a line or misses a cue. Just like the conductor, Chris has to be sensitive to these kinds of problems, and catch up as best he can. It doesn't happen all that often and I'd guess that fewer than five percent of those in the audience ever notice when it does.

above: *The view from the supertitle booth with monitors and carousel trays;* and right, *Chris at work.*

below: *Tech rehearsal for* The Conquistador. *John David Peters and Milt King prepare the stage.*

The Stage Manager is part psychologist, part master scheduler, diplomat, and a tough-as-they-get general. She works with the director, conductor, crew heads, and administration, but there's only one person actually in charge of the show. From the first downbeat to the final curtain call, the opera must run smoothly from the audience side of the curtain, no matter how hectic it gets backstage.

Stage Manager Mary Yankee Peters and her two assistants rarely work less than 12-hour days (and usually more), in running all the rehearsals (and keeping them moving – I thought early on Mary should have a tape made of "Quiet, please!" and play it in an endless loop). They also schedule singers for rehearsal, coaching sessions, costume fittings, and publicity appearances. There is a huge amount of paperwork to be kept: union timekeeping requirements; lists of every item needed on stage; cue books; and the usual round of seemingly endless meetings and follow-up.

right: Mary's backstage station has two television monitors: one shows the front view of the full stage, the other shows the conductor, as seen on all the backstage monitors used by the singers.

Mary has two announcing systems: one goes out over the headsets to all crew members and is used to call lighting and scene change cues; the other is the backstage loudspeaker to call singers to their places.

The Stage Manager's cue book is the master guide for running the show. A thick notebook, it holds lists of all cast and crew for the show, their call times and phone numbers, as well as containing a singing score with floor plans of each scene and all the variations, with the placement of each piece of furniture and every prop, no matter how often they get moved. The score is marked with different colored tags indicating cues for curtain, scene changes, lighting changes, 5-minute and 2-minute warnings to the end of an act, and when to call everyone to their entrances. In a complex show there can easily be more than 500 of these tags. Mary creates the book as rehearsals progress.

You have to be more than a little detail-oriented, like Mary, to be able to do this job. She also has the ability to maintain a cool head – a sense of humor helps her out too. Add to that a great appreciation for opera, and you have a premier stage manager.

LA TRAVIATA
by Giuseppe Verdi

below: Act I, *Brindisi*. Alfredo (Jorge Lopez-Yañez) and Violetta (Deborah Riedel) drink to love and life. Deborah, a wonderful acting singer, engaged the audience as she revealed the full range of Violetta's emotions.

opposite, above right: Act II. Giorgio Germont (Richard Zeller) convinces Violetta to renounce her love for his son.

opposite, below right: Act IV. Alfredo (Jorge Lopez-Yañez) weeps in despair when he learns Violetta is dying. Doctor Grenvil (David Downing) watches from the shadows.

Taking the Lead

the principal singers

The principal singers are the most visible part of the opera company. They come into town for a month of rehearsals and performances, then go on to their next engagement – some singers may be at home for only a week or two every year. They have a shorter rehearsal period than actors in a play, but like actors, they are concerned with dialogue, blocking, diction (often in foreign languages), characterization, choreography, swordplay, and interaction with the others onstage. They also engage in the physical effort of singing. Producing and projecting the sound is hard work and is the reason for days off in between opera performances. It's obvious to everyone in the opera world that the voices are not amplified in any way, but many in the audience aren't aware of that. No microphones, no pre-recorded high notes – and an audience of 3,000.

The talent of a great voice alone is not enough to guarantee a successful career in opera. Today, a singer's life can revolve around airline schedules, recording contracts, and video appearances. A singer needs the personality, the drive, the commitment to focus on the work without being distracted – along with the sense to know which roles are right for the voice, which are not, and an ability to say "no." But it begins with the voice. Think of how many world-class voices there are in any generation of singers – you can almost name them all. A very short list, indeed.

Before rehearsals begin, the singers have already learned the music and text, whether they are new to a role or whether they have many performances behind them. In Carmen, there were both. Tenor Richard Leech was taking on Don José for the first time, while mezzo-soprano Adria Firestone had performed Carmen more than 100 times... 104, 110, she can't remember. Director Jim de Blasis has "no idea" how many Carmens he's directed – too many, no doubt, as it's not his favorite opera. He was frustrated by a shortened rehearsal period that gave him only two weeks before dress rehearsals began. Jim was pleased, though, to find that he had been given a cast of actors: not singers who were pretty good actors, not "good actors... for opera singers," but artists who were passionately interested in finding the truth of their characters.

Principal rehearsals were filled with a friendly "butting heads" atmosphere of lively discussions, provocative questions, and an intense respect for each other's work. The two protagonists, Adria and Richard, challenged each other to dig deeper, to find a better way to convey to the audience who Carmen and José were. With Jim, they formed an intense, intelligent triumvirate, committed to finding the best Carmen possible.

opposite: La Traviata
above: *During a break, director Wolfgang Weber talks with bass-baritone David Downing (Doctor Grenvil) while mezzo-soprano Carter Scott (Flora) and Maestro Richard Bonynge discuss music.*

far left: *Tenor Jorge Lopez-Yañez (Alfredo) and soprano Deborah Riedel (Violetta) listen to director Wolfgang Weber. Spanish-born, Jorge started out following in his father's footsteps as a matador, but lasted only a short time. With the love of danger and the thrill of living on the edge, he says being a tenor is remarkably similar...*

right: Carmen – *Soprano Cynthia Clayton (Micaëla) and tenor Richard Leech (Don José) listen to their director, Jim de Blasis.*

this page: Carmen, *Act I* Seguidilla. *Director Jim de Blasis with Adria Firestone (Carmen) and Richard Leech (Don José).*

I was glad to hear the Opera would be performing the dialogue version of Carmen. *I think it's stronger than the sung/recit version and I simply like it better. This decision is made long before rehearsals begin. Both Adria and Rick fought with the dialogue, in part because it wasn't completely set until the end of the first week. In the middle of blocking, one or the other would stop, frustrated, trying to remember which lines were cut and which were left in. Often they would simultaneously break into English, paraphrasing – not translating – to get at the meaning of the individual words and the intent underneath the phrases. With this clearly understood, the blocking fell into place and they were able to add the French text on top of that. It's an actor's technique, one rarely seen in opera rehearsals... in* Carmen, *it happened every day.*

Richard Leech has long been known for his acting ability, almost as much as for his thrilling voice. How does he go about creating the dramatic aspect of his role? For one thing, he asks questions: "Is he deliberately ignoring her (during the Habanera*) or is he truly oblivious?" – the manner in which he portrays José ignoring Carmen would be different, depending on the answer here. Or, "the kiss for Micaëla, does it start to be a real kiss, or is it always intended to be completely innocent?"*

Carmen *rehearsals were exciting to watch. They were always lively, rarely contentious, filled with intelligent discussion and enough laughter to break up the normal workday tension.*

above: *Adria Firestone (Carmen) with Richard Leech (Don José) in the Act I* Seguidilla...
... and with Louis Otey (Escamillo) at the end of the Toreador song in Act II.

Adria Firestone brought the experience of a hundred Carmen performances – her tote bag holds scores of the opera in French, English, and German versions – but for the most part, she was able to let go of preconceptions about how to play the role. There were times when you could see the conflict, the puzzlement over something Jim was asking for. She would be willing to try it, then you would see the understanding as she worked through it, sometimes as it was presented to her, often with modifications... and finally you would see in her face and body an acceptance of this new aspect of Carmen, one that she embraced and made her own. And always there was the willingness to listen, to try, to learn. This is fairly typical of American singers, but Adria embodied it more fully than anyone else.

As an example, in Act II, Carmen dances for Don José accompanied only by her own singing and castanets. Jim had José seated, straddling a chair, and then asked Adria to keep the dance close to him. As in very close... Clearly, Adria was accustomed to using much more of the stage for this, a bit of a showpiece for her dancing. "No, no," Jim insisted – and he was adamant – "don't ever move more than three feet away from him."

Adria tried it out, but kept asking for more space. She worked through it again... and again, effectively a lap dance, in keeping with the seductive nature of the music. Adria stopped yet again and said "But Jim, if I'm just in the one spot on stage, won't the audience be bored?" Jim, more wily veteran than kindly director at this point, looked around to the five or six of us in the rehearsal hall and (all innocence) asked "Are you bored? Is anyone bored?" "No!" we cried. Adria adopted the staging and gave a strong, sexy performance of the dance. This scene was hotter-than-hot, all the emphasis placed right where it needed to be, on the sizzling obsession between José and Carmen.

Adria was an actress before she became a singer, and it shows in her multi-layered portrayal of Carmen, both playful and sultry with none of it appearing to be an act. Later in the season, Adria created the role of Doña Francisca in The Conquistador, with the same intense attention given to her acting.

"It is always a challenge to work with new colleagues, conductors, and directors. They all have a different way of looking at this gypsy... and I take all I know of the character and bring whatever facet, new or in an undiscovered combination to the moment, meeting another viewpoint...

"Carmen has so many guises and depths that I am constantly driven to search more deeply for the truth. She is, in a word, totally fascinating."

– Adria Firestone

There's rarely enough rehearsal time to spend on details such as little sword fights... so the singers are often on their own. (A show with complex or lengthy sword fights will usually have a fight director.) In Act II of Carmen, there is a brief bit of swordplay between Don José and Zuniga. Richard Leech, who often plays characters with swords, worked out the sequence himself and showed it to James Butler, below; Louis Otey, another stage fight veteran, shared his experience and advice. Stage Manager Mary Yankee Peters keeps watch to make sure they're not disrupting the rest of rehearsal, and that no one gets hurt. They eventually move into another part of the basement to keep working on the choreography. The precisely timed moves are designed for safety but are executed with punch and intensity, making it look very real. And when they later show the fight to director Jim de Blasis, it meets with full approval.

"As a singer, the role of Don José gives me a wide range of styles, from the duet with Micaëla to the passionate music in the last half of the opera. And dramatically, the role has pensive moments all the way up to the ultimate rage – and that creates all sorts of opportunities dramatically. There are corners and sharp edges to find as an actor. He's not just 'the guy-in-love,' like so many of the characters I play."

– Richard Leech

opposite and right:
Carmen, *Act III*, at the smuggler's camp; Richard Leech
with Adria Firestone; and with Beau Palmer and
Stephen Powell (Remendado and Dancaïre) and Louis
Otey (Escamillo).

below: Carmen, *Act II*
The end of the Flower Song

The daytime rehearsals are for the principals – chorus
and supers are added during the evening. Often while
waiting to make an entrance during the afternoon
sessions, Rick Leech would softly sing the chorus parts.
He started out in the chorus as a teenager at Tri-Cities
Opera and received all his training there – music,
acting, stagecraft, makeup – moving into principal roles
several years later. "I grew up on stage," he says.

As the rehearsals move into the final week, the intimacy of the rehearsal
hall is traded in for the main stage, upstairs. Sets, lights, costumes,
makeup, and orchestra are added during dress rehearsals. The layers help
make the performance come alive – but they also put distance between
the singers and the audience. Richard uses this week of adding layers as
a means of stepping back from the personal involvement with his
character, the intense involvement he's been cultivating in the rehearsal
hall. Rather than reliving the agony of Don José's life, he now needs to
be slightly removed so he can control the techniques of singing and
stagecraft, and project the character's emotion to the audience. That's
what acting is all about.

"One of the things about having some success in a
career is I can choose where to work – and San Diego is a
home to go to. I can trust that a company will be put
together, that the people are about the same thing I'm
about – working towards the same product, with the
same passion – without being jaded or grinding it out. To
have a place where you know the process is genuine...
that makes it very satisfying to come back."

– Richard Leech   119

All artists are linked by the processes we go through – trials and explorations, doubts, fears, failures, discoveries, and creative breakthroughs.

When I described what it is I do as a photographer, Rick Leech said "But you've just described singing – that's exactly what I do." As a photographer, I learn and train and practice so that technique becomes subconscious, second-nature to me. When it all comes together, it's as if I'm surrounded by a slow-motion bubble. Everything seems to slow to a crawl, giving me the time I need to become centered, focusing me, not just the cameras. Like an actor, I effectively strip myself down, letting go of barriers, letting go of everything to get to the emotional core of who I am in order to truly "see." Yet, a part of the brain is still reserved to hold onto the technique, making sure it's working for me, capturing the emotion of what I'm seeing. Photographer DeWitt Jones says we actually make photographs of what's four inches behind the viewfinder, not what's four feet in front of it.

A singer does the same thing – letting go of the obsession with technical details just enough in order to interpret and project the character emotionally. It's what we all do as artists – no matter the medium we use to communicate our vision, we all control technique as a tool that we use in order to capture the emotion and present it. Technique alone without the vision, without the personal imprint of the artist on the work, is not enough.

Maestro Richard Bonynge and tenor Richard Leech.

La Traviata
Soprano Deborah Riedel as Violetta – Act I, "Sempre libera"

Baritone Richard Zeller as Giorgio Germont – Act II, "Di Provenza"

lower right: *Director Wolfgang Weber with Richard Zeller*

In rehearsals for La Traviata, *director Wolfgang Weber emphasized the difference in social standing between the courtesan from the* demi-monde *and the scandal-conscious elder Germont, and wanted the scene played with an anger and contempt close to the surface. Richard Zeller was eager to do the job as the director asked... but he was having a lot of trouble reconciling this interpretation with the tenderness of the music, a typically lyrical Verdi father-daughter duet. Conductor Richard Bonynge was having the same difficulty, and finally stepped in to say that this goes too far, it goes completely against the music. Richard Zeller's instincts were good, but as a young singer, he was unsure about just how to approach the director on this; Maestro Bonynge, with considerably more experience, had no such qualms.*

By the time they got to final dress rehearsal, the tenderness was again prominent in the duet... but underneath, there remained a tension between Germont and Violetta, giving their interaction a darker dramatic edge than the languid (sometimes slightly boring) quality often present in this scene. For example, when Violetta finally gives in to Germont's mandate, she asks him to embrace her as a daughter. She runs to him and throws herself in his arms, but Germont, visibly disturbed, merely suffered the embrace and did not return it.

Both Richards were right about the dramatic intensity of the scene having strayed from the musical intent. But Wolfgang was right, too. He saw these characters as people living in a tangible world with real human (rather than real operatic) emotions. Ultimately, the music dictates the interpretation, but the fact that they stretched it this far – too far – in rehearsal allowed them to find something new. The creative differences here led to a creative solution, which gave a far better result in the final performances than without it.

121

The artists who appear with San Diego Opera come from – and perform – all over the world.

above: *American bass-baritone David Downing works in a musical rehearsal for* The Passion of Jonathan Wade. *David is a high school music teacher in the Los Angeles area and performs frequently with San Diego. It's not strictly a repertory company, but there are people who fit in well, and they tend to be asked back year after year.*

In Turandot, *Chinese soprano Ai-Lan Zhu had sung only two performances as Liù several years before, so although it wasn't a debut role for her, it wasn't very familiar, either. Canadian tenor Richard Margison was performing his first Calaf; it will no doubt become a signature role for him. American bass Kevin Langan is a veteran in the role of Timur. A alumnus of the Merola Program in San Francisco, Kevin performs all over the United States, and frequently with San Francisco Opera. It turns out I had seen his mainstage debut there, in a lavish production of* Samson et Dalila, *many years ago. Small world...*

right: *Ai-Lan takes a break.*

opposite page, top: *Act I, "Non piangere, Liù." Richard Margison and Ai-Lan Zhu.*

opposite, right: *Timur in Act I (lower image) and after Liù's death. Note that Kevin is not quite looking at Ai-Lan... his character is blind, and Kevin maintained that quality in every rehearsal. In performance, he wore loops of netting glued from his eyebrows to just below his eyes. What the audience saw was an opaque film over his eyes, but Kevin could still see the conductor.*

Tosca *staging rehearsal.*

Nelly Miricioiu is a fine actress (and without the qualifier "... for an opera singer"). While she certainly brings her own ideas about how to portray Tosca into rehearsal (and that's part of her job), she was always willing to listen to the director's plans and try them out in the exploring manner most common among American-style singers. Her discussions with director Bliss Hebert were thoughtful and based on what was best for the character and for the scene, rather than being driven by ego or vanity. Nelly's voice is more lyrical, less heavily dramatic, than is often heard from a Tosca, giving a heartbreaking tenderness and vulnerability to the role. Her "Vissi d'arte" during Sitzprobe left me stunned with its simplicity, and in tears.

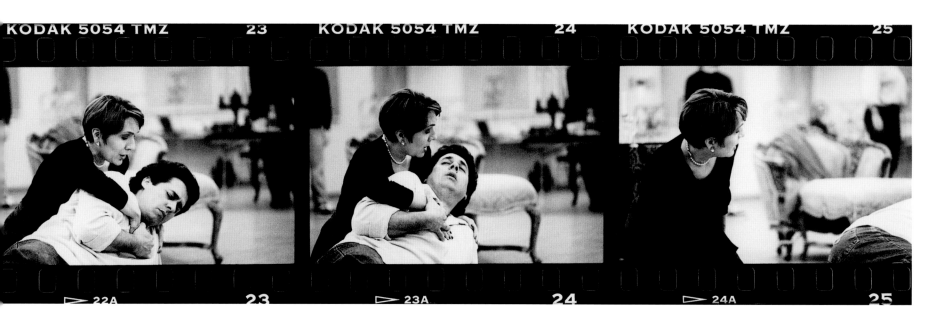

Romanian soprano Nelly Miricioiu and Puerto Rican tenor César Hernández as Tosca and Mario in Act II. After he has been tortured, Mario asks Tosca if she told Scarpia anything. "No, amore," she reassures him... only to have Scarpia immediately contradict her.

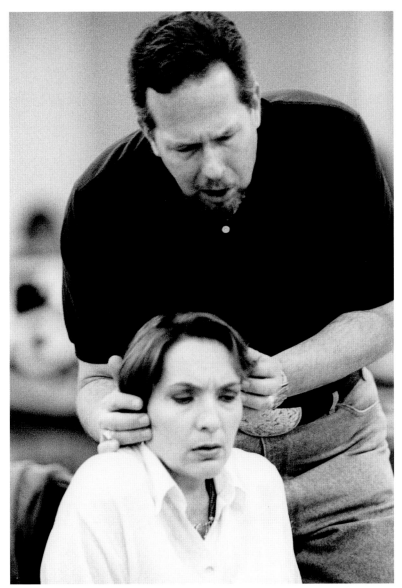

Bass-baritone James Morris and soprano Nelly Miricioiu rehearsing Act II of Tosca.

Both singers have performed these particular roles many times, and had also worked with each other in San Diego several years before, playing four heroines and four villains in the 1985 production of The Tales of Hoffmann.

left: *Scarpia describes in graphic detail the form of torture being used to "persuade" Tosca's lover.*

right: *"Questo è il bacio di Tosca!"*

125

Jim Morris arrived late in the rehearsal process due to a conflict in his schedule. He and director Bliss Hebert (who have worked together frequently) walked through Act I on the set (at left) and spent the rest of the day working on Act II with the other principals. They would walk through a short portion of each scene, usually with questions from Jim: "Don't you think I should...?" Bliss would smile, shake his head, and go on. Then they'd walk through it with the piano, nobody doing much singing, until the next segment.

Jim would say: "Umm, what if I did this here...?" or "I think it would be really effective at this point if..." Bliss would listen, and move on. Finally Jim just laughed and said "I'm not saying another word – you just tell me where you want me to be!"

These questions and discussions were very good-natured (Nelly had asked all her questions in the weeks before) and while Bliss was happy to listen to what a singer has to say and incorporate some of those suggestions, there's also no question as to whose opinion will prevail. The responsibility for what takes place on stage is, after all, his, and not the singers'.

Whether Jim agreed with all of the director's choices was not entirely possible to tell; but in every single performance on stage, he executed the blocking, characterization, and every detail in exactly the way they had worked out in the rehearsal hall. That may not sound too unusual, but many singers will nod and smile... and once the director has left town (after opening night), their own "preferred" bits often start to creep back into the performances.

Not so with Jim Morris – and his spine-chilling portrayal of Scarpia was more than appreciated by the audiences.

left: Sitzprobe *is the first time the singers add the component of the orchestra to the rehearsal process. It's very different hearing this sound – and this volume – after two and a half weeks with the piano in the rehearsal hall. If the music is new (as was the case with* The Conquistador*) or if a singer is new to a role, the adjustments here are critical. In* Carmen, *tenor Richard Leech, working on a first-ever Don José, asked for several repetitions of the final phrase of* The Flower Song, *the last part of "Carmen, je t'aime..." where the voice and the orchestra fuse into one delicate sound. The timing and the breathing could only be refined at this time – after this, it's just one more part of rehearsals and the performances.*

It's not just about singing...
American soprano Michèle Crider made her United States debut as Aïda after a successful (and ongoing) European career. She didn't seem particularly bothered by all the media attention. Below, she's involved in costume and makeup for a publicity shoot with makeup designer Terry Baliel and photographer Ken Howard (and about a dozen other people, too). Michèle was very down to earth about it. She says "All I can do is the best I can. On any given night, I do the best job I possibly can. There isn't any more." Later in the year, Michèle made debuts at San Francisco Opera and the Metropolitan Opera.

left: *Tenor Bruce Fowler and a quiet moment in a usually lively rehearsal hall for* The Italian Girl in Algiers. *In the previous year, Bruce had been involved in three operas that had him riding a bicycle... that might be a new world record.*

below: *Piano tech for* Cinderella, *with mezzo-soprano Margaret Lattimore and tenor Bradley Williams as Cinderella and the Prince. Below, they are looking to escape the crowd at the ball... then [something funny happens]... and they have a short break.*

An emergency replacement for Manhua Zhan, who was ill, Maggie Lattimore arrived from New York on the third day of rehearsal and proceeded to dazzle the entire company with her warm personality and seamless fit into the role. She was a perfect "fix" for this production.

Big names sell big tickets...
The one-night-only gala concert event of 1997 was headlined by superstar tenor Plácido Domingo. Flying in for a couple of days between Wagner nights at the Met, Domingo delivered a concert of their dreams to an ecstatic audience. Showmanship – and that voice! – along with the San Diego Opera Orchestra and Spanish soprano Ainhoa Arteta, made it a night to remember. Encores included "Là ci darem la mano" and "Granada."

The first opera I ever saw onstage was a student dress rehearsal at the Civic Theatre – San Diego Opera's 1966 production of Faust. *A cancellation had resulted in a last-minute replacement for the title role, a relatively unknown tenor by the name of Plácido Domingo... I'd remembered seeing the opera, but not this part of the story until I was well into working on this project. Full-circle, here, as Domingo and Arteta rehearse the Act II duet from* Faust.

These days, Maestro Domingo wears many hats – singer, conductor, artistic director – and he arrived with full entourage of family, secretaries, and people to handle his various tasks. He was dictating instructions and answering questions while warming up before the concert. But when he was offstage, I watched his face light up as he carried his infant granddaughter around the backstage hallway, crooning Spanish songs as she, a wide-eyed audience of one, listened in wonder.

The Italian Girl in Algiers *was a fun, slightly zany production with a wonderful cast. It proved to be a welcome break between the drama of* Carmen *and the intensity of* The Conquistador.

left: *Vivica Genaux as Isabella enchants Taddeo, played by Reinhard Dorn, making his United States debut. Reinhard was strong vocally and unleashed a dynamic stage presence in the generally thankless role of the would-be-suitor. It was a perfect ensemble cast – no weak links.*

Vivica Genaux, the (very) young mezzo soprano, very much on the rise, made her company debut as Isabella, Rossini's Italian Girl in Algiers. (General Director Ian Campbell decided to cast her for this, halfway through hearing her professional debut two years earlier.) Later in the year, she made a surprise debut at the Met on two days' notice.

Vivica specializes in Rossini and Handel ("even the serious stuff is stylized") and loves the lightness of it, the fun. She also sang in the production following this one, The Conquistador, a good change for the voice – too much Rossini can get you away from breathing, she says. But The Conquistador rehearsals, with their intensity and darkness, were sometimes depressing for her. "Those other composers, Puccini and so on, there's just too much testosterone there!"

The Passion of Jonathan Wade

below right: *tenor Joseph Evans*

right: *mezzo-soprano Débria Brown*

The Italian Girl in Algiers
above left: *The Italian Girl makes her entrance in a lifeboat on wheels. Vivica Genaux is terrified of the pirates, while supernumerary Boat Person Richard Francella crouches next to her. At far left, super Boat Captain Bob Borntrager is in fear of the men's chorus. And no wonder: there's David Schmidt (right, white shirt) and Joe Sundstrom (at left behind Vivica, with glasses and sword) encroaching with cat-like tread; Catherine Patacca (center back) is the extremely dismayed super Shipwrecked Companion.*

left: *Mezzo-soprano Ava Baker Liss as Zulma in The Italian* Girl in Algiers.

131

Carmen:

Tenor Richard Leech effects part of the visual transformation of Don José from Act I...

... to Act IV.

133

Backstage, La Traviata, *Act II.*
Assistant Stage Manager Kathleen Smith
(with book) waits to hear the Stage
Manager's cue over her headset. She gives
Richard Zeller (Germont, at right) his cue.
He will walk onstage and appear in the
garden, then turn left to enter Violetta's
house through the French doors. A
propman, just to Kathleen's left, stands by
in the unlikely event of a problem with
the doors.

right: *Reading reviews for
Tosca – César Hernández as Mario
(after the Act III execution, clearly)
and Alan Fischer as Spoleta (wearing
the hat), check one of the reviews,
while Roberto Gomez (Sacristan)
hovers in the background. Good
reviews are posted on every call
board backstage, for the crew as
much as for anyone else; bad ones
are ignored. Many singers don't read
them at all. The audience response
each night is the only review really
worth having.*

below*: Curtain calls are the
performers' reward for what they've
accomplished, a measure of where
they've been – "in boca al lupo!"*

left: Carmen *curtain call for the two
principals, from the house.*

right: Tosca, *from backstage. Nelly
Miricioiu and César Hernández
leave the stage; prop men hold the
curtain open for them. The red
velvet curtain weighs 650 pounds.*

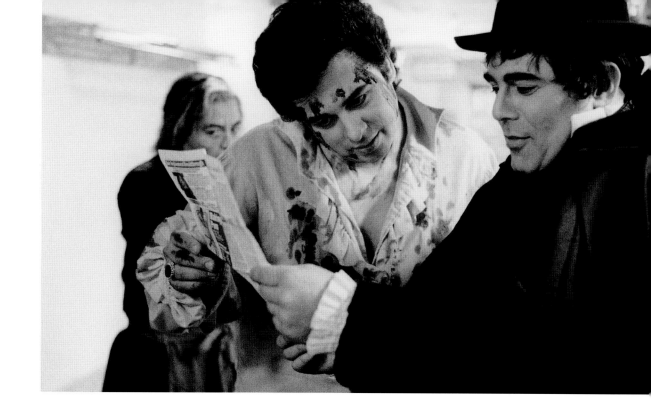

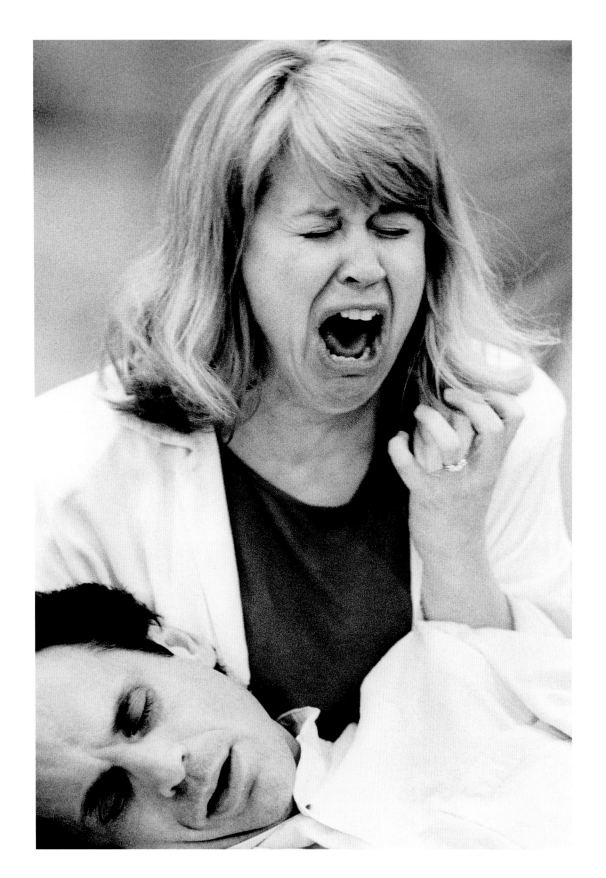

"This isn't just
about the Civil War.
It's anywhere now...

"It's Bosnia. It's
Ireland – it speaks
to us today."

Kenneth Montgomery
conductor,
*The Passion of
Jonathan Wade*

The Passion of Jonathan Wade
Sheryl Woods as Celia
Erich Parce as Jonathan

Carlisle Floyd's powerful music and dramatic libretto explore the aftermath of war and the lives of survivors on both sides during occupation. With an entire cast of singer-actors committed to their roles and to the piece, rehearsals were sometimes an overwhelming experience. In the final scene of the opera, Jonathan is assassinated and dies in Celia's arms – the first time I saw this in rehearsal, I couldn't move. I was numb. There are moments like this in the rehearsal process that affect you, not always when you'd expect them... this was one.

Later in the day and with Sheryl's permission, I shot closeups throughout the entire scene ("I'll be oblivious by then..." she said). At the end she sat there on the floor for almost five minutes before she could get up for notes from the director and conductor. Erich sat and spoke with her a bit, mostly just held her hand, and Débria Brown, tears running down her face, sat with an arm around Sheryl's shoulders and talked with her.

It was never quite as moving for me on stage, though; perhaps because of the distance from the audience, but perhaps because of the power found in the minimalist aspects of the rehearsal hall. No costumes, no lights... just a piano and the desire of the performers to communicate.

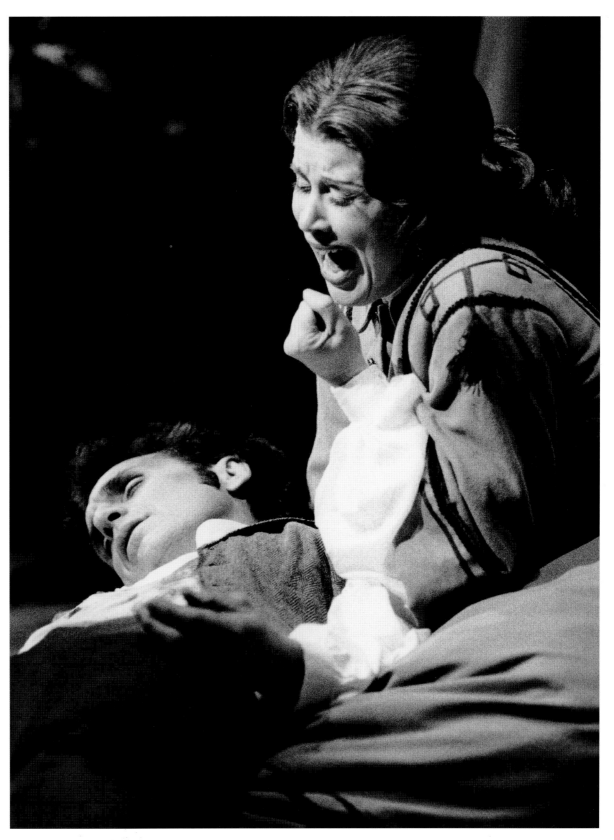

137

below: Act I. Don José (Richard Leech) with Micaëla (Cynthia Clayton), the innocent village girl his mother wishes him to marry. Cynthia found a way to balance the innocence without becoming a simpering nonentity.

right: Act I. Don José (Richard Leech) with Carmen (Adria Firestone), the *Bohémienne* who has captivated his very soul. Richard was performing the first Don José of his career, while Adria was giving her more-than-100th performance as Carmen.

opposite left: Act IV. Carmen shouts at José to strike her down or leave her alone... *"Eh bien, frappe-me donc, ou laisse-moi passer!"*

opposite center and right: Adria Firestone, a stage actress before she became a singer, is also a dancer and has studied with the flamenco master, Carlos Saura, in Spain.

CARMEN
by Georges Bizet

"I find new layers to Carmen in every production – the minute she loses her fascination for me is when I stop playing her. I have to. If I'm not fascinated by her, how can I make you be fascinated?"

– Adria Firestone, mezzo-soprano

"You find as you remove the protective masks from yourself as an actor, that it frees up the instrument. There is no way a singer can keep masks up and still give a good vocal performance."

– Richard Leech, tenor

"Un seul desir,
un seul espoir...
Carmen,
je t'aime!"

Don Jose (Richard Leech)
at the end of the Act II
Flower Song, with Carmen
(Adria Firestone)

"Vous pouvez
m'arrêter...
C'est moi qui l'ai tuée!
Ah Carmen, ma
Carmen adorée!"

Don Jose (Richard Leech)
at the end of opera with
Carmen (Adria Firestone)

in the Spotlight –
one Singer, two Roles

baritone Erich Parce

In the spring of 1996, Erich Parce performed back-to-back leading roles with San Diego Opera: the heroic and tragic title role in Carlisle Floyd's *The Passion of Jonathan Wade* (*at right*) and the silly, foppish Dandini, the Prince's valet, in the Rossini comedy *La Cenerentola*, or *Cinderella* (*below*). Written nearly 150 years apart, the musical styles of the operas are as opposite as the dramatic challenges of portraying these characters.

As part of the overall look at the Company and the singers, I had wanted to use my cameras to follow one particular singer capturing what he or she would be going through in preparing and performing a role. In pre-season meetings, it was suggested that Erich would be a good subject for this. I thought it was a great choice; Erich was agreeable and tolerated the endless invasion of cameras with a wonderful sense of humor.

In the summer of 1997, we sat down to reflect on his experience, not only with these two roles, but as an opera singer and performer in general. Our conversation was about opera, singing, and art... and Erich's own words address this in a more direct way than would be possible if I distilled or interpreted what he had to say.

mlh: At the beginning... what do you start with when you're looking at a role for the first time, do you look at the music first? do you look at the words first? or do you find that you can't separate them?

Erich: I read the script first, I read the libretto. I think that's, for me, the most telling. I mean, if it engages you, just the words first, half the battle is over. Then the next step is how well the music fits with the words. Does it enhance it? And then step three is: [starts to smile] let's hope it's vocal in terms of...

mlh: [starts to laugh]

Erich: ...is it singable music?

mlh: Right. And singable for you.

Erich: yes.

right: Erich consults with conductor Kenneth Montgomery during a break in rehearsal for *Wade.* Robin Stamper, the rehearsal pianist, looks on. It's a far more demanding job than just playing the right notes at the appropriate time. The pianists for each show had their own distinct personalities and styles.

In a work like *Wade,* the singers frequently relied on Robin to play not only the accompaniment but also their individual pitches. In effect, he was trying to provide a viable substitute for the whole orchestra during the rehearsal process. And because Robin is such an accomplished pianist as well as a skilled accompanist, his own flair often contributed as much of a sense of artistry to the rehearsals as did the singers.

below: On another break, Erich works on finding some pitches himself. "Breaks" for all principal singers, the director, the conductor, and the production team always end up being spent on working out some problem rather than sitting around and relaxing.

mlh:	I would assume that there are certain directions you take with your role choices, that suit your voice, sit in your voice better than others.
Erich:	And at least with 20th-century opera, with the modern style of acting, too. You can put up with the prepos-tos..., -posterous-ness of... [laughs]
mlh:	the..? [a lot of laughing]
Erich:	Prepostocity?... [more laughing]... you know, some of these really stupid plots from the bel canto era, because that didn't matter. That was about singing, you go to hear singing when you go hear that. And if so-and-so can't recognize them... then it's the this and the that and all of it in Così fan tutte and all those things that make you say, "Give me a break...!"
mlh:	But that's okay.
Erich:	But that's okay. Because that's not the name of the game. But that is the name of the game in this century. If you're working with 20th-century music but a 19th-century story, you have to decide – since you're using 19th-century language, do you use a 19th-century acting style?
mlh:	ah yes, sure.
Erich:	Everything a little bit straight up and down and...
mlh:	declamatory.
Erich:	... declamatory, and you know, like this [indicating facing forward, face frozen, rigid spine]. Or do we go with modern-style acting within that language. If that is what you opt for, then you've still got to wear the costume well. They wouldn't slouch on a chair like this in those costumes.
mlh:	right.
Erich:	And so you try to find the blend. And I think... I think that becomes important for modern audiences. That if you're going to do something, you want to grab the audience – you've got to choose the right acting style with the right book.

145

mlh: *What do you go through as a singer when you're faced with a situation like you had in San Diego in '96? The back-to-back roles that were so very different. They were both ones that you knew…*

Erich: *First time in* Cenerentola.

mlh: *You're kidding?*

Erich: *And that was difficult, because during* Wade *I wanted to work on* Cenerentola, *and it was almost impossible just because of the musical and vocal differences.* Wade *was a lot of, kind of heavy-metal singing,* Cenerentola *was all high coloratura singing. And the voice just never felt right in the whole first couple weeks of rehearsal.* Cenerentola *just comes right off the back of that… that was a tough change. I mean, as Callas used to say, "I can sing Wagner and I can sing Donizetti but I need three weeks."*

mlh: *right! [laughs]*

Erich: *To reshape the voice. Because the muscles have to kind of let go of one and start into the next. And I felt a lot of that. That was hard. And I felt kind of, oh you know, out of the water a little bit the first couple of weeks of* Cenerentola. *But it came in and found its way.*

above left (rehearsal) and *right* (performance):
Jonathan Wade, the party scene of Act I. Wade
encounters the hostility of the townspeople as
he tries to walk the fine line between duty and
justice. Lucas Wardlaw (Joseph Evans, in frock
coat to the left of Jonathan) is one of the
instigators.

Erich: Something else too, it's just… you tend to live a role, especially when you're on your own in a
        hotel room. And one of the weirdest things was to leave that same apartment, to leave it as
        Jonathan Wade, and to come back in as Dandini…

mlh: [laughs]

Erich: It was a different apartment. That sounds really stupid, but it was so true, because I did
        everything different. I mean, Dandini just bounced off the walls, you know. As Wade you came
        home and you just… [choking sounds]

mlh: oh yeah! [laughs]

Erich: ..you know? And I'd laugh about that on my own, I'd walk into the apartment and think,
        this is not the same apartment.

mlh: "I don't belong here…"

Erich: No…

mlh: … who is this person? Could I have another room, please? [laughs]

Erich: [laughs] But I almost needed… I should have changed apartments, to let the character
        change better, especially when there are long periods like that, five weeks.

mlh: I didn't know this was your first Dandini. Did you feel… I mean, in an ideal situation I
        think you would have wished for a little more breathing room to approach it.

Erich: You know, the hardest thing I felt about the Dandini, and yes, part of that is my own fault, just
        booking shows when they're back-to-back like that. And you don't… I mean if you don't
        put in the lead time those couple, three weeks ahead of time, to really sink into the show… or if
        you've done a show before, it's a different story.

mlh: sure, of course.

Erich: But when you're out on stage, especially in rehearsal trying to remember words, you can't give
        a hundred percent to the character, to the singing… and it's hard especially if every one else has
        done it before and they know you're struggling along. You hate to be put in that position. And,
        you know, the first couple of weeks I felt a bit of that. But those are all parts of the operatic world
        in terms of, well, you've got to do that, and sometimes...

mlh: Well, here's the job offer...

147

left, top: Artists' Roundtable: On the Thursday before dress rehearsal week, each production presents a panel discussion open to the public, with the director, conductor, and major principal singers taking part. They discuss the particular production and the rehearsal process, the historical context of the opera and its musical style, and other background information that can help the audience more fully enjoy the performance. In the opera world, it's a rare treat to have the composer available to give an inside perspective on the work. Carlisle Floyd and Erich answer questions from the audience.

left, center: Erich in his dressing room before a performance, with Marianne Flettner, Artistic Administrator for the Company. Marianne is the primary liaison between the artists and Administration and before each performance, she delivers paychecks to the artists. For this, tenor Patrick Power gratefully dubbed her "the carrot lady."

left, bottom: Erich at makeup call with Makeup Artist Sandra Davis.

below: Erich and Carlisle Floyd on opening night of *Wade*.

opposite page: Cinderella in rehearsal and performance – the Dancing Tables sequence. At left, Erich with drumstick, and soprano Evelyn de la Rosa (Clorinda) with flounder. At right, Tisbe (Carter Scott), Dandini, Clorinda, and the Prince (Bradley Williams) get caught up in the excitement... or try to remember what they're supposed to do first.

Erich: ...even the Plácido Domingos of the world come in and they don't know note one of the show. And they hand them a coach and they learn it. And you hate to do that. I felt that way a little bit with it, I would have loved at least one more week. One week to sing, and it would have changed everything.

mlh: Yes, always another week... but I think that you had good support with both shows. And with knowing the people there.

Erich: Right... first of all, you couldn't ask for two better casts. When you've got a Débria Brown, where you can just fall into her arms and disappear. I mean, every time you passed her, you got this hug that would last you a year, you know? And would kind of change your life, that kind of a person. And Sheryl... There is nobody in the business like her.

mlh: She's extraordinarily powerful on stage. That production [Jonathan Wade] was very strong and it took me a long, long time before I started to get it out of my head.

Erich: But, that really, I mean... that... that makes all the difference, not only in the shows and the performance, but in the business, in your life. If you're working with people that you trust, that feed you, that you can feed in that way... things blossom – wonderfully. And both those shows had that.

mlh: Cenerentola... it was kind of a perpetual-motion production, wasn't it? especially for your character...

Erich: You know, having worked with Linda [Brovsky – director] before, I really trusted her, in that Linda will not do anything that doesn't work. She may push you absolutely to the limit, you know...

mlh: That's what rehearsal is for...

Erich: ... and that's what it's for. And if it doesn't work, she'll back off. But – if she can get that hundred and ten percent, and get the wackiness, and the singing and everything else, more power to her. Because she's thought it out well. We had a good time with the energy, with all the nut stuff that she gave us to do, which was great. And I really, really found that helped, too.

mlh: Oh yes, so you liked that? Towards the end of the rehearsal period there were... [laughs]... a few complaints.

Erich: Well, I know that... I know it was hard for Karen [Keltner – conductor] in the pit. 'Cause there were many moments, I mean, you just see her... [laughs] "... is anyone looking?" That kind of thing, where's the concentration? as we're doing figure-eight dances and kicks and jumping and flying arms and...! But it's a trade-off. You can do the big ensembles when you stand and sing and listen to beautiful music, or you can – when it's a nuts ensemble, like these are – you can play it.

mlh: It was nuts – great fun.

Erich: I mean the whole thing with the moving the tables and the... it was hysterical. I couldn't believe – you know, we went into rehearsal, and... and...you want us to do what?! The banquet, and the huge tables full of food, and we danced with the tables. And they're on wheels and it was all choreographed – anytime we were not singing, we were eating the food. And moving the tables. And everything was choreographed so that, I mean, you'd... the chicken leg would go over and the napkin would go up and you'd move the table and then it's like... oh, it took forever to....

mlh:	Didn't it take two full days to rehearse that sequence that lasted, what? a minute and a half or two minutes? [laughs] But the audience response to that show was terrific.
Erich:	It's wonderful...
mlh:	I mean, they loved it.
Erich:	And that's where I've really got to give Linda credit, she went for it. I mean, that was... these words mean something and you may be doing absolutely stupid things, but the character – it fits the character. Go for it. You know, don't apologize for what you sing here, do it. And it works when you do that. If it's a good show. And that's why Cenerentola has popped to the top, it does work.
mlh:	And then you went directly to Denver to do Mozart?
Erich:	Right... Così fan tutte [laughs][sort of]. I was rehearsing that during Cenerentola, flying to Denver in between every show.
mlh:	How often does that happen to you? That sort of road block, traffic jam...?
Erich:	Well you hope not often, but maybe once a year you end up flying back and forth and rehearsing the show and coming back... But I, I really felt I kind of cheated Cenerentola a bit, on both ends of that. At the beginning and at the end when I was performing, after opening night I flew to Denver. So it wasn't like it ever really even settled in.
mlh:	Let's see, here I should ask you what is the thing you like least about your work and it's probably the same thing that everybody says, and that's the...
Erich:	The traveling! [laughs]
mlh:	... traveling!
Erich:	Yeah. Well, yes and no. The first couple nights in a new town are wonderful. But eventually every hotel room looks the same, they all have the same channels [laughs]. That's got to be it, just not having the home base. You know, you feel like you're kind of uprooted all the time. When I've been away for a couple of months, I really look forward to going to soccer games and hearing violin practice again.

above: Costume Designer Allen Charles Klein works on Colonel Wade's uniform in a costume fitting. Historically accurate details on every single costume in the opera, whether worn by a principal singer or by a super who stood at the edge of the stage for two minutes, gave one a sense of looking at old daguerrotype photos, a feeling of actually living in this time and place.

right: Erich with Sheryl Woods in *Wade* rehearsal. "There is nobody in the business like her."

opposite top: Working out details in the rehearsal room and in the hallway before a performance (with Julian Patrick looking on). Erich and Sheryl have performed these roles before, not only opposite each other but with other singers as well. Both continued to search throughout the rehearsal process and each night during performances, too, for the best ways to convey the emotion to the audience. They had an intelligent and deeply emotional bond with each other; their collaboration and mutual respect was visible in every scene they had together.

opposite, lower right: Jonathan Wade, Act III, Jonathan and Celia.

mlh: *Okay.* Jonathan Wade.

Erich: Jonathan Wade... *there's wonderful catharsis in the work. A role like this, huge amounts of things come up.*

mlh: *yes...*

Erich: *... huge amounts. I mean, the first time working through the show with Carlisle in Miami, where he really went for how do you feel, you know, as opposed to just getting it up on stage. And we... there were times we just broke down at the end of rehearsal, sobbing, all of us in a pile on the floor. There were a couple of moments with Débria, where all of a sudden – and she didn't know it was in there, inside – the whipping scene…*

mlh: *oh yes...*

Erich: *... You know, the first time she was cool with all of that. Then all of a sudden one day it just surfaced, something that had been down in there. And she just went to another world and lost it, you know. It happened to all of us so many times in that show, in particular. And that means it's a great show, if it can take you to those places because it takes the audience there. One of the greatest things with that show, one of the greatest things with my career, I think, was the night we did it for the kids. Those kids were so into that show. They didn't come thinking that they had to… that they were coming to see a Puccini, as so many of the adults did, wanting to hear Puccini.*

mlh: *Right, not having that preconception...*

Erich: *Right, which is what opera should be... And so they loved the music. They thought it was fabulous, you know, and they were screaming and yelling and into it… And one moment that sticks out so vividly in my mind is the moment when Jonathan is shot. And it's a – well, you know – it's a shocking moment. Comes out of nowhere… and the scream from the audience, en masse, because the kids didn't know they had to be quiet. And that even happens some nights with the adult audiences. But it was an en masse scream, and people yelling, "NOOO!" And I found that really shocking, because all this… what I'm feeling on stage … and all of a sudden to have this wave of energy just hit me in the face. And you realize... boy, this works. This works. Carlisle wasn't there, but I called him right away and I said, "That's affirmation. That's it. You have a great show."*

mlh: *Was that the first time you did it...*

Erich: *... for kids? yeah. You know, that will change the lives of a lot of these kids. They will come see operas, they will talk about this show ...*

mlh: *They'll* think.

Erich: *..they'll think, yes.*

mlh: Tell me what you like best about your work, about being an opera singer.

Erich: Getting to be someone else... what comes with that exploration, what comes with the rehearsal of that. Being with other people as someone else. I mean all of those things that liberate people to find out what's inside them. And then what that does off stage in terms of friends, in terms of these kind of little mini-lifetimes that we spend with a group of people, where, you'll never do that show with that group again, basically. You really treasure those moments.

mlh: So for you, it's the blend of all of it, isn't it? all the members of the cast, the production team, the conductor... and the staging and the acting and the singing ...

Erich: Yeah, it is. I mean, I'm the first one to admit that there are a thousand singers out there that can out-sing me. And I try my best always to put all of those pieces together. And if they want the stand-and-sing singers, I'm probably not going to be in that cast. But my philosophy is to make pure musical theater in the operatic sense. Even in Cenerentola, which I think we found pretty well [laughs]...

mlh: Sometimes you don't always get that in the rehearsal process. But in the best situation, everybody is working towards the same goal. I think with a show like Wade, it almost demanded that everybody was committed, was working at the same level.

Erich: Right... What makes a show not work, I guess, is when everyone doesn't do that. But you've got a couple people who are, and they're constantly being pulled out of it. Other people are standing around telling jokes and you're down there dying, or something. You know, that's a tough process. And it's... it's sometimes hard with opera because so much of opera is over the top. To just delve into this over-the-top stuff. But when you do, it works. Partially because of the medium, partially because you've got the huge sets and the orchestra and this and that and... and that's so... it's all there. You're watching more than life.

mlh: So. You'll be back for another of Carlisle Floyd's works...?

Erich: Of Mice and Men, right.

mlh: Good. And you've done that before, or no?

Erich: I never have.

mlh: No?

Erich: I've been aching to do that – I've never seen it. But I've gone through the score and all, many times now, and I just... every time I open that book, it's: Here we go!

above: Erich standing at *Sitzprobe* for *Cinderella*.

right: Erich leaving the dressing room hallway for his first entrance as Wade.

right: In the aftermath of the Civil War, Celia Townsend (Sheryl Woods) is in mourning for her mother and fiancé. Deep in her own grief, she finds herself strangely touched by similar losses suffered by Colonel Jonathan Wade, a Union Army officer assigned to restore order as part of the occupation.

above: Lucas Wardlaw (Joseph Evans) is a Southern gentleman caught in the complexity of trying to rebuild his shattered life.

below: The riot scene. Celia (wearing a white veil) is inside, while Nicey (Débria Brown, lower right) is stunned by the violence.

"Shall I resolve to live again,
To open my life, my heart once more?
Has this stranger come to deliver me?

"An alchemist has touched my grief.
Will he turn it into joy?"

– Celia

THE PASSION OF JONATHAN WADE
by Carlisle Floyd

"I don't like the word 'villain' – Enoch Pratt is not a villain, Lucas Wardlaw is not a villain – they're both men who have a particular background, maybe they're after something that conflicts with their job, or the situation they find themselves in when their whole world has changed.

"Actually, I don't consider Jonathan Wade to be a 'hero,' because he has the same kinds of good and evil, dark and light, within him."

– Carlisle Floyd

"Anything of great value – creation, a new idea – carries its shadow zone with it. You have to accept it that way... every action has an implicit share of negativity.

"There is no escaping it. Every positive value has its price in negative terms and you never see anything very great which is not, at the same time, horrible in some respect.
"The genius of Einstein leads to Hiroshima."

– Pablo Picasso

above: The Wedding Scene. Nicey (Débria Brown) sings a song of blessing based on an old Negro spiritual, the most purely lyrical music in the opera.

154

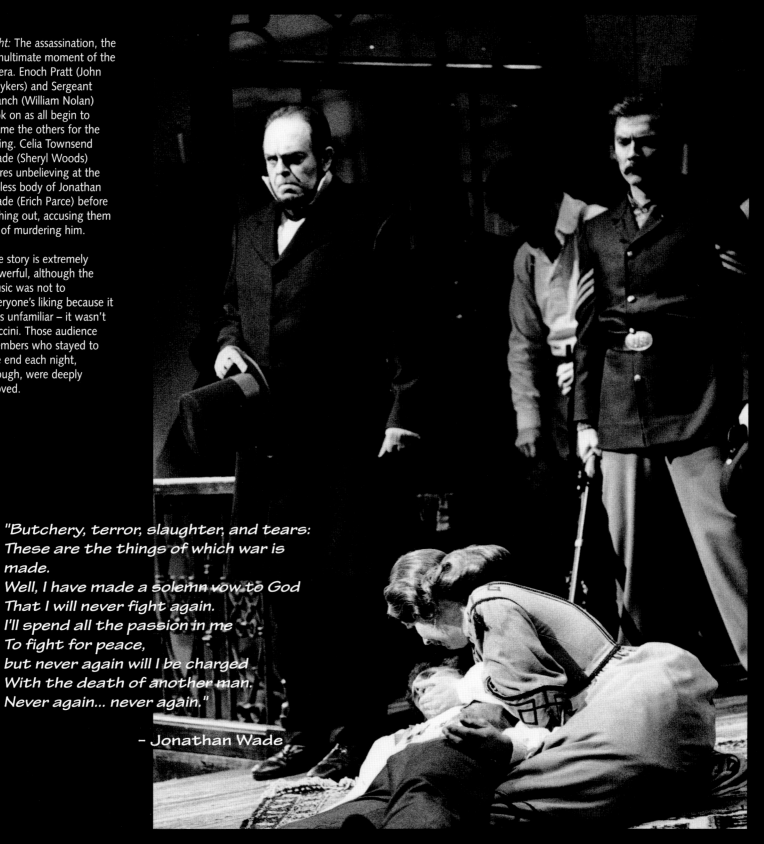

right: The assassination, the penultimate moment of the opera. Enoch Pratt (John Duykers) and Sergeant Branch (William Nolan) look on as all begin to blame the others for the killing. Celia Townsend Wade (Sheryl Woods) stares unbelieving at the lifeless body of Jonathan Wade (Erich Parce) before lashing out, accusing them *all* of murdering him.

The story is extremely powerful, although the music was not to everyone's liking because it was unfamiliar – it wasn't Puccini. Those audience members who stayed to the end each night, though, were deeply moved.

"Butchery, terror, slaughter, and tears:
These are the things of which war is
made.
Well, I have made a solemn vow to God
That I will never fight again.
I'll spend all the passion in me
To fight for peace,
but never again will I be charged
With the death of another man.
Never again... never again."

– Jonathan Wade

155

the Business of Art

administration

"I think if there's one thing that I try to instill all the way down through the staff, it is that they are responsible for what they do; they are a very important part of the machine. We're analyzing our data like any business. That was not done in this company when I arrived. I'm fascinated by figures, and they give you hints about where to go.

"We're forced, in the way I do business, to look three and four years down the track and also look back at where we've gone. So when I'm thinking of what can happen here, I'm looking at the history… That to me is Management 101. There's nothing clever in that."

– Ian Campbell

San Diego Opera is opera for five months at a time, but it's business 365 days a year... what you see on stage happens only after the publicists, ticket sellers, and fundraisers have done their jobs. This is Administration. The people who work here include former singers, actors, and arts administrators – and many have worked in other performing arts organizations. Every single one of them feels that this company is special… and that kind of attitude comes from the top.

Ian D. Campbell, General Director of San Diego Opera since 1983, sits at the top. His energy, experience, and vision have led the Company into financial stability while returning a creative sensibility to the repertoire. That kind of achievement requires some kind of genius... and that's what the Company has in Ian Campbell.

There are no secrets at San Diego Opera. Ian's open-door communication policy means that the flow of information is constant, both ways. The better informed and more involved staff members are, the better they are at doing their jobs; Ian looks for a "fire-in-the-belly" attitude when hiring. He doesn't second-guess his staff... but nothing happens in the Company that doesn't bear Ian's fingerprints.

above: *Ian and composer Carlisle Floyd discuss both past and future productions of Floyd's work.*

right: *Celebration! Board President Faye Wilson (at left) and others led a campaign to raise a $50,000 birthday gift to the Company for Ian's 50th. A membership challenge later doubled that amount.*

158

left: Ian's weekly radio program combines selections from opera, song, and musical theatre with information about upcoming productions. It's a way for the Company to widen the San Diego Opera audience and reach those who are unable to attend performances. Tape-delay radio broadcasts of the productions have been on the air for years... but the Opera recently went live with broadcasts of all Sunday matinees.

below: Personal contacts and networking are key to how Ian does business. He keeps up to date with singers, agents, directors, and conductors by phone and e-mail.

Much is made of Ian Campbell's uncanny ability to find talented young singers. The usual reason given is the fact that Ian was a singer himself before moving into administration. While there's no question that his knowledge of singing allows him to listen with technical understanding, that alone isn't enough to explain why he's able to assemble the casts he does. He hears more than 200 singers each year, in audition and performance, from San Diego to Europe. He usually concentrates on smaller companies in Germany, Italy, and the United States, listening to the voices, assessing language skills, looking for stage presence – in German it's Ausstrahlung, imperfectly translated as "radiance" – all of which need to be part of the "package." It requires a certain detachment and analytical ability to be able to fill roles for upcoming seasons. He needs to know how a particular voice will match up with those already cast, how a singer is likely to sound three years ahead, and how their fee will fit into the total budget. He shows the same skill in finding conductors, directors, and designers, so it's not just his musical background that explains his artistic successes.

"I think my favorite part is planning it," he says, "not in seeing it happen, because I hire other people to do that. I enjoy working out the budget with staff, making sure it can happen, overseeing the planning, getting all of the ingredients together.... But once it's on, in fact once it's here, I'm pretty well done with it."

The list of what Ian does in any given week is daunting. He attends rehearsals, negotiates contracts, gives speeches, meets with civic leaders, reports at Board meetings, holds auditions, conducts press conferences, records his radio show, appears at fund-raising parties, supervises staff, prepares to direct an upcoming opera, plans repertoire... You sometimes have to remind him what year it is – he's always in another year, on another calendar. He may tell you that what he does is nothing more than hard work and common sense – but Ian Campbell's sense in guiding and shaping the Company is far from common.

Everyone in Administration was enthusiastic about my project, asking how the shooting was going, showing interest and support. When it was time to document the work that goes on in the Administrative offices, everyone suddenly became camera-shy. I spent four consecutive days coaxing and bribing people into letting me close with the cameras... but I found no one was shy when it came to talking about what they do. They spoke of their admiration for the artistic achievements of the Company. They were enthusiastic about the future and about their role in those plans. They often showed me pictures and lists and flow charts of upcoming events. Most of all, they were excited, fulfilled, content, and challenged – glad to be part of the team.

top left: *Connie Taluban, Receptionist. Usually your first contact when you call the office, Connie reveals a warm concern for every person she speaks to. In this way, she has been "The Voice of the Opera" for more than ten years.*

center left: *Lisa Kalal, Associate Director of Development (Corporations and Major Gifts) is one of the tireless members of the Development Department. Most of them on this team have been working together for three, five, or more years (rare in this kind of high-stress job). They occasionally rotate titles and responsibilities to avoid creative burn-out.*

lower left: *Lillian R. Parra, Bookkeeper. Lil has been with the Company longer than anyone else in the Administrative offices and – like the rest of them – loves what she does.*

center: *Bruce Viggars, Volunteer. While there is a pool of volunteers who regularly help with everything from filing to mailings, Bruce is one of two full-timers, working primarily in Marketing and Development. Elizabeth Otten, the other full-time volunteer, can be found in the Education Department. Both are former school teachers, and their writing and editing skills – along with their energy and commitment – are of enormous value to the Company.*

far left: *Ron Allen, Director of Production, used to do crossword puzzles, but now has more than enough satisfaction in this job, what with the problem-solving and putting together of puzzle pieces. Ron supervises everything that eventually ends up on stage and he's involved on a daily basis with the sets, lights, and costumes of the current production. He's also planning, budgeting, and coordinating the acquisition of productions for future seasons, so he's another one who seems to exist in several years at the same time.*

near left: *Chris LaZich, Annual Fund Director, has an ability to remain cool and calm (a shared staff quality) in the sometimes-frantic Development Department.*

below: *Assistants in the Development Department hold an impromptu meeting in the hallway: Angie Chan and Joanie Merriman.*

"We may not be the ones on stage," Public Relations Manager Stephanie Thompson says, *"but we help make it happen."*

One of the first things I noticed when I started meeting people in the Company was an almost-tangible spirit of teamwork and camaraderie throughout the Administrative offices. It seemed a bit too good to be true at first; I used to work in theatre and one of the reasons I left was a frustration with the unprofessional attitudes and out-of-control egos. At San Diego Opera, everyone in Administration knows that they are an integral part of the team. Each person's job is important, each person's contribution is acknowledged. This is an organization where initiative and creative thought are not only encouraged but expected.

The backgrounds of people who come to work for San Diego Opera encompass theatre and opera company management, teaching, computers, economics, marketing, journalism, singing, and acting. They are fluent in several languages including French, Italian, Spanish, Arabic, German, and English (both the Australian and American versions).

They like people, music, and the arts. They also appreciate being part of the team and making a contribution to the end product, the creative aspect of the work, the complexity of handling different aspects of their jobs, variety, challenge, learning, the high standard of work the Company does, and the fact that everyone is accountable for what they do.

Work days are long, especially during the performing season, and the pressure can build up... but they all derive great satisfaction from working for the Company and with the people there. "It's the best," is a comment I heard all the time.

far left: *Michael Murphy, Director of Administration, in a meeting with Todd R. Schultz, Director of Marketing & Public Relations.* "What the audience experiences is why I work here," Michael says. "Everything I do affects the audience experience."

left: *Kerry Hogan-Bean, Assistant to the Director of Administration. What this title actually means... Kerry coordinates, assists with, and handles a bit of everything.*

right: *Backstage with Resident Conductor and Music Administrator Karen Keltner... who adds another task to a long list. This one is fun: finding the best technique to use in pinning a rosebud boutonniere to composer Carlisle Floyd's lapels. Marianne Flettner, Artistic Administrator, is the consultant.*

"You know where I think it starts? As in any business, at the top... in this case it's Ian. And what's the next step out? this is going to sound funny, but it's Marianne. Then you get to the director, the conductor, and if Ian has put those pieces together so that they all fit, you've got magic... You really see that if it works well from the top, then it's right down to the people changing the sets and everything else. It's smooth."

– Erich Parce, singer

This company, like all opera companies, plans the upcoming seasons at least three, often four years in advance. This is primarily dictated by the need to contract world-class singers, directors, and conductors – they're booked three to five years ahead.

The broad outlines of operas that might be performed are sketched some five years ahead of time. The plans shift, grow, and change as the big pieces are put in place first: a major singer, a particular production, a certain conductor, a world premiere. Different productions are reviewed in terms of the design and the direction, availability is checked, budgeting is worked out, and contracts begin to be signed. A few of the principal singers will not be determined until much later in the process, perhaps only two years ahead; smaller roles are usually filled one year in advance.

Long-range plans involve more than just the next three or four seasons. The Development Department works on five-, ten-, and twenty-year projections in their fund-raising efforts. The Education Programs are building a future audience, looking a generation or more ahead. Upcoming operas are selected to balance audience favorites (which generate excitement and revenue) with less-familiar works which help the audience experience something new. They need to be challenged as well as soothed and the Company needs to be stretched artistically in order to grow and stay viable for the future.

They're always facing forward, trying to see how the Company can best fit in with the community... it's not just about presenting operas and recitals this week or next month. The reach is wider – the vision is far greater.

above: *Todd Schultz, Director of Marketing and Public Relations, puts in some evening work time when the phones are quiet. The Company's five-opera season allows staff to give a high degree of attention and care to each production, which helps provide stylistic continuity. As a result, everyone works long hours, especially during the hectic weeks of the season; I would often find three or four of the staff in their offices after a performance, unaware of the time.*

right: *General Director Ian Campbell reports to The Board of Directors. Ian conducts the same open-access policy of information with the Board as he does with his staff. The better informed the Board is, the more clearly they're able to determine the direction for the Company. They have come to trust Ian and the information he and staff present, precisely because there are no secrets. That mutual trust is one of the reasons the Board recently extended Ian's contract through the year 2012. It's also one of the factors that has allowed the Board to support some big strides forward in the artistic caliber of the Company.*

Reaching Out

the education & outreach program

above: *Artists' Roundtable for* Tosca. *Tenor César Hernández and soprano Nelly Miricioiu are – delightedly – sharing the story of the first time they worked together. Nelly was singing* La Traviata *in Italy and, by the middle of Act I, it was clear her tenor was quite ill. César had dropped by the theatre to visit his friend (the tenor) when the stage manager caught up with him backstage, demanding: "Can you sing Alfredo?!" Nelly was already in the middle of "Sempre libera" and wondering what would happen, when from the wings "this glorious voice!" sang "Amor è palpito..." César sang the rest of the performance from the orchestra pit while the other tenor went through the motions on stage. They had a wonderful time working together on Tosca, too, and their offstage rapport carried over onstage.*

San Diego Opera's Education and Outreach Program is the largest of its kind in this country, reaching approximately 100,000 people each year. Lectures, performances, and educational activities for audiences of all ages are conducted throughout most of the year. The San Diego Opera Ensemble, a group of six young singers and a pianist, conducts Spring and Fall tours covering all of San Diego County and parts of Baja California, Mexico. They present four different programs that go to schools, colleges, convalescent homes, prisons, and special events such as private parties, fundraisers, and store openings.

opposite page:
left: "San Diego Opera Spotlight," a television program airing during the season, sets up to tape an interview with Sharon Ott, director of The Conquistador. The program presents interviews with the artists in a behind-the-scenes look at each opera.

center: Backstage tours of the theatre are an important part of the outreach program – people love to see how (and where) the magic is made. Docent Ruth Ledermann (at left) leads a group of the curious.

right: During intermission at the Student Dress Rehearsal for Turandot, Director of Education and Outreach Adam Eisenberg (left) and Ping, Pang, and Pong speak to the audience of high school students. That's Beau Palmer (Pang) with the microphone, encouraging the students to finish school and follow their dreams.

this page: Opera on the Concourse – Free outdoor concerts allow the principal artists to sing some of their favorite songs and arias while entertaining the lunch-time crowds on the plaza. They are always fun concerts – most memorable for me were Syliva Wen's Chinese folk song; Sheryl Woods' "What a curse for a woman is a timid man;" by Gian Carlo Menotti; an Irving Berlin Medley sung by Patrick Power; Maggie Lattimore's "I'm a Stranger Here Myself;" and most of all, a heartbreaking "Joanna" from Sweeney Todd, sung by bass-baritone David Downing.

below left: Bass Walter Du Melle concludes the aria "Ha! Wie will ich triumphieren" from Mozart's The Abduction From the Seraglio.

below right: From the Cinderella cast, soprano Evelyn de la Rosa and bass Kevin Langan sing "Là ci darem la mano" from Don Giovanni.

above: *Puppets and puppeteers in* Papagayo, *an opera written for very young children by Edward Barnes from the story by Gerald McDermott. The puppets, designed by Lynne Jennings, are quite large, some of them the size of a small child. Their operators – all volunteers – meet with the audience after the performance. The children are enchanted. It makes no difference to them that the puppet characters sing rather than speak. And the kids send fan mail... the walls of the Education office are decorated with colorful drawings of the opera and thank-you letters written in crayon.*

The outreach programs are geared to all ages. For the adults, there are lectures and presentations on everything from the background of a particular opera to a look behind the scenes of the Company. These are held all over the County in a variety of community and college settings, presented by experts in related fields as well as by docents. The Artists' Roundtable discussions, Opera on the Concourse, and the radio broadcasts are all under the umbrella of the Education Department, along with several other programs. I had intended to photograph a little bit of everything they do, but I couldn't keep up with them.

The Ensemble is the main performing arm of the Outreach Program. Six young singers with classical training and professional experience are selected during a competitive audition process each year. They perform any of four different programs, twice a day, six days a week, for three months in the fall and again in the spring. Although it's a performance program rather than a singers' training program, there are plenty of learning opportunities and the singers are often cast in minor roles in the mainstage productions. In spite of their demanding schedule, the Ensemble members are upbeat and optimistic about the program; many of them go on to have solo careers in Europe and the United States.

During an intensive two-day rehearsal for a recording session of excerpts from The Conquistador, the singers worked with composer Myron Fink and conductor Karen Keltner, both of whom provided additional input on this new music. I watched and photographed during most of those rehearsals. The music is challenging and these singers worked as hard to learn this as they did in learning all the other programs together. Their faces often reflected puzzlement and frustration, and they were sometimes skeptical when they got it right. Their Music Director, Chris Allen, Myron, and Karen were patient and encouraging throughout the rehearsal process.

Ensemble musical rehearsals for The Conquistador. *Many months before opening night of the world premiere opera, excerpts were performed for thousands of people in different venues.*

right: *Soprano Carolyn Scimone works on the Ghost Aria.*

top: *Tenor Mark Hernandez, with the Sword Aria.*

above: *Soprano Barbara Divis.*

left: *Master Class for the Ensemble singers. Maestro Edoardo Müller pushes soprano Catherine Ireland to a new level of achievement. While it's helpful to learn just where a singer is at this particular point in her development, there's also value in hearing her do something that's wrong for her and knowing or finding out she can do better or different. There's a fine line between striving to get more out of the voice and knowing when to stop. A young singer's voice may not be ready to take on certain roles and it's important to understand the balance so as not to ruin the voice early on.*

Maestro Müller was very direct in assessing the arias the singers presented to him, as he needed to be, for how can they learn if they're not being told the truth? He had a dozen practical suggestions for each of them to work on the sound of the voice, the language, the quality of the tone... At the conclusion of the two-day class, the singers and the observers all felt it was a shame Maestro is so busy with his conducting – he'd make a great vocal coach. He says "With humility, you always learn."

The Ensemble learns several programs each year, including an abridged version of a full opera, a collection of arias and duets, the very popular childrens' show The Magic is You!, *and a speciality program.*

right: *The Ensemble warms up with Music Director Chris Allen (at piano) for a performance of* Opera For Our Time, *a program of excerpts from 20th-century operas, including those of Puccini, Stravinsky, Britten... and Myron Fink's* The Conquistador.

Programs for arts education are often the exception rather than the rule in many California schools, victims of slashed budgets. Unfortunately, it's the children who are the real losers, for exposure to any kind of art gives them a better education. Now it's left to corporate sponsors and arts organizations to provide programs from the outside.

With the Company's outreach programs, teachers are given study guides that suggest classroom projects and outside activities connected with the opera presentation. If you were to attend any of these performances and watch the reactions of the children, you would see how hungry they are for anything that challenges them. Oh yes, they laugh in "strange" places and don't respond to things the way you "expect" them to (the sight of little kids covering up their ears for the soprano's high notes is a treat to watch!)... but they're involved with what's going on. Occasionally they were more interested in what I was doing with the cameras, but that interest faded quickly as the performance recaptured their attention.

Programs for younger children include presentations such as The Magic is You! (a charming story that conjures up Carmen, Musetta, Figaro, and Brünnhilde to help an everyday fellow believe in his dreams). There's also an interactive program called "Opera For Kids... By Kids!" This is six weeks of training by a music director, stage director, and technical director resulting in a performance with everything handled by the elementary school students. They sing, act, run the lights, make the scenery and costumes, apply makeup, hand out posters, get stage fright... They learn to be part of a group effort and are rewarded by achieving something they never thought they could. This is the kind of experience that builds audiences for the future of opera and the arts in general. You can well imagine what it does for the children's lives.

above: *School children have a chance to question the Ensemble members – Tijuana Project Coordinator Bella Sanchez is with student Argentina Servin, who has a question following a performance. The questions most often asked: How did you know you wanted to be a singer? How long have you been studying?*

right: *Elementary school audiences are delighted with the SDO Ensemble's performance of* The Magic Is You!*...*

top :*... with Carmen, Musetta, and the Wizard.*

the Reason for it All

the audience

The lights go down, the curtain goes up, the music begins... and I'm a voyager to another world. When I'm a member of the audience, I become part of a new group. Tonight's performance is different from any other before or after because I am there.

We are there.

As the audience, we respond with admiration, laughter, tears, deep silence, and applause, our individual reactions blending into one.

above: *Audience members mingle at an Education & Outreach performance held in the Museum of Man.*

right, bottom: *Audience members sample some exotic desserts during intermission.*

right, top: *At a gala post-curtain dinner, an unknown waiter and "Mozart" contemplate each other.*

The plans, the rehearsals, the contributions from all members of the Company are complete. The opera shows up on stage, not as a theoretical exercise but as an opportunity to reach those eager to be entertained, enlightened, enchanted. Tonight the audience may meet a painter, a gypsy, a princess, a soldier or a lover... they might visit a mythical kingdom or a battlefield or a banquet...

... they're at the opera.

After all the work, all the rehearsals, all the contributions from the artists... the performance is incomplete without the participation of the audience.

It is the reason we do what we do.

It is, quite literally, why.

above: *There are 84 standing room tickets available for each performance... for Aïda, the line began forming in mid-afternoon, winding out the lobby doors onto the plaza.*

above right: *A sea of empty seats in the Civic Theatre seems to me a world of possibilities, a promise that almost anything can happen the next time they are filled with a new audience.*

right: *Mezzo-soprano Cecilia Bartoli accepts the gratitude of a delighted audience, following a recital of French and Italian songs. The joy reflected on this man's face is the reason for it all.*

Epilogue

The challenge of capturing artists on film during the creative process is so great, that many books of this kind avoid the problem altogether, becoming mere collections of posed performance photographs. But such books fail to generate the emotional charge we see in these images from Martha Hart's cameras, or the candor of her fascinating thoughts from behind the lens. When this project was first discussed several years ago, Martha made it clear that her view would be unique, and she has kept her promise. She has created a special record of an exciting time by way of her personal observations, and yet in it we find something that touches each of us. It is a story told in many chapters, one which I know you will look at again and again.

Martha has made images that invite us into another world. We have seen the usually unseen: the stagehands, costumers, make-up artists, carpenters, painters and administrators whose primary function is to make the performing artists' path to the stage that much easier. As you explored this intriguing book, I am certain you shared in the excitement, the passion, and the plain hard work which is required to bring opera to the stage. I hope you have developed a healthy respect for the remarkable army of people who make it possible. While they rarely receive the public recognition or adulation that the artists on stage do, they are the backbone of any opera company. These people, each of them artists, contribute greatly to bringing these masterpieces of music to life at every rehearsal and performance.

The images and thoughts which make up the lion's share of this volume record almost two years of San Diego Opera's life. So much is here: the triumph in the creation of a world premiere; the thrill of the return to San Diego of a superstar tenor after an absence of thirty years; the sense of discovery as we witness the debuts of exciting young artists who will become tomorrow's audience favorites; and the wonder of a child's first experience of opera.

This look at two seasons of San Diego Opera tells part of the story, but the history and performance chronology which follow will serve to give you an even greater feel for the heritage of this Company. The quality of performances and casting, including an extraordinary number of United States debuts and many singers' first-ever portrayals of significant roles, are factors contributing to the high regard the Company enjoys in this country and around the world.

Here, in the most complete story of San Diego Opera's work ever printed, are all the productions we have performed with the names of the singers, conductors, directors and designers who gave those works life. The casual reader, who may be most interested in the photographs, will recognize that the Company has developed substantially and that it will continue to do so in the future. The more passionate reader will be able to explore in greater depth, discovering the range of operas given and the hundreds of fine artists who have appeared here.

But no book can tell all the story of opera. The full story is told in the darkness of the theatre itself, as 3,000 people at each performance look into their hearts, souls and minds, experiencing emotions so often hidden in our most modern of worlds. Here they may choose to suffer with Tosca, to go to the guillotine with the Carmelite nuns, to find true love with Tamino, or to lead a less respectable life with Don Giovanni. Whatever the choice, it is entirely personal and subjective, as the glory of this most miraculous of performing arts takes over all their senses and they relive forgotten emotions.

All of us know these feelings, and return to opera again and again. Our experience is different, our responses enhanced with every hearing, every year, and our hearts cry out for more.

Ian D. Campbell
General Director
San Diego Opera

Nights of Glory: A History of San Diego Opera
by David Gregson

In the Beginning – 1952 to 1965

If frequency of performance is an accurate index of popularity, then *La bohème* is the all-time favorite of San Diego Opera audiences. It was the first opera the company ever presented, and since that time locals have marked the passage of the years in stagings of Puccini's beloved romantic tragedy. *La bohème*s connect the past and present like so many tear-stained musical milestones: 1965, 1968, 1974, 1979, 1985, 1990 and 1995. But the *La bohème* that helped celebrate the San Diego Opera's 30th Anniversary season was either the seventh or eighth production of the popular masterpiece, depending on how you count. In a very real sense, our local opera company has not one, but two beginnings, the first occurring not in 1965, but in 1952.

In 1952, a newly formed group calling itself the San Diego Opera Guild managed to bring a production of the prestigious San Francisco Opera to town. With much hoopla and press fanfare, the show opened for a one-night stand in one of the very few local venues large enough to accommodate such an extravaganza, San Diego High School's Russ Auditorium.

But while the venue was quaintly provincial, the performance was not. Excitement was high, for right here in our humble little city, better known for its tourist beaches, aircraft factories and military installations than for its culture, was a major-league *La bohème*, starring soprano Dorothy Kirsten and tenor Jan Peerce, both gigantic American celebrities at the peak of their popularity.

That remarkable evening had been the result of numerous ladies' club luncheon meetings dating back to 1947, when a San Diego Committee of the Opera Guild of Southern California was informally shaped, with prominent socialite Mrs. Edgar A. Luce as chairman. Every fall since 1937, Los Angeles had been hosting an extensive out-of-town "second" San Francisco Opera season at the enormous Shrine Auditorium. In 1949 Mrs. Luce began discussions with San Francisco Opera representatives about the possibility of importing productions to San Diego during those annual Los Angeles visits. With the help of the Los Angeles-based Opera Guild of Southern California, the San Diego Opera Guild was officially established on January 20, 1950, at a tea given by Mrs. William Paxton Cary. Mrs. Luce was made president.

After the Guild's second imported production in 1953, a flawlessly cast *The Barber of Seville* with Giulietta Simionato, Cesare Valletti, Frank Guarrera, Salvatore Baccaloni and Nicola Rossi-Lemeni, conducted by Tullio Serafin, one of La Scala's greatest maestros, the visiting company abandoned the acoustically atrocious Russ Auditorium for the Fox Theater, today's Copley Symphony Hall. The San Francisco Opera continued its San Diego visits there for 12 consecutive fall seasons.

From 1954 to 1955, one annual presentation was all our local Guild could manage, but from 1956 to 1957 the seasons expanded to two operas each, and from 1958 to 1965 the yearly offerings swelled to three. Performances invariably took place in late October and/or early to mid-November.

During those memorable seasons, the greatest international opera stars came to town. Today their names are the stuff of legend: Elisabeth Schwarzkopf, Victoria de los Angeles, Anna Moffo, Leonie Rysanek, Licia Albanese, Joan Sutherland, Leyla Gencer, Pilar Lorengar, Blanche Thebom, Ettore Bastianini, Jess Thomas, James McCracken, Jon Vickers, Franco Corelli, Mario del Monaco, Tito Gobbi, Geraint Evans and Robert Merrill, just to name a few.

Because her *La bohème* helped start it all, and because she was a glamorous woman and a compelling artist, particularly in Puccini operas, Dorothy Kirsten was a big favorite with local audiences. They could not get enough of this uniquely American diva, and she sang here five more times.

In 1954 the American soprano came to town to portray Tosca, one of her trademark heroines. Goaded into a jealous fury by tenor Brian Sullivan's Cavaradossi and reduced to sobs by baritone Robert Weede's menacing Scarpia, Kirsten thrilled her audience. The next year she exacted more tears as Puccini's tragic jilted geisha in *Madama Butterfly*. Tenor Giuseppe Campora was the dastardly Lieutenant Pinkerton, Margaret Roggero the Suzuki, and Louis Quilico, Sharpless.

1959 witnessed one of Kirsten's specialty roles outside the Puccini repertoire, Fiora in Montemezzi's *L'amore dei tre re*, an opera once hailed as a masterpiece, but seldom performed today. Giuseppe Zampieri was Fiora's lover, Avito; Guarrera was Manfredo, Fiora's husband; and Giorgio Tozzi, the vengeful old blind king, Archibaldo.

San Diegans saw Kirsten next in 1960 in her second *Tosca* here, with Zampieri and Mario Zanasi, Silvio Varviso conducting. The diva's final performance here (outside of a 1965 concert sponsored by the Guild) came in 1963 with *The Queen of Spades*, co-starring Regina Resnik, Janis Martin, James McCracken, John Shaw and Thomas Stewart, conducted by Leopold Ludwig. Kirsten's stature as San Diego's favorite diva was never rivaled until 1970, when Beverly Sills began her long love affair with San Diego Opera audiences.

Albanese's touchingly vulnerable Marguerite and Siepi's charismatic Méphistophélès were just two highlights of a stunning *Faust* in 1956. By today's standards, the singers might constitute something close to a "dream cast." Peerce was the eponymous hero, Cornell MacNeil the Valentin, Margaret Roggero the Siebel, with Jean Morel conducting. This was followed by a delightful 1956 *Così fan tutte* with Schwarzkopf's incomparable Fiordiligi, superbly matched by Nell Rankin as sister Dorabella. Patrice Munsel was the sprightly Despina, Richard Lewis and Guarrera were the two boyfriends, and Lorenzo Alvary the mischievous Don Alfonso.

In 1957 the most famous and controversial opera star on the planet was Maria Callas. Miraculously, she was slated for a performance of *Lucia di Lammermoor* at the Fox Theater that year, but the diva's problems with San Francisco Opera director Kurt Herbert Adler ultimately resulted in the cancellation of her contract. This was a crushing disappointment to many devout Callas worshippers (who knew her largely from her many recordings on Angel Records). Adler enlisted a relatively unknown Turkish soprano, Leyla Gencer, as "La Divina's" replacement.

On October 31, 1957, San Diego got Gencer, not in *Lucia* but in *La traviata* (with Jon Crain and Robert Merrill), but her unique vocal style and histrionics went largely unappreciated, probably due to the disappointment over the absence of Callas. Once more, the season had begun with a slight let-down: soprano Herva Nelli, more distinguished for rumors of having been Toscanini's mistress than for her singing, was the heroine in a lackluster *Aida*, remarkable only for mezzo-soprano Blanche Thebom's electric performance as Amneris.

Gencer came to town for the following 1958 season in *Manon* with Lewis, Alvary and Quilico, conducted by Jean Fournet. Few in the audience that year had a hint of what the future held in store for the diva. Today Gencer is a cult figure rivaled only by Callas and Magda Olivero in the wide, weird and wonderful world of "pirate" – make that "private" – recordings. Collectors would kill for recordings of those San Diego performances, if any exist.

The first three-opera season of the San Francisco Opera came in 1958. It began with the Gencer *Manon* and continued with a scintillating *The Marriage of Figaro* with Schwarzkopf, Eugenia Ratti, Cecilia Ward, Katherine Hilgenberg, Rolando Panerai and Giuseppe Modesti, conducted by Adler; and *The Force of Destiny* with Leonie Rysanek, Ward, Pier Miranda Ferraro, Weede, Arnold van Mill and Richard Wentworth.

1959 saw *Carmen* starring Vickers as Don José, with Gloria Lane as his gypsy lover; plus the Kirsten *L'amore dei tre re* and a thoroughly Italianate *Otello* with Mario del Monaco, Gabriella Tucci, and Giuseppe Zampieri, conducted by Francesco Molinari-Pradelli. The 1960 season brought *Der Rosenkavalier* with Schwarzkopf, Kurt Böhme, and Hertha Topper, Varviso conducting; and *La sonnambula* with Moffo, Sylvia Stahlman, Janis Martin, Nicola Monti and Tozzi, Molinari-Pradelli conducting.

Joan Sutherland exploded onto the international scene in 1961, and San Diegans saw her *Lucia* at the Fox on November 3, with Renato Cioni as Edgardo, Molinari-Pradelli conducting. "La Stupenda's" performance left audiences and critics gasping for breath. "The voice itself is one of the modern seven wonders," wrote *San Diego Union* music critic Alan Kriegsman. Twelve years later, Sutherland would appear again in San Diego, not with the San Francisco Opera, however, but with our very own San Diego Opera.

The 1960s began with the San Francisco Opera at the Fox Theater and ended with the San Diego Opera in the present Civic Theatre. November 9 brought more excitement with Gre Brouwenstijn, Fritz Uhl, and sensational newcomer Marilyn Horne as Marcellina in *Fidelio*. "She bids fair to emerge at the top of the heap in the future," correctly prophesied Kriegsman, who was also ecstatic after a November 16 *Rigoletto* with MacNeil and Mary Costa.

Operatic life went on at the Fox with an amazing *Don Giovanni* with Evans, Schwarzkopf, Lewis, sets by Franco Zeffirelli, and Ludwig conducting; *Il trovatore* with Elinor Ross, McCracken and Bastianini; and a *Cav*-and-*Pag* bill starring Evans, Sandor Konya, Wilma Lipp, Glade Peterson and Irene Dalis, directed by Tito Capobianco. Kriegsman found Capobianco's direction "obvious, but unpretentious and wholly effective." Thirteen years after Kriegsman's assessment of the man's work, Capobianco would be made artistic director of San Diego Opera.

Remarkable productions continued in 1962: *Don Giovanni* with memorable leading ladies Victoria de los Angeles, Schwarzkopf, and Jolanda Meneguzzer, plus Tozzi and Evans, Ludwig conducting; and *Il trovatore* with Elinor Ross, Sona Cervena, McCracken, Bastianini, John Macurdy, Molinari-Pradelli conducting. An alternately thrilling and hilarious *Falstaff* came in 1963 with Evans' incomparable impersonation of the fat knight, plus Mary Costa, Thomas Stewart, Janis Martin, and Janos Ferencsik conducting. The season was fleshed out by the aforementioned Resnik-Kirsten-McCracken *Queen of Spades*; and *The Valkyrie* with Vickers' matchless Siegmund, Otto Edelmann's imposing Wotan, Amy Shuard as Brünnhilde, Siv Ericsdotter as Sieglinde, and Ludwig conducting.

1964, the last SFO season at the Fox, saw Tito Gobbi's brilliant *Gianni Schicchi* on a double bill with *Carmina Burana* featuring the then very popular Mary Costa. Resnik, Lorengar, and Vickers were heard in *Carmen*. The year closed with McCracken's celebrated Otello, partnered by Lorengar as his long-suffering bride, Desdemona; Molinari-Pradelli conducted.

One of the profound ironies of our local cultural life is that the Fox Theatre, now glamorous and respectable in its expensively refurbished state, was reviled at the time as being inappropriate for so highbrow an undertaking as grand opera. During the days of the San Francisco Opera's visits, the Fox auditorium's acoustics were only marginally better than those of Russ. You could not make out any words, no matter what the language. Nor was the place ideally equipped for large stage shows – and who wanted to sit in seats stuck with chewing gum and redolent of rancid buttered popcorn?

The embarrassment of having to attend high art/high society functions in a lowly movie theater eventually resulted in a campaign to build a new civic auditorium. When the actual designs for such a building were finally unveiled in 1962, the seating capacity was calculated with the San Francisco Opera's visits in mind. There were, in fact, some objections to plans for such a capacious hall. "How far should three yearly performances of the San Francisco Opera dictate our needs?" queried *The San Diego Union's* critic, Kriegsman.

But the visionaries who dreamed and fought for our present Civic Theatre were numerous in the San Diego Opera Guild, as well as in the local press. Bruno Ussher, a *San Diego Union* music critic before Kriegsman, was vociferous on the subject for several years. Guild member Mrs. George Roy Stevenson summed up the issue, saying, "Only with the possession of appropriate and necessary facilities, now sadly lacking, will our citizens know the happy and beneficent experience of developing their cultural life as they deserve."

By the mid-'60s, Los Angelenos had finally built their long-dreamed-of Music Center. Its crowning jewel, the Dorothy Chandler Pavilion, turned out to be a theater with only half the seating capacity of Shrine Auditorium. Audiences were eager to frequent their more intimate temple to the arts and quickly lost all interest in going to the cavernous Shrine to take in any event more cultural than a three-ring circus. San Francisco Opera's management, however, much preferred the larger revenues of the huge conventioneers' venue. The Pavilion meant smaller crowds and dwindling profits, and soon the company threatened to stop coming to Los Angeles altogether. Since the SFO's San Diego visits had always been a mere side-junket stemming from the much larger Los Angeles season, our local opera season seemed doomed.

But the San Diego Opera Guild was prepared for this worst-case scenario. What the Guild had really wanted for some time was its own San Diego company in a brand new theater. When problems up north resulted in the San Francisco Opera's determination not to come to southern California anymore, the Guild took a deep breath and began to face the future on its own. In the spring of 1965, a spanking new San Diego Opera company presented its very own production of *La bohème*. A new era began and, in the fall, the great northern company that had kindled San Diego's passion for opera, paid our city one final, spectacular visit...

The Adams – Herbert Era (1965 to 1971)

Tickets started at $3.50 and rocketed upward to an outrageous top of $7.50, but they were nearly all gone the day after they went on sale in April 1965. The purchasers were in for a double treat, because the opening night of *La bohème* on May 6, San Diego Opera's very first opera production, would take place in the 2,945-seat Civic Theatre of the recently completed Charles M. Dail San Diego Community Concourse.

The interior of the theater at the time was a depressing battleship gray. Abstract bronze decorations looking like enormous melting ashtrays encircled the proscenium arch.** But these minor aesthetic blemishes hardly dashed the spirits of the glittering assembly. Here at long last was San Diego's very own Temple of Art, an auditorium especially designed for opera, theater and concert events. For the many dedicated citizens who had planned and raised funds for so long, it was a sweet victory, an achievement to savor. The city itself seemed finally to have "arrived." No longer condemned to walk the tacky platforms and foyers of a movie palace, muses and patrons alike could strut their stuff with heads held high.

This gala opening night boasted no one to equal soprano Dorothy Kirsten and tenor Jan Peerce, who had sung Mimì and Rodolfo during the 1952 *La bohème*, the glorious San Francisco Opera import that inaugurated operations of the San Diego Opera Guild. Indeed, none of the singers approached the stature of the numerous internationally famous stars to whom San Diegans had become so joyously accustomed during 14 years of visits by the august northern opera company.

Yet from the instant conductor Walter Herbert lunged into the exuberant opening chords of Puccini's beloved warhorse, the audience could tell this was not going to be just another amateur night in some hick town. The performance was surprisingly proficient, with soprano Maralin Niska and tenor Nicholas De Virgilio as the two bohemian lovers, and a locally bred luminary, soprano Margery MacKay, as Musetta. The Old Globe Theatre's popular and gifted designer, Peggy Kellner, had created extremely literal sets which delighted the audience and performers alike, while San Diego State

*** Note: Those decorations were never to be forgotten by any of us who ever attended a performance at the theatre during those years. It may be of interest to know that the "crumpled copper jello molds" (as my family dubbed them) were actually part of the acoustic engineering plan for the Civic Theatre. They were not the designer's first choice (nor second, nor third), but rather a committee decision – one clearly lacking in several aspects... The reason I know this: three years after the Civic Theatre opened, the sound engineer on the architectural design team, Junichi Tanida, joined a new architectural partnership. The junior partner, James Murry Hart, would later be my father-in-law.*   *–ML Hart*

College professor William Adams impressed with his inventive stage direction. Opening nighters pronounced the crowd scenes especially effective.

"No one really expected this to be the *Bohème* to end all *Bohème*s," said *San Diego Union* music critic Kriegsman, who did concede that the production was "uncommonly handsome and well integrated." Whatever its faults and strengths, however, this was the *Bohème* that began what would soon be recognized as one of the finest regional opera companies in America.

Just the year before this gala opening night, while the prestigious San Francisco Opera was offering what turned out to be its final season in the Fox Theatre, a committee for a San Diego Spring Opera had been formed, with Lowell Davies as production chairman. Plans were drawn up for a home-grown *La bohème* in May 1965, to be followed later in November by the regular three-opera season of SFO imports. In fall 1964, the San Diego Opera Guilders were still awaiting the completion of the Civic Theatre, where they hoped to stage San Diego Opera's first production. The 1964 fall program covers featured an architect's rendering of the new building.

Auditions for the chorus started in January '65. Soprano Lee Venora was engaged to sing Mimì, but she was released from her contract when the Los Angeles Civic Opera offered her $14,000 to sing in *The King and I*. Since Ms. Venora's San Diego salary was to have been a paltry $1,200, her defection may be easily understood. New York City Opera soprano Maralin Niska was signed on as Ms. Venora's replacement.

Plans for the new opera company also included some startlingly new aesthetic and economic philosophies. Musty conventions and elitist foreign languages were to be given the old heave-ho. "Opera in English" became the buzz phrase. "Outmoded operatic traditions which have cobwebbed realization of the composer's dramatic intentions" were to be discarded, according to a Guild brochure.

The Civic Theatre
San Diego, California

183

The reformers also wanted colorful productions, singers who could act as well as display well-trained voices – and all of this for low ticket prices the common man could afford.

Under the leadership of newly appointed artistic director, Walter Herbert, who had already helped establish opera companies in New Orleans and Houston, San Diego Opera hoped to develop "an ensemble style" buoyed by lavish amounts of extra rehearsal time. "Community opera," said Herbert in a *San Diego Union* interview at the time, "is opera originating in a community and being performed in that city for its citizens as opposed to a traveling company set up to play in several of many different cities."

Despite this refreshing new view, the Guild brought down the San Francisco Opera for one final fall season. The three farewell productions were star-studded extravaganzas, starting on November 10 with Puccini's Wild West show, *The Girl of the Golden West*, directed by Lotfi Mansouri, conducted by Francesco Molinari-Pradelli, and featuring the exciting singing actress Marie Collier as pistol-packing Minnie, and the sensational singing tenor hunk, Franco Corelli, as her outlaw boyfriend, Dick Johnson.

On November 17 came Wagner's *Lohengrin,* designed by Oliver Smith and conducted by Horst Stein, with famed Heldentenor Jess Thomas as the Grail Knight and soprano Hildegarde Hillebrecht as Elsa. Annamaria Bessel was the Ortrud, Chester Ludgin the Friedrich von Telramund. Then, on November 24, the glory years of SFO in San Diego came to a festive end with Johann Strauss Jr.'s *Die Fledermaus*, starring Mary Costa, Reri Grist, Brian Sullivan, Richard Lewis, Thomas Stewart, Andrew Foldi, and the inimitable Sona Cervena as a wonderfully world-weary Prince Orlofsky.

It was sad to see the San Francisco Opera go – forever – but the impressive success of San Diego Opera's *Bohème* left both the Guild and the community on a "high" which carried them into the uncertain future. In February 1966, the Guild did in fact bring the Metropolitan Opera National Touring Company to the Civic Theatre for a single performance of *Madama Butterfly*, but after that San Diego Opera focused entirely on creating its own productions.

In late spring 1966, San Diego Opera audiences enjoyed their first two-opera season: *Faust* (May 19 and 21) and *The Barber of Seville* (June 2 and 4). At first, *Faust* seemed doomed. Mallory Walker, who was to have sung the leading role, was taken ill and replaced by an unknown entity. The city's leading newspaper thought his name sufficiently obscure as to be unfit for a headline: "Mexican Tenor To Replace Ill Faust Here," mysteriously announced *The San Diego Union*. This ho-hum personage unworthy of introduction turned out to be none other than Plácido Domingo.

Who knew? Few people could have suspected they were about to hear one of the great voices of the century. But poor Plácido! Although he knew the title role in *Faust* backwards and forwards, he could only sing it in the original French, not the English required by the San Diego Opera's new reforms. Since English was being sung by all the other cast members, the future superstar was shown off to disadvantage. Periodically Domingo attempted to interpolate English phrases, but his heroic efforts proved somewhat ludicrous. In the aria "Salut demeure chaste et pure," he sang the first phrase in French, but submitted the second to a spontaneous English translation: "O hail you house so pure and love-lee." And so it went.

The biggest thrills that night came from the sensational vocalism and dramatic talents of Norman Treigle as Méphistophélès. Treigle was to return here many times and soon became San Diego's most beloved operatic visitor, second only to Beverly Sills. Others in the cast were Raymond Gibbs (Wagner), Dominic Cossa (Valentine), Carol Todd (Marguerite), and Mary MacKenzie (Martha). In unusual casting, tenor Melvin Brown was an actual male Siebel in place of the usual mezzo-soprano *rôle travesti.*

Stage director Adams emerged as a subject of controversy from the very start. During Marguerite's prayer scene, the unlucky heroine was menaced by semi-naked muscle men who appeared to be writhing through a sort of "Goblins A Go-Go" number. The pop-art finale represented Marguerite's apotheosis through blinking Las Vegas-style lights that swirled up from her body as if about to form the name of a hotel casino. Ten million stars emerged and a choir of angels floated on fluffy clouds.

The disputes over Adams' glitzy productions were to hound the director for years until, in December 1971, he quit in a huff just before a performance of *The Barber of Seville.* But Adams' first *Barber,* in fall 1966, was also spiced by the director's knack for comic gimmickry. A lively and colorful production, it featured a boisterous Richard Fredricks as Figaro and sweet-toned Anne Elgar as Rosina.

In the third season, 1966-1967, Adams and Herbert put San Diego on the operatic map, if there is such a thing. The United States premiere of Hans Werner Henze's *The Young Lord* rightly attracted the attention of all the nation's critics. Although the season had begun with a largely forgettable *Aida,* featuring the Met's utilitarian backup diva, Lucine Amara (and sung in Italian, apparently out of deference to her), *The Young Lord* was truly a coup for Adams and Herbert. San Diegans were privileged to hear a major new opera before it reached New York City.

The production, designed by Klein and Kellner, was a critical and public sensation. Audiences were surprised at the accessible nature of the score and delighted by the opera's biting satirical story concerning a rambunctious monkey groomed for a place in high society. The opera was also the beginning of San Diego Opera's reputation for attempting major productions of unusual operas.

The Young Lord was followed in May by a *Tosca* notable for the reappearance here of Domingo as Cavaradossi. This time Domingo had learned his part in English – a fact that belongs in every book of opera trivia! Audiences were more taken with the fabulous tenor this time around, and rumblings about his being the next Björling or Di Stefano began to be heard among the cognoscenti. Needless to say, talk about Domingo overshadowed the performances of Eileen Schauler as Tosca and Chester Ludgin as Scarpia.

Felicia Weathers was the degenerate demoiselle of Richard Strauss' *Salome* which opened the 1967-68 season. Local audiences, unfamiliar with Straussian dissonance and violence, liked the princess' fiery song and dance, but did not like having to attend a one-acter without an intermission suitable for socializing. The physical production was memorably hideous, full of garishly colored stalactites and stalagmites – or were they supposed to be melted candle drippings? No one knew.

However, Bizet's *Carmen* came next, with plenty of intermissions and loads of familiar tunes. But the gypsy chestnut arrived in what was, for the time, a truly unusual incarnation – the Opéra-Comique version with spoken dialogue – all English, of course. Shortly following this additional San Diego "first," the Metropolitan Opera followed suit, with the sensational Marilyn Horne in the title role. San Diego's cast was less memorable, though Maralin Niska was a notable Micaëla.

Described uncharitably by one member of the audience as a "Calgon Bath Oil commercial," a production of Mozart's *The Magic Flute* continued the 1967-68 season, with William Blankenship (Tamino), Rita Shane (The Queen of the Night), Thomas Palmer (Papageno), Heather Thomson (Pamina) and Thomas O'Leary (Sarastro). With its myriad marble walls and columns, the show seemed to be taking place in a giant bathroom.

The 1968-69 season opened with Peter Glossop in *Rigoletto*, continued with a Lee Venora-John Stewart *La bohème*, and concluded with a rarity, Massenet's *Don Quixote*, a production designed to show off Treigle, but which showcased instead bass-baritone Michael Devlin because of Treigle's unexpected cancellation. The operas that followed in the 1969-70 season were a double bill of *Pagliacci* and Carl Orff's *The Moon* (not as successful a pairing as one would have hoped); *Tannhäuser* with Janis Martin, Klara Barlow, John Reardon, and Richard Martell; and another *Faust* with Treigle, John Walker, Heather Thomson and Marvellee Cariaga.

And then there was the event of the season – the event of all seasons! On the cusp of her rise to superstardom, American soprano Beverly Sills arrived on the scene to play all four heroines in Offenbach's *The Tales of Hoffmann*. Treigle would portray the quadruple villains. It was the beginning of San Diego's love affair with Sills and a glorious moment for the Adams-Herbert regime. Certainly no one could foresee that less than a year remained before Adams would storm out the exit, never to return.

The End of an Era (1970 to 1975)

"It was an unfortunate thing," San Diego Opera artistic director Walter Herbert told *Opera News* in March 1973. "Dr. Adams is a brilliant man, and I like him very much. But he was famous for his gimmicks, and after the 1971 *The Barber of Seville* dress rehearsal, several board members asked him to tone things down. He refused, they insisted, and he resigned." A speech professor at San Diego State College, where he had been active in a program that produced children's opera at local schools, William J. Adams became a major mover and shaker in the foundation of San Diego Opera. He was the company's principal stage director for 17 out of the 20 productions before his departure. His glitzy show-biz style may have grown out of his experience directing outdoor musical comedies for the Starlight Opera in Balboa Park, and much of the success of the fledgling San Diego Opera must be attributed to the Adams' colorful crowd-pleasing style. Ironically, the same imaginative flamboyance led to his downfall.

Adams' resignation left Herbert temporarily in total artistic control. Often affectionately acknowledged as the "Father of San Diego Opera," Herbert was the company's orchestra conductor from day one. Born in Frankfurt in 1902, he developed an early interest in music, going on to study with Arnold Schönberg in Vienna. At the invitation of Margaret Ridout, Morley Golden's co-chairman of the Opera Guild's Survey Committee, Herbert came to San Diego from Louisiana, where he had helped found the New Orleans Opera. A dynamically talented man, Herbert was to guide the inexperienced San Diego orchestra through dozens of opera scores, both strange and familiar, with amazing assurance and polish.

Together, Herbert and Adams were the creative team responsible for the distinctive style of a vital new institution; yet a major artistic milestone in the company's history found Adams sitting on the sidelines. This was the 1969-70 season's *The Tales of Hoffmann,* which brought the sensational singing actress Beverly Sills to San Diego for the very first, but not the last, time. A tremendous critical and audience success, *Hoffmann* was directed by Bliss Hebert, a former general director of the Opera Society of Washington.

Hoffmann paired Sills with Norman Treigle, who played the four male heavies to her four heroines. Walter Herbert had discovered the great basso singing musical comedy in New Orleans. Treigle then went on to work at the New York City Opera, where he developed strong friendships with two of the leading artists there, stage director Tito Capobianco and Beverly Sills. Sills and Treigle appeared together in some of the NYCO's most celebrated productions, notably Handel's *Julius Caesar*, which catapulted Sills to international stardom. After that, Sills could have sung almost anywhere she wished; it was out of respect for Treigle and Herbert that she was prevailed upon to star in a regional opera production.

Despite the artistic triumph of *Hoffmann*, the 1970-71 season was a time of financial crisis. One of the San Diego Opera's principal contributors, the Combined Arts and Education Council (COMBO), was in a dry spell. At least $65,000 was needed for the season's opener, *La traviata,* but COMBO was so broke there was a serious doubt about San Diego Opera's future.

Fortunately, a group of ladies including Margaret Ridout, Becky Wilson and Madie Hall came riding to the rescue like triumphant Valkyries. They raised enough money for a season of two operas: *La traviata* with Mexican soprano Gilda Cruz-Romo and a lovely *Madama Butterfly* featuring African-American soprano Felicia Weathers, with sets and costumes by Ming Cho Lee, a designer whose beautiful but budget-conscious designs were familiar to NYCO audiences.

Though Weathers had not won many hearts with her 1967 impersonation of Salome, as the jilted geisha Cio-Cio San she captivated audiences with her sensitive singing and delicate characterization. As for tenor Chris Lachonas as her faithless husband Lieutenant Pinkerton, "better seen than heard" was one critical assessment. Herbert, as usual, conducted, but the talented assistant director of the Old Globe Theater, William Roesch, directed in place of Adams.

The two-opera season of 1970-71 was slim pickings indeed, but the 1971-72 season rallied with five – three full operas plus a double-bill of one-acters. The October opener was Puccini's *Turandot*, starring soprano Klara Barlow and tenor Richard Cassilly. "A tacky roadshow version of 'The Land of Smiles' set in a tarnished cardboard replica of Grauman's Chinese Theater," wrote *Los Angeles Times* music critic Martin Bernheimer. Adams' hand was apparent in the colorful and noisy crowd scenes.

By December, Adams' enemies were ready for the kill, yet opera-goers accustomed to today's anything-goes directorial approaches would be puzzled by the controversy that swirled around *The Barber of Seville*. The cast was more than competent – John Stewart (Figaro), Joy Clements (Rosina), Andrew Foldi (Dr. Bartolo) and Michael Devlin (Don Basilio), with Marvellee Cariaga, later an imposing Wagnerian for the company, as a memorably amusing Berta. But it was the staging that everyone talked about. Adams contrived at one point to have cannon fire cause the ceiling to fall down on the singers in a great cloud of dust. Audiences loved the children, policemen, musicians, townspeople and animals cavorting about the stage, but the fun and games offended some influential board members, and Adams' fate was sealed.

Once Adams was out of the picture, William Roesch rose instantly to the position of production coordinator and the 1971-72 season sailed along fairly smoothly. There was a truly memorable *Boris Godunov* with Treigle – although it was memorable chiefly for Treigle's performance rather than anything else. The rest of the casting was weak and the physical production disappointingly skimpy.

The season concluded in April with yet another Treigle star turn – *Gianni Schicchi*, conducted by Herbert and directed by Bliss Hebert, with Carolyn Lewis as Lauretta, sets by Davis West, and costumes recycled from some Old Globe Shakespeare productions. The Puccini masterpiece was part of a double bill with Menotti's *Help, Help the Globolinks!*, a work that apparently failed to inspire its producers. One critic attacked the diffuse, erratic staging and the poorly integrated electronic sound effects, and suggested that Menotti's opera, however weak, was probably better than its production.

Felicia Weathers returned to San Diego for *Aida*, the 1972-73 opener. The company's second go at this staple of the repertoire generated a great deal of audience and patron excitement, but it was soon eclipsed by Herbert's attempts to do something to grab the attention of the world. Herbert had commissioned Alva Henderson to compose an opera based on Euripides' *Medea* to fit the talents of the dramatic mezzo-soprano Irene Dalis, then at the peak of her powers.

International interest was focused on this new American opera based on a Greek tragedy. Dalis was convinced she was creating the title role of an American masterpiece, though to date Henderson's name seems to have eluded the operatic Pantheon. To get in the mood for her part, Dalis paid a call on Dame Judith Anderson, one of the great dramatic actresses to play *Medea* on the stage. Dalis' intense performance clearly reflected the depth of her emotional and intellectual commitment. However, Ms. Dalis fell ill after the opening performance, and Marvellee Cariaga took over the role for the following two performances. Gounod's setting of *Romeo and Juliet* followed in February, with Eileen Shelle and Raymond Gibbs as the star-crossed lovers.

A return visit from the now adored Beverly Sills concluded the season. As Marie in *The Daughter of the Regiment,* her natural comedic skills and brilliant coloratura assured rave reviews. Spiro Malas was Sulpice, and Grayson Hirst sang Tonio, Marie's ardent admirer. Directed by Lotfi Mansouri, this original production introduced wonderfully designed sets by Beni Montresor that were later used by the San Francisco Opera and many other companies.

The 1973-74 season began with Treigle's gratifyingly diabolic cavorting in Boito's *Mefistofele.* The basso proved he could not only sing but could also move like a dancer. This was followed by a pedestrian *Carmen* with Ann Howard. San Diego audiences savored Treigle yet again as the eponymous hero of Mozart's *The Marriage of Figaro*, with Johanna Meier superb as the Countess, and fine performances by Joy Clements (Susanna) and Susanne Marsee (Cherubino).

San Diego Opera's first brave foray into *Ring* territory was meant to show the company had at last really come of age. George London, formerly one of the greatest Wotans to bestride the clouds at Bayreuth, was employed to direct *The Rhinegold* in an English translation by Andrew Porter. The cast was more than respectable, including David Ward (Wotan), Marvellee Cariaga (Fricka), Howard Fried (Mime) and Andrew Foldi (Alberich). Though *The Rhinegold* contains two and a half hours of music, it is, in fact, a one-act opera – so the management thoughtfully (and controversially) inserted a whopping intermission to placate patrons unaccustomed to Wagnerian rigors. An anti-climatic *Tosca* starring Marisa Galvany closed out the season's activities.

Then came "La Stupenda" – Australian soprano Joan Sutherland. The international furor she stirred has no equal today. Everyone in San Diego was a-dither to hear her in *Lucia di Lammermoor*, conducted by her husband, Richard Bonynge. All the seats in the Civic Theatre were sold out a month in advance for this highlight of the 1974-75 season, and a fourth performance had to be added.

This *Lucia* was the event to end all events, even in Sills country. Sutherland was the biggest name ever to have appeared on a San Diego Opera roster. With Franco Tagliavini (Edgardo) and John Darrenkamp (Lord Enrico Ashton), the opera was sung in Italian – contrary to Herbert's policy of all operas in English.

There can be no question that the *Lucia* thoroughly overshadowed *Manon*, the 1974-75 season opener. The opera's namesake was the charming (and underrated) Catherine Malfitano, who would later sing this role in many major venues around the world, including the Metropolitan Opera and the Opéra-Comique in Paris. Raymond Gibbs was Chevalier des Grieux.

After the exhausting excitement of *Lucia*, the season somehow managed to go on with the sort of unusual fare that was helping to make the company famous – in this case Frank Corsaro's production of Delius' *A Village Romeo and Juliet*. Utilizing 400 slides and 4,000 feet of 16mm film projected on three separate scrims, the production was advertised as a multi-media event. The technical show, however, seemed to overwhelm the opera. *San Diego Union* critic Don Dierks found it "oozed gently without climax or incident." Patricia Wells was Vreli-Juliet, John Stewart sang Sali-Romeo, and David Holloway the Dark Fiddler.

San Diego Opera's second *Ring* installment, *The Valkyrie*, directed by Ghita Hager and featuring Johanna Meier (Sieglinde), Jon Andrew (Siegmund) and Anna Green (Brünnhilde), enjoyed a moderate success. The *La bohème* with Karan Armstrong and Raymond Gibbs that closed the season is remembered today mainly for the sad fact it marked Walter Herbert's final work for the company he helped to build. Herbert died in September – the second shattering death of 1975. Only 47 years old, the great Norman Treigle had died in New Orleans on February 18. It was truly the end of an era.

Herbert's death, however, had not been wholly unexpected. He had been suffering for several years from arterial problems as well as increasing deafness. For some performances, an extra conductor was stationed in the wings in case Herbert was unable to make it through the entire evening. With his retirement imminent, board officials had been searching for a new artistic director for some time. Tito Capobianco, the man they chose, was ready to become the San Diego Opera's new guiding light the day Herbert died.

Capobianco came from the New York City Opera to San Diego to be "in residence" for the 1975-76 season. Getting the acclaimed director and producer was widely regarded as something of a coup. Capobianco's work with the San Francisco, Berlin, Hamburg and Sydney, Australia, opera companies had earned him a reputation for innovation and excitement; however, the first full season planned entirely by the Opera's new general director did not occur until 1977-78. During the already scheduled 1975-76 season, Capobianco worked on his plans for the future.

1975-76 proved to be one of the most exciting seasons in the history of the young company. William Roesch directed an effective *Il trovatore* to kick off the season, and Capobianco's first work as stage director was seen in Dvořák's *Rusalka*, at that time a rarity, but today more and more frequently performed around the world. The opera was conducted by Theo Alcantara and featured Kathryn Bouleyn as the Water Nymph of the title, Spiro Malas as the Water Spirit, and Gwendolyn Killebrew as both Ježibaba and The Foreign Princess. Santo Loquasto designed abstract sets with luminous discs evoking the surface of a fairyland water world. Critics complained about the large cuts in the score.

The Dvořák work was followed by San Diego Opera's third *Ring* effort, *Siegfried*, featuring an underwhelming 65-piece orchestra conducted by Kenneth Schermerhorn. As in the case of *Rusalka,* Wagner's score was pruned of nearly 30 minutes of music. This editing invited the almost universal scorn of the press, as did the papier-maché rock-scapes of John Naccarsto. Tenor Alberto Remedios, however, immensely impressed critics as Siegfried. The cast included Marvellee Cariaga (Brünnhilde), Paul Brook (Mime) and Noel Tyl (Wotan).

It would be difficult to forget Johanna Meier's glorious Marschallin in Richard Strauss' *Der Rosenkavalier*, but the return of Beverly Sills tended to wipe out all other thoughts. "Here is the blood and bone, the fever and fire of grand opera and its grand passions – as religious vows are violated," was the lurid promise of a season subscription brochure describing Bellini's *Norma*, one of the main selling points of the 1975-76 season. It was San Diego Opera's first ever production of the *bel canto* masterpiece and what a cast! "La Sills" as the Druid priestess; mezzo-soprano Tatiana Troyanos as her bosom friend and rival in love, Adalgisa; and John Alexander as the fickle Roman warrior, Pollione. Superbly sung, the opera was further enhanced by polished orchestral playing under the leadership of conductor Sir Charles Mackerras.

Without question, Capobianco had arrived at a very good time. San Diego Opera had reached its artistic pinnacle. Now it only remained to see what Capobianco's magic touch could do to make things better.

The Capobianco Era (1976 to 1983)

In 1975 Tito Capobianco ended an eight-year association with New York City Opera to become Artistic Director of San Diego Opera. He was already one of the best known opera stage directors in the world. New York had seen 23 of his productions, both at the New York City Opera and at the Metropolitan. Before that he had impressed critics and audiences in Hamburg, Australia, San Francisco, Paris, and Berlin. A native of Argentina, he had begun his career with the Teatro Argentino in La Plata and the Teatro Colón.

When Capobianco arrived here, the board that hired him was expecting great things – world premieres, famous stars, brilliant productions. It got all these, plus much more than it had bargained for. Capobianco wanted to produce familiar repertory alongside obscurities nobody had ever heard of. Not only that, he wanted to put on an annual Verdi Festival during the summer months when the Old Globe Theatre was thought to be the only cultural activity capable of luring San Diegans off the beaches. Finally, Capobianco wanted to establish a San Diego Opera Center to train young singers and conductors.

In January of 1977, Capobianco was promoted from Artistic Director to General Director, replacing Kenneth K. Caswell. Capobianco's visionary schemes disturbed some board members, yet his talent and charismatic personality won many supporters. His aura of knowledge, his "European" demeanor and handsome Latin looks suggested a storybook impresario – Anton Walbrook, perhaps, in the classic film *The Red Shoes*. A smooth dresser, Capobianco was a walking fashion plate for clothes created by his versatile wife, designer/choreographer/assistant director Gigi Denda. He brought a sense of glamour and excitement to the job.

When Capobianco first arrived in San Diego, he was officially "in residence" for the 1976-77 season, but it was not until 1977-78 that audiences saw the first full season planned entirely by the new general director. This got off to a splashy start the only way it could in "Bubblesville" with San Diego's adored Beverly "Bubbles" Sills, this time as Hanna Glawari, the heroine of Lehár's operetta *The Merry Widow*, a production later televised nationally.

Since Capobianco was planning to do away with San Diego's official policy of performing all operas in English, more and more productions were performed in the original languages. *The Merry Widow* was in English, but the first season's *Carmen* was sung in French and *Madama Butterfly* in Italian, although *Don Giovanni* cropped up in English along with Rossini's *Cinderella* and Verdi's *Falstaff,* starring Spiro Malas as the fat knight. The surprise big hit of the season with audiences and critics alike was the rarity of Prokofiev's *The Love for Three Oranges*, a colorful English-language production conducted by Calvin Simmons.

The Verdi Festival began in August 1978 with a modestly titled "Prologue to a Festival," consisting of Verdi's *Requiem*, a Civic Theatre showing of the movie *Verdi's Life*, and a fully staged production of *Aida*, starring famed African-American soprano Martina Arroyo in her San Diego Opera debut. Tenor Carlo Bini was her heroic lover, Radames, and mezzo-soprano Carol Wyatt in her United States debut as her jealous rival, Amneris. Twenty-year-old soprano Aprile Millo, far in advance of her years of glory as one of the Met's reigning divas, was cast as the High Priestess.

Arroyo brought mature musical sensibility to her role, but Bini's contribution was much less polished; nevertheless, Capobianco continued to cast Bini in leading roles, year after year. The handsome Neapolitan tenor gradually became a divisive factor among opera fans, many of whom dreaded seeing his name in the season-ticket brochures.

Two of the most artistically significant events of Capobianco's regime occurred during the 1978-79 season: a revival of Ambroise Thomas' *Hamlet*, unseen in an American professional production since 1920; and the world premiere of *La Loca*, especially composed by Gian Carlo Menotti to suit the unique vocal and dramatic talents of Beverly Sills.

"An occasion for discovery and rare pride," was *Los Angeles Times* critic Martin Bernheimer's verdict on *Hamlet*. Audiences afforded the two stars enormous ovations: popular American baritone Sherrill Milnes for his glorious vocalism and dramatically intense characterization, and soprano Ashley Putnam for her superbly nuanced and accurate coloratura in Ophelia's mad scene. Andrew Porter's English translation here and there reconstructed Shakespeare's text from the deconstructed English of the Carré-Barbier libretto.

The composition of *La Loca* (later renamed *Juana La Loca*) was a cliffhanger in local newspaper headlines right up until the day of the premiere, June 2, 1979. A notorious procrastinator, Menotti was still writing music hours before the first performance. Eight copyists worked around the clock for several weeks, and Menotti himself was finally incarcerated in a local hotel room until he could complete Act Three. Miraculously, the opera went on and was a tremendous success, particularly for Sills, who thrilled audiences with her partially improvised mad scene. The rest of the season included *Rigoletto*, *Così fan tutte*, *Manon Lescaut* and everybody's favorite double feature, *Cavalleria Rusticana* and *Pagliacci*.

Fans were delighted when they received their season brochures announcing the second Verdi Festival season of 1979. Internationally acclaimed tenor Carlo Bergonzi was scheduled for two events: a Verdi concert with New York City Opera regular soprano Diana Soviero, and a leading role in Verdi's epic *I Lombardi alla prima Crociata,* unheard and unheard-of in those dark days long before the Met's 1992 revival. The 11-scene extravaganza also brought to town two more famed singers – Dutch soprano Cristina Deutekom and bass Paul Plishka. An enormous critical success, *I Lombardi* was followed by *La traviata,* with *Hollywood Squares* comedian Charles Nelson Reilly as director, and Soviero as a polished though not deeply moving Violetta.

Sills had always been first in the hearts of San Diego Opera audiences, but suddenly along came the great Luciano Pavarotti to sing with Soviero in *La bohème.* All the 1979-80 season tickets were sold on the basis of the tenor's irresistible allure. The old 1975 production looked tired and worse for wear, but the opera was a triumph with press and patrons.

Pavarotti may have been the major marketing ploy, but the season leading up to his *La bohème* could stand very well on its own. It had begun with an impressively cast Verdi *Don Carlo* with Luis Lima (in his San Diego debut as Carlo), Anne Evans, Paul Plishka, and Juan Pons. Mozart's *The Abduction from the Seraglio,* with Benita Valente as Constanze and Gianna Rolandi as Blondchen, enjoyed Nathaniel Merrill's outstanding stage direction. An English-language production of *The Tales of Hoffmann* had Barry McCauley as Hoffmann, Michael Devlin as the four villains, and Ashley Putnam as the four ladies. Boito's *Mefistofele,* first performed with Norman Treigle in 1973, came around with Robert Hale in the title role. In May, Sills earned her usual round of *bravas* in a sprightly *Don Pasquale* with Giorgio Tozzi, Richard Fredricks, Rico Serbo and Melvin Lowery.

If the third Verdi Festival of 1980 had any faults, they belonged to the composer's librettist for *Giovanna d'Arco*, Temistocle Solera. His Joan of Arc does not seem at all like the familiar figure of legend. She charges into battle like an Amazon and then dies from her wounds rather than in the fires of martyrdom. However, soprano Adriana Maliponte successfully turned *Giovanna* into a recognizable human being. Then conductor Calvin Simmons whipped melodramatic fire into *Il trovatore*, while Martina Arroyo brought expressive dignity to the role of Leonora.

Today we regularly enjoy the spectacle of the world's three most famous tenors acting like the greatest of pals, but the idea that all great opera stars must by nature be savage rivals still enjoyed currency back in 1980. But when Joan Sutherland and Beverly Sills sang together on the same stage in *Die Fledermaus* during the 1980-81 season, a few fans may have been disappointed to discover the great American and Australian divas got along famously. The event itself, however, was more exciting than the actual singing. The part of Adele was Sills' farewell to opera at age 51. As Rosalinda, Sutherland was in noticeably better voice than her supposed rival. Alas, some premeditated swapping of the parts of Rosalinda and Adele failed to materialize.

The 1980-81 season had opened with Richard Strauss' *Elektra* in English, directed by Regina Resnik and featuring a truly high-voltage performance by soprano Pauline Tinsley in the leading role. The season was rounded out with *Werther* with John Brecknock, Katherine Ciesinski, and Pamela Hicks; *Tosca* with Arroyo, Bini, and Richard Fredricks; *Lucia di Lammermoor* with Gianna Rolandi, Barry McCauley and John Bröcheler; and a revival of the successful *The Love for Three Oranges*, once again conducted by Simmons.

"Verdi The Beginner" could have been the title of the 1981 summer festival. Audiences got two exotic rarities penned when the composer was still a young man – *Nabucco* and *Un Giorno di Regno*, his only comic work other than his mature masterpiece *Falstaff*. In *Un Giorno*, Simmons' conducting and Capobianco's direction combined to bring the piece an irresistible effervescence. Andrew Porter provided the English translation for this story of a Polish king who eludes his enemies by allowing someone else to assume the regal identity. In *Nabucco*, Deutekom assayed Abigaille's dramatically angular arias and baritone Kari Nurmela was the Babylonian king. This Festival was also notable for a misguided attempt at performing Verdi's heavyweight *Requiem* outdoors on a golf course in Rancho Bernardo.

The first novelty of 1981-82 was Carlisle Floyd's masterful and moving *Susannah*, directed by the composer and conducted by Christopher Keene. Patricia Craig was the unjustly persecuted title heroine, and up-and-coming basso Samuel Ramey was her persecutor, the hypocritical Rev. Olin Blitch. The second novelty was Riccardo Zandonai's steamy piece of decadent *verismo*, *Giulietta e Romeo*, starring Cassolla in her United States debut and the ubiquitous Bini. The season included *Andrea Chénier* with Cassolla, Bini, Justus; *Faust* with Pamela Meyers, Susanne Lodato, John Brecknock, J. Patrick Raftery, Robert Hale; *The Barber of Seville* with RoseMarie Freni, Bruce Reed, Raftery, Paul Plishka; and *Turandot* with Deutekom as the icy princess and the inevitable Bini her determined suitor.

Several outstanding sopranos were "discovered" during the 1982 Fifth Annual Verdi Festival: June Anderson, Rosalind Plowright and Josephine Barstow. *Il corsaro*, based on Lord Byron's sensational 19th-century rhymed romance *The Corsair*, featured some glorious singing in a lackluster production. Plowright, fresh from her success in the English National Opera's *Mary Stuart*, glowed as the hero's lover, Medora. June Anderson as Gulnara, the impressionable harem girl, revealed the magnificent voice that would eventually become in demand throughout the world's leading opera houses. Barstow proved herself a formidable singing actress as Amelia in a visually stunning *A Masked Ball,* with innovative touches such as a ghostly materialization of the fortuneteller Ulrica in the last act. A "Verdi Jubilee" completed the Festival with Shirley Verrett joining Anderson and Plowright and others in a program of arias.

Sutherland and Milnes were the big drawing cards for the 1982-83 season. The rarity this time was Chabrier's *Gwendoline* in French with Plowright again, and Raftery as Aral, Leader of the Danes. The production had striking sets and costumes by Beni Montresor, and – memorably – dozens of wigs that made everyone redheaded. There was also *Madama Butterfly* with Arroyo, and *La Périchole* in English, with Leigh Munro.

No one who saw Milnes in Saint-Saens' *Henry VIII* will ever forget the way the baritone limped about the stage feigning the monarch's celebrated case of gout. Because of a throat infection, however, Milnes was unable to complete the run and his part was taken over by baritone William Justus. Brenda Boozer was Anne Boleyn, Deutekom was Catherine of Aragon. *Aida* starred Gilda Cruz-Romo, Rachel

Gettler in her United States debut and Adriaan van Limpt; and Sutherland won more fans with her portrayal of the tragic actress in Cilea's *Adriana Lecouvreur* conducted by Bonynge.

During the years he remained in San Diego, Capobianco saw most of his grand projects realized. In 1977 he inaugurated his training program for singers at the San Diego Opera Center. Over a three-year period the program attracted distinguished instructors including Licia Albanese, Sherrill Milnes, Louis Quilico, Beverly Sills, Burt Lancaster, and Lee Strasberg. In the summer of 1978, Capobianco kicked off the Verdi Festival, and, in the 1980-81 season, he announced the creation of a Young American Conductors Program.

Unfortunately, not one of Capobianco's brilliant brain children was fated to survive. An expensive extra burden on subscribers to the regular season, the Verdi Festival was poorly attended; a former board president refused to buy tickets to it. The Festival had already started running into financial problems during its second season, and, when board members finally took a really close look at the books, they felt they had to cancel the 1983 festival season (the fourth). Devastated by this challenge to his authority, Capobianco accepted an offer as General Director of the Pittsburgh Opera, and left town. He called the Verdi Festival his "legacy to San Diego," yet it did not long outlive his departure – nor did the San Diego Opera Center.

Capobianco's defection caused the San Diego Opera to lose some of its strongest supporters; nevertheless, Board President Mrs. Frank T. Weston managed to write to Capobianco, "Your performance has raised our company from a regional/national entity to international stature."

On July 14, 1983, after a search committee reviewed the dossiers of 55 applicants, 37-year-old Australian emigrant Ian Campbell was selected as the San Diego Opera's new General Director.

The Campbell Era (1983 to present)

Opera lovers worldwide want to know: "Who's singing in San Diego this year?" They know that San Diego is a magnet for today's freshest and best singers. Ever since Ian Campbell assumed the general directorship of the company in 1983, San Diego Opera has been a showcase for marvelous new talent. Of course, there are still those curmudgeons who refuse to buy tickets unless there's a mega-star tenor or soprano in the cast – but when the book is fully written on The Campbell Era, his hiring of important new artists will be remembered as one of the finest achievements of his administration. Campbell's success as a vocal talent scout may have something to do with the fact that he himself is a singer. After he received his BA degree from the University of Sydney, he contemplated a law career, but the world of opera got him instead. He started out in the chorus of the Australian Opera, and, in 1967, became a principal tenor specializing in character roles. At the end of his seventh season with the company, he decided to shift into management. He served for two years as Senior Music Officer for the Australia Council, and in 1976 he was appointed General Manager of the State Opera of South Australia at Adelaide. When New York's Metropolitan Opera beckoned in 1982, Campbell emigrated from his homeland to become Assistant Artistic Administrator of America's leading opera company.

Campbell was familiar with our city before he arrived here in 1983 to take over as General Director of San Diego Opera. Campbell had visited San Diego on a 1980 tour of American opera companies, and in 1981 he appeared as a guest lecturer at the Opera Center. When Capobianco's sudden defection to Pittsburgh left the Opera's directorship open, Campbell practically assessed his opportunities for significant advancement at the Met and decided to apply for the San Diego job. A special search committee hired Campbell after conducting personal interviews with seven of 55 applicants.

The new General Director arrived here under difficult circumstances. He had to deal with two full seasons of opera and a Verdi Festival already committed and planned without the necessary financial underpinning. Even though the San Diego Opera was not experiencing a deficit at the time, Campbell could see serious financial problems were imminent. Unfortunately, many board members, who had been great admirers of Capobianco and had not wanted him to leave, were reluctant to believe the warning signs. For a fee of $30,000, the board hired The Shaver Company, a group of financial consultants, to work with Campbell on the budgets.

The deficit predicted by Campbell occurred two years later – about $750,000 on a budget of about $3 million. By then the company had already begun to undergo some radical restructuring. In the 1985-86 season, Campbell reduced the number of mainstage opera productions from the six of the previous season to four, and compensated for this move artistically by instituting a new recital program and by producing a chamber opera (Peter Maxwell Davies' *The Lighthouse*) at the Old Globe Theatre.

Before Campbell could realize his own artistic schemes, however, he had to steer 14 of Capobianco's projects to completion, sometimes taking the praise, sometimes the blame. Unfortunately for Campbell, the 1983-84 season was one of superstar cancellations. Handsome rock-star-turned-Heldentenor Peter Hofmann canceled *Lohengrin* and got married; the opera went on with William Neill in the title role. Then baritone Sherrill Milnes canceled a revival of Capobianco's production of Ambroise Thomas' *Hamlet*; Justus took over as the Danish prince, with Gianna Rolandi his Ophelia. And finally, mezzo-soprano Teresa Berganza failed to materialize for *Carmen*; Rachel Gettler, Campbell's wife at the time, played the tempestuous gypsy heroine, under the terms of a former contract with Capobianco.

Despite these disappointments, the season turned out fairly well. There was a lively *Cinderella* with Ann Murray and John Aler, followed by *Anna Bolena* with Katia Ricciarelli (a bit droopy as Anna), and a solidly cast *Don Giovanni* in English with Michael Devlin (Don Giovanni), Stuart Burrows (Ottavio), Faye Robinson (Donna Anna), Marianna Christos (Elvira) and Melanie Sonnenberg (Zerlina), conducted by Christopher Keene.

Campbell had been with the company almost a year when the sixth and final Verdi Festival rolled around in June and July of 1984 with *I Masnadieri* starring Joan Sutherland, and *Simon Boccanegra* with Martina Arroyo, Nicola Ghiuselev and Milnes. Despite the presence of these big stars, attendance was very poor – only 68 percent of six performances were sold – at a time when Milnes was getting almost $18,000 per night, and Sutherland and her husband, Maestro Richard Bonynge, $35,000. Still, Campbell worked hard to promote the performances and later could claim the ticket sales were a record high for the Festival.

The 1984-85 season began with a tautly dramatic *Peter Grimes* (with Richard Cassilly), and continued with *La traviata* with soprano Rosalind Plowright, replaced at one matinee performance by Rosario Andrade. The audience's enjoyment of the opera was enhanced by a recent innovation that would gradually become a regular feature of San Diego productions – supertitles that projected the opera's text above the proscenium. Other operas produced were *Hansel and Gretel, The Merry Widow, La bohème* (with Hei-Kyung Hong), and, as a farewell tribute to the defunct Verdi Festival, the composer's very first opera, *Oberto.* Campbell wanted to cancel it, but it had been contracted too far in advance.

Campbell's first season (1985-86) began with a triumph, a brilliantly cast production of Offenbach's *The Tales of Hoffmann,* with the multiple heroines and villains sung by Nelly Miricioiu and James Morris (both near the beginning of their careers), Luis Lima as Hoffmann, and Judith Forst as a memorable Muse/Nicklausse – a part larger than usual thanks to the wonderful Fritz Oeser edition Campbell chose for this production. A pleasant English-language *Eugene Onegin* directed by Covent Garden's John Copley was followed by the same director's very well staged and intelligent *The Marriage of Figaro.* Lotfi Mansouri directed and Michelangelo Veltri conducted Verdi's *Otello* with Giuseppe Giacomini (replaced by Richard Cassilly on February 14, 1986) and Ilona Tokody (Desdemona) and Silvano Carroli (Iago).

Campbell's first attempt at chamber opera at the Old Globe Theatre was a tremendous artistic success, one of the most original opera productions ever staged here. Set in Edinburgh and the Outer Hebrides in 1900, *The Lighthouse* tells the story of the mysterious disappearance of three lighthouse keepers, sung in this production by Michael Ballam, Harlan Foss and James Butler. Memorable for its interesting lighting effects, the production was directed by the Old Globe's Jack O'Brien. Opera Center graduate Karen Keltner conducted.

Unfortunately, chamber operas at the Old Globe did not bring the box office success Campbell had hoped for. After a second try in the 1986-87 season – Gian Carlo Menotti's two masterful one-act operas, *The Telephone* and *The Medium* – Campbell regretfully rescinded his scheme. Although superbly directed by the composer himself and skillfully conducted by Keltner, the double bill did not stimulate tremendous interest in chamber opera. As Madame Flora in *The Medium,* mezzo-soprano Beverly Evans gave a riveting performance. Nadia Pelle was Monica, and the composer's son, Francis Menotti, appeared in the mute role of Toby. Amy Burton and Wayne Turnage did charming work as Lucy and Ben in *The Telephone.*

Campbell's recital program, one of the most significant additions the general director has made to the yearly opera schedule, was launched in the 1985-86 season with a program of songs by soprano Renata Scotto at the Old Globe. Campbell reasoned that the high fees of big-name stars gave the Opera two choices: either go without hearing the stars at all, or bring them here for a single recital, usually with piano. Stars coming on this economical and often highly artistically satisfying plan have included Sutherland (with orchestra); Siegfried Jerusalem; Kiri Te Kanawa; Carol Vaness; Tatiana Troyanos; Håkan Hagegård; Robert White (in "Homage to John McCormack"); Marilyn Horne; Carol Neblett with Thomas Pasatieri; Hans Peter Blochwitz singing Schubert's song cycle *Die schöne Müllerin;* Dmitri Hvorostovsky in his West Coast recital debut; Hermann Prey singing Schubert's *Winterreise;* Delores Ziegler; baritone Thomas Hampson and tenor Jerry Hadley in a highly enjoyable duet recital; the delightful Italian mezzo-soprano Cecilia Bartoli; and the young American mezzo Vivica Genaux. In addition, there have been the big revenue concerts, encompassing each of "The Three Tenors" – the Luciano Pavarotti show at the Sports Arena (1992), José Carreras at the Civic Theatre (1993) and Plácido Domingo at the Civic Theatre (1997).

Shortly after his arrival here, Campbell also began restructuring the Opera's educational activities. He decided to dissolve the Opera Center and its programs for the training of singers and conductors and to refocus attention on educational outreach programs. (Philanthropist Muriel Gluck has donated more than $2 million since 1994 to further develop these programs.) Because San Diego City schools are no longer offering any exposure to classical music, Campbell feels reaching local students is absolutely critical if there are to be any audiences for opera in the future.

But winning over young people was not the only problem Campbell had to face since his arrival here. Adults, it seems, also need wooing. Campbell found he had to rebuild the support of an audience that had been dropping off after the retirement of Beverly Sills. People would go to hear Sills or some other famous singer, but would not show much interest in the opera company as a whole. Nevertheless, Campbell felt he had to banish the star system if the company were to survive economically. For one thing, the star system has a built-in absurdity: The average Southern California ticket buyer only recognizes a handful of names – Pavarotti, Domingo, Sutherland, Norman – but the names of other international stars, like Freni, Marton or Gedda, draw blank stares.

As Campbell phased out the star system, his choice of repertory became significantly more conservative: *Tosca, Norma, The Flying Dutchman, The Barber of Seville* and so on. However, Campbell also scheduled operas that had not been done here before – *Eugene Onegin, The Elixir of Love, Fidelio, Dialogues of the Carmelites, The Passion of Jonathan Wade, Macbeth*. The idea was to keep the audience coming, while at the same time broadening tastes.

Meanwhile Campbell's genius as a talent scout produced an impressive list of "discoveries:" sopranos Hei-Kyung Hong, Susan Dunn, Deborah Riedel, Nelly Miricioiu, Susan Graham, Renée Fleming, Marilyn Zschau, Nova Thomas, Sabine Hass, Ilona Tokody, Barbara Bonney, Sylvia Wen, Michèle Crider; mezzo-sopranos Delores Ziegler, Susanne Mentzer, Judith Forst, Dolora Zajic, Stefania Kaluza; tenors Antonio Barasorda, Hans Peter Blochwitz, Gregory Kunde, Vladimir Popov, Gary Lakes, Luis Lima, Ramón Vargas, Fernando de la Mora, Richard Leech, Jonathan Welch, César Hernández, Siegfried Jerusalem; baritones and bass-baritones Roger Roloff, James Morris, Michael Devlin, Jeffrey Wells, Jeffrey Black, Silvano Carroli, Ferruccio Furlanetto, Haijing Fu, David Malis and Louis Otey.

Each opera season under Campbell has had its distinct highlights. In the 1986-87 season, it was a new production of Wagner's *The Flying Dutchman,* directed by Bernd Benthaak and conducted by Matthias Kuntzsch and starring Roloff (Dutchman), Hass (Senta) and Jerusalem (Erik). A well-cast *Norma* with Cristina Deutekom (Norma), Ziegler (Adalgisa) and Barasorda (Pollione) had the misfortune of being the same physical production that had featured the potent pairing of Sills and Troyanos back in 1976 – a fact that invited odious comparisons. Hermann Prey, somewhat past his prime, appeared in a fine *Barber of Seville* with a brilliant, though very well traveled, three-story set. An excellent *Porgy and Bess,* directed by Jack O'Brien, was a welcome revival of the 1976 Houston Grand Opera production.

1987-88 brought a wonderfully intense *Faust* with great performances from Leech (Faust), Soviero (Marguerite), and Furlanetto (Méphistophélès), directed by Francesca Zambello. The 1989 season's Banana Republic-ish, postmodern *Fidelio* from Houston Grand Opera offended many patrons with its updated political statement, but it was still musically and visually memorable with Hass (Leonore), Arthur Korn (Rocco), and Tom Fox (Pizarro). And Leech thrilled his swelling fan club as Edgardo in *Lucia di Lammermoor*, with Gail Dobish as Lucia.

The 1989-90 season came in October with *Boris Godunov* as part of the city's Russian Festival with Alexander Morozov an imposing Boris; but by far the greatest artistic success was Poulenc's deeply moving *Dialogues of the Carmelites* with Maureen Forrester (Mme. de Crissy), Nova Thomas (Blanche), Cheryl Perrish (Sister Constance), Heather Begg (Mother Marie), and Carol Neblett (Madame Lidoine), conducted by Bonynge, directed by Hebert, and featuring sets by Günther Schneider-Siemssen. *La bohème* successfully returned in January of 1990 with Tokody and Dennis O'Neill. And "The Great Richard Wagner Concert" offered thrilling performances by Johanna Meier (Sieglinde), Lakes (Siegmund) and John Macurdy (Hunding), with Heinz Fricke conducting the San Diego Opera Orchestra.

The 1991 opener, *Così fan tutte,* was a delight, with Vaness (Fiordiligi), Forst (Dorabella), Bonney (Despina), Keith Lewis (Ferrando), Hågegard (Guglielmo), and Peter Strummer (Don Alfonso). A superb but underrated production of Benjamin Britten's *Albert Herring* starred Barton Green (Albert) and Susan Graham (Nancy). The premiere of Carlisle Floyd's *The Passion of Jonathan Wade* came along in April. Overwrought and lacking the concision of his masterpiece, *Susannah, Wade* is nonetheless a significant reworking of an opera by a major American composer.

A wonderful *Der Rosenkavalier* with cut-out sets by Allen Charles Klein was a highlight of 1992, with Putnam, Mentzer, and Barbara Kilduff. Campbell courageously brought San Diego another Britten work, *The Rape of Lucretia,* with Robert Tear (Chorus), Rita Cullis (Female Chorus), Otey (Tarquinius), and Melanie Sonnenberg (Lucretia), conducted by Keene. 1993 was notable for *The Barber of Seville* with Magritte-like sets and first Black and then Malis as beefcake Figaros, with Ziegler (Rosina), François Loup (Bartolo) and Kevin Langan (Basilio).

Wonderful singing distinguished *Don Giovanni* with Furlanetto (Don Giovanni), Dean Peterson (Leporello), Rita Cullis (Anna), Patricia Schuman (Elvira), Emily Manhart (Zerlina), and Blochwitz (Ottavio) conducted by Edoardo Müller. And Leech melted hearts in *Werther* with Jean Rigby and Jeanine Thames, Bonynge conducting.

The 1994 season brought an astonishingly high standard of vocalism evenly distributed across the repertory: *Eugene Onegin* with Renée Fleming, Black, Blochwitz; *Rigoletto* with Fu, Sheryl Woods, de la Mora; *Rappaccini's Daughter* (a striking production!) with de la Mora, Encarnación Vázquez; *La sonnambula* with Riedel, Vargas, Wen, and Julien Robbins; and finally *The Tales of Hoffmann* with Jerry Hadley and Louis Otey.

The 1995 30th Anniversary Season began with a beautiful production of *Rusalka* featuring Fleming in fabulous voice, the San Diego debut of Neil Rosenshein as The Prince, and the basso tones of Mark Doss as an appropriately lugubrious Water Spirit. *Lucia di Lammermoor,* although a physically uninteresting production, was saved by the incomparable sound of Vargas, whose confidence and stage presence had increased dramatically since his 1994 debut here. Haijing Fu returned as Enrico, and Martile Rowland made her debut in the title role.

The national touring production of Houston Grand Opera's revival of *Porgy and Bess,* with San Diego Opera as a co-producer, swept through the Civic Theatre next, leaving audiences with the impression of a fabulous set, exciting music and gorgeous voices – unfortunately, the words were often unintelligible due to the amplification (required by Houston) and the lack of supertitles. Verdi's

Macbeth followed with a stunning new production designed by Davis West, with impressive Timothy Noble making his debut in the title role and the return of Plowright as his Lady.

The highlight of the season was surely *La bohème.* However used to this opera San Diego audiences think they are, this production directed by a young woman, Lesley Koenig, a former Metropolitan Opera resident director, was fresh, honest and touching in its simple desire to communicate Puccini's characterizations without obfuscation. Koenig also had a brilliant young cast to work with – Leech, in his fourth San Diego Opera appearance, as Rodolfo, the debut of Patricia Racette as Mimì, the remarkable Mark Oswald debuting as Marcello, and Rosemary Musoleno as a vivacious, but not vulgar, Musetta. In the often-overlooked roles of Schaunard and Colline were Jeff Mattsey and Yanni Yannissis, whose humor and sensitivity shone. It was no suprise that all five performances sold out before opening night, or that audiences shot to their feet for standing ovations after each curtain (most with tears in their eyes following Leech's impassioned final cry).

The 1996 season began in September with a beautiful and original recital of French and Italian songs by one of the newest superstars in the opera firmament, Italian mezzo-soprano Cecilia Bartoli. Anyone who had previously suspected her voice is too small to be heard in a large auditorium was quickly disabused of that widely circulated myth. The audience was entranced by her sharply articulated runs, sumptuous tone and ebullient personality.

In January's *Tosca,* soprano Nelly Miricioiu and bass-baritone James Morris brought dramatic intensity to the adversarial relationship of the opera's eponymous heroine and the evil Baron Scarpia, with conductor Edoardo Müller giving a taut reading of Puccini's popular score. Donizetti's *The Elixir of Love* in February was supported by the solid vocalism of the principals: Deborah Riedel, Sylvia Wen, Patrick Power, David Malis and Andrew Shore in his United States debut, although the comedy never really caught fire. Much more successful was Rossini's *Cinderella,* energized by superb ensemble playing and a charming central performance by mezzo-soprano Margaret Lattimore, stepping in at the last moment to replace an ailing Manhua Zhan.

The brightest highlights of the season, however, were the revival of Carlisle Floyd's *The Passion of Jonathan Wade* in March and the United States debut of African-American soprano Michèle Crider in Verdi's *Aida* in April. Though Stefania Kaluza's Amneris (also a U.S. debut) was probably the strongest performance in a variable cast that included Lando Bartolini, Mark Rucker and Andrew Wentzel, it was Crider's performance as the Ethiopian slave girl that attracted the most attention. She revealed a promisingly powerful, possibly major-league voice, but her wide vibrato and sometimes tentative high notes were cause for concern.

The 1996-97 season presented tenor Richard Leech in an earnest and not altogether unpleasant first try at Don José in Bizet's *Carmen.* The fiery gypsy lady here was Adria Firestone, raw of voice but with all the right moves and plenty of stage charisma. Rossini's *The Italian Girl in Algiers* showcased mezzo-soprano Vivica Genaux, looking like a *Vogue* model and tossing off fancy coloratura as if it were as easy as you please. Zack Brown's clever sets and costumes combined with Leon Major's imaginative direction to create some memorable stage pictures incorporating some unusual props. In one scene, for example, everyone rode bicycles.

The world premiere of Myron Fink's *The Conquistador* in March was San Diego Opera's most important undertaking of the year, with tenor Jerry Hadley surpassing himself in his creation of the title role. The ambitious work, commissioned by San Diego Opera, proved to have a surprising, almost unexpected theme of religious persecution and anti-Semitism. Campbell assured the piece received sterling vocal and dramatic treatment. The singers included Elizabeth Hynes, Kerry O'Brien, Genaux, Firestone, Beau Palmer, John Duykers and Louis Otey. This exciting event, however, was followed by a somewhat routine *La traviata*, despite the generally commendable participation of Riedel as Violetta, Jorge Lopez-Yañez as Alfredo and Richard Zeller as Germont.

The season ended with such an impressively world-class production that it almost obliterated memories of everything that came before. Drenched in great washes of vibrant color, the sets for this production of Puccini's *Turandot* were created by internationally renowned painter/set designer David Hockney, and the singers under the deft direction of San Francisco Opera's general director, Lotfi Mansouri, were top notch – every single one of them. Soprano Jane Eaglen was sensational as the "ice princess" of the opera's title. She found herself in superb company: tenor Richard Margison as Calaf, soprano Ai-Lan Zhu as Liù, Stephen Powell, Beau Palmer and Joseph Hu as Ping, Pang and Pong, and Kevin Langan as Timur.

At press time, upcoming seasons promised more great vocal performances from returning favorites such as Leech, Genaux, de la Mora, Hadley, Racette, Furlanetto, Gilfry and exciting newcomers like Kristine Ciesinski, Robert Hayward, Alan Woodrow, Rosemary Joshua, Emily Magee, Peter Seiffert, Eva Johansson, Ruxandra Donose and Sondra Radvanovsky.

San Diego is a singer's place and will remain so as long as Campbell has his way. Each voice that exists is unique and challenges our prejudices and preconceptions. We all need to learn to listen. In San Diego, we are listening to the future of opera.

Music Critic for San Diego Magazine, *David Gregson is a freelance writer on classical music, whose work has been widely published in various national publications.*

San Diego Opera Chronology
1965 - 1997
PERFORMANCES

* United States debut   *m = matinee performance*   *(numbers in parentheses indicate the dates on which substitute artists performed)*

1965

La Bohème   Giacomo Puccini
May 5m, 6, 7, 8, 1965
Maralin Niska (Mimì), Margery Mackay (Musetta), Nicholas Di Virgilio/John Craig (7) (Rodolfo), Neil Gilbert Oehl (Parpignol), Benjamin Rayson (Marcello), William Beck (Schaunard), Harold Enns (Colline), Charles Gonzales (Benoit), John Powell (Alcindoro), Raymond Gibbs (customs guard); Walter Herbert, conductor; William Adams, director; Peggy Kellner, designer

1966

Faust   Charles Gounod
May 19, 21, 1966
Carol Todd (Marguerite), Melvin Brown (Siébel), Mary MacKenzie (Marthe), Plácido Domingo (Faust), Dominic Cossa (Valentin), Raymond Gibbs (Wagner), Norman Treigle (Méphistophélès); Walter Herbert, conductor; William Adams, director; Larry Kane, sets

The Barber of Seville   Gioachino Rossini
June 2, 4, 1966
Patricia Velsir (Berta), Anne Elgar (Rosina), Gene Bullard (Almaviva), Richard Fredricks (Figaro), Richard Wentworth (Bartolo), John A. Ford (Basilio), Raymond Gibbs (Fiorello), Morgan Lane (Ambrogio), George Endsley (officer), R. Lee Owens (notary); Walter Herbert, conductor; William Adams, director; Jack McCullagh, sets

1966-67

Aida   Giuseppe Verdi
November 3, 5, 1966
Lucine Amara (Aida), Jean Stone (high priestess), Irene Kramarich (Amneris), Giovanni Gibin (Radames), Joshua Hecht (Amonasro), John A. Ford (Ramfis), Edward Baird (King), Leonard Johnson (messenger); Walter Herbert, conductor; William Adams, director; Mario Cristini, sets

The Young Lord   Hans Werner Henze
February 17, 18, 1967
United States Premiere
Norma Lynn (Luise), Louise Parker (Begonia), Claramae Turner (Baroness Greenweasel), Gwen Curatilo (Mrs. Harethrasher), Margot Blum (Mrs. Hoofnail), Carol Toscano (Ida), Lizanne Wilson (parlormaid), Glenn Cole (Lord Barrat), Kenneth Riegel (Wilhelm), Ken Remo (Amintore), John Ellsworth (Sir Edgar), Richard Fredricks (secretary), Gimi Beni (Burgomaster), Orville White (Harethrasher), Lloyd Hanna (Sharp), Howard Fried (von Mucker), Louis MacKay (lamplighter), Lee Owens (Monsieur la Truiare), Morgan Lane (Meadows), Ray Collymore (Jeremy); Walter Herbert, conductor; William Adams, director; Allen Charles Klein, sets; Peggy Kellner, costumes

Tosca   Giacomo Puccini
May 4, 6, 1967
Eileen Schauler (Tosca), Paula Chastain (shepherd), Plácido Domingo (Cavaradossi), Howard Fried (Spoletta), Chester Ludgin (Scarpia), Gimi Beni (Sacristan), Eugene Brundage (Angelotti), Alan Pitt (Sciarrone), Louis MacKay (jailer); Walter Herbert, conductor; William Adams, director; Jack Montgomery, sets

1967-68

Salome   Richard Strauss
November 10, 11, 1967
Felicia Weathers (Salome), Claramae Turner (Herodias), Andree Jordan (Page), Judith Owens (slave), Arturo Sergi (Herod), Chris Lachona (Narraboth), Joshua Hecht (Jochanaan); Howard Fried, Raymond Gagan, Raymond Manton, Morris Crisci, Alan Pitt (five Jews); Harold Enns, William Bahrt (Nazarenes); Tony Lind, Robert Lynch (soldiers); Louis MacKay (a Cappadocian); Walter Herbert, conductor; William Adams, director; Peggy Kellner, designer

Carmen   Georges Bizet
March 14, 16, 1968
Maralin Niska (Micaëla), Sylvia Davis (Frasquita), Dorothy Krebil (Carmen), Dorothy Dallas (Mercédès), William Olvis (Don José), Ken Remo (Remendado), Norman Treigle (Escamillo), Alan Pitt (Zuniga), William Leyerle (Morales), Robert Glover (Dancaïre); Walter Herbert, conductor; William Adams, director

The Magic Flute   Wolfgang Amadeus Mozart
May 2, 4, 1968
Rita Shane (Queen of the Night), Heather Thomson (Pamina), Sylvia Davis (Papagena); Janet Pavek, Barbara Patton, Donna Peterson (three ladies); William Blankenship (Tamino), Howard Fried (Monostatos), Thomas Palmer (Papageno), Thomas O'Leary (Sarastro), Harold Enns (speaker/first priest), Leslie Cozzens (second priest); Sam Baris, Bruce Bolger, Louis MacKay, Jr. (three spirits); Walter Herbert, conductor; William Adams, director; William Barbe, costumes

1968-69

Rigoletto   Giuseppe Verdi
October 17, 19, 1968
Anne Elgar (Gilda), Yvonne Garcia (Countess Ceprano/page), Roxana Cherico (Giovanna), Dorothy Dallas (Maddalena), Michael Trimbel (the Duke), Jamison Gill (Borsa), Peter Glossop (Rigoletto), Alan Pitt (Marullo), Gilbert Sloan (Ceprano), Alan Gilbert (Monterone), Harold Enns (Sparafucile); Walter Herbert, conductor; Rexford Harrower, director; Lorenzo Ghiglia, designer

La Bohème   Giacomo Puccini
November 14, 16, 1968
Lee Venora (Mimì), Peggy Bonini (Musetta), John Stewart (Rodolfo), Lee Owens/Jack Craig (Parpignol), Richard Fredricks (Marcello), Raymond Gibbs (Schaunard), Harold Enns (Colline), Gimi Beni (Benoit), Fred Rigby (Alcindoro), Alan Pitt (customs guard); Walter Herbert, conductor; William Adams, director; Peggy Kellner, designer

Don Quixote   Jules Massenet
April 24, 26, 1969
Nedda Casei (Dulcinea), Lila Deis (Pilar), Dorothy Dallas (Inez), Ken Remo (Rodriguez), Gene Bullard (Juan), Andrew Foldi (Sancho Panza), Michael Devlin (Don Quixote), Forrest Gantz (bandit chief); Francisco Aguirre, John Hermann (servants); Walter Herbert, conductor; William Adams, director; Glen Holse, sets

1969-70

Pagliacci   Ruggiero Leoncavallo
October 9, 11, 1969
Judith de Paul (Nedda), Robert Nagy (Canio), Ken Remo (Beppe), Julian Patrick (Tonio), Raymond Gibbs (Silvio); Jack Craig, Tony Avendano (villagers); Walter Herbert, conductor; William Adams, director; Robert Darling, sets

The Moon   Carl Orff
October 9, 11, 1969
Ken Remo (narrator), Julian Patrick (St. Peter), Louis MacKay (farmer), Tony Avendano (mayor); Alan Pitt, Raymond Gibbs, Howard Fried, Orville White (four fellows); Walter Herbert, conductor; William Adams, director; Robert Darling, sets

Tannhäuser   Richard Wagner
November 13, 15, 1969
Klara Barlow (Elisabeth), Janis Martin (Venus), Kathleen Knight (shepherdess), Richard Martell (Tannhäuser), Perry Price (Walther), Val Stuart (Heinrich), John Reardon (Wolfram), Harold Enns (Hermann), Alan Pitt (Biterolf), Eugene Brundage (Reinmar); Walter Herbert, conductor; William Adams, director; John Naccarato, sets

Faust   Charles Gounod
February 19, 21, 1970
Heather Thomson (Marguerite), Perry Price (Siébel), Marvellee Cariaga (Marthe), John Walker (Faust), Bernard Turgeon (Valentin), Robert Austin (Wagner), Norman Treigle (Méphistophélès); Walter Herbert, conductor; William Adams, director; Jack McCullagh, designer

The Tales of Hoffmann   Jacques Offenbach
April 23, 25, 1970
Beverly Sills (Olympia/Giulietta/Antonia/Stella), Nancy Williams (Nicklausse), Christina Krooskos (voice of Antonia's mother), Jean Cox (Hoffmann), Nico Castel (Andrés/Cochenille/Pitichinaccio/Frantz), Ron Nelem (Nathanael), Norman Treigle (Lindorf/Coppélius/Dappertutto/ Dr.

201

Miracle), Alan Pitt (Hermann/Schlemil/Crespel), Robert Caruso (Luther), Howard Fried (Spalanzani); Walter Herbert, conductor; Bliss Hebert, director; Allen Charles Klein, designer

---

1970-71

La Traviata   Giuseppe Verdi
November 11, 13, 15, 1970
Gilda Cruz-Romo (Violetta), Dorothy Dallas (Annina), Gwen Jones (Flora), William Blankenship (Alfredo), Ron Stevens (Gaston), Seymour Schwartzman (Germont), Chris Webb (Douphal), Eugene Brundage (Grenvil), Roger Winell (Marchese d'Obigny), Louis McKay (Giuseppe); Walter Herbert, conductor; William Adams, director; Davis West, sets; Franco Zeffirelli, costumes

Madama Butterfly   Giacomo Puccini
March 24, 26, 28m, 1971
Felicia Weathers (Cio-Cio-San), Marlena Kleinman (Suzuki), Sharon Atack (Kate), Chris Lachonas (Pinkerton), Howard Fried (Goro), John Robert Dunlop (Sharpless), Tom Masuko (commissioner/ Yamadori), Desmond Vaughan (registrar), Michael Gallup (Bonze); Walter Herbert, conductor; William Roesch, director; Ming Cho Lee, sets/costumes

---

1971-72

Turandot   Giacomo Puccini
October 20, 22, 24m, 1971
Klara Barlow (Turandot), Esther Hinds (Liù), Richard Cassilly (Calaf), William Royal (Altoum), Howard Fried (Pang), Edgar Stone (Pong), John Fiorito (Ping), Thomas Simmons (Mandarin), Raymond Michalski (Timur); Walter Herbert, conductor; William Adams, director; Davis West, sets; Catherine Hand, costumes

The Barber of Seville   Gioachino Rossini
December 1, 3, 5m, 1971
Joy Clements (Rosina), Marvellee Cariaga (Berta), John Stewart (Almaviva), Thomas Palmer (Figaro), Andrew Foldi (Bartolo), Michael Devlin (Basilio), Ellison Glattly (Fiorello), Morgan Lane (Ambrogio), Thomas Simmons (officer); Walter Herbert, conductor; William Adams, director; William McCullach, sets; Peggy Kellner, costumes

Boris Godunov   Modest Moussorgsky
February 23, 25, 27m, 1972
Constance Haldeman (Xenia), Nedda Casei (Marina), Edna Garabedian (innkeeper/nurse), Nico Castel (Prince Shuisky/simpleton), Gene Bullard (Gregory), Norman Treigle (Boris Godunov), Thomas McKinney (Stchelkalov), Samuel Van Dusen (Pimen/Varlaam), Michael Gallup (Nikitich/officer), Howard Fried (Missail), Tom Nelson (Fyodor), John McClellan (a boyar/Khrustchov); Walter Herbert, conductor; Jacobo Kaufmann, director; Ming Cho Lee, sets; Bess Dimitri, costumes

Gianni Schicchi   Giacomo Puccini
April 26, 28, 30m, 1972
Carolyn Lewis (Lauretta), Jeanne Garson (Nella), Lila Stuart (Ciesca), Marvellee Cariaga (Zita), Perry Price (Rinuccio), Tom Nelson (Gherardino), Howard Fried (Gherardo), Norman Treigle (Gianni Schicchi), Thomas Simmons (Marco),

John Fiorito (Betto), Samuel Van Dusen (Simone), Alfred Dennis (Spinelloccio/notary), Don Watts (Pinellino); Walter Herbert, conductor; Bliss Hebert, director; Davis West, sets; Peggy Kellner, costumes

Help, Help, the Globolinks!   Gian Carlo Menotti
April 26, 28, 30m, 1972
Margaret Immerman (Emily), Marvellee Cariaga (Newkirk), Sarah Fleming (Euterpova), Howard Fried (Timothy), John Fiorito (Stone), Thomas McKinney (Tony), Alfred Dennis (Lavendar-Gas), Samuel Van Dusen (Turtlespit); Walter Herbert, conductor; Bliss Hebert, director; Davis West, sets; Bess Dimitri, costumes

---

1972-73

Aida   Giuseppe Verdi
October 18, 20, 22, 1972
Felicia Weathers/Alpha Floyd (20, 22) (Aida), Barbara Park (high priestess), Sandra Warfield (Amneris), Jon Andrew (Radames), Eugene Holmes (Amonasro), Michael Devlin (Ramfis), Don Watts (King), Jamison Gill/Gerald Whitney (20)/David Caylor (22) (messenger); Walter Herbert, conductor; Ross Allen, director; Mario Cristini, sets

Medea   Alva Henderson
November 29, December 1, 3m, 1972
World Premiere
Irene Dalis/Marvellee Cariaga (1,3) (Medea), Marvellee Cariaga/Joyce Jones (1,3) (Nurse), Glade Peterson (Jason), Samuel Van Dusen (Creon), Thomas McKinney (Tutor); Walter Herbert, conductor; Ghita Hager, director; Robert Darling, sets/costumes

Romeo and Juliet   Charles Gounod
February 7, 9, 11m, 1973
Eilene Shelle (Juliet), Julia Shelley/Barbara Park (9, 11) (Stephano), Joyce Jones (Gertrude), Raymond Gibbs (Romeo), Howard Fried (Tybalt), John Fiorito (Mercutio), Thomas Simmons (Gregory), Charles Curtis (Duke of Verona), Samuel Van Dusen (Capulet), Michael Devlin (Friar Lawrence); Charles Rosecrans, conductor; James de Blasis, director; Henry Heymann, sets; Suzanne Mess, costumes

The Daughter of the Regiment   Gaetano Donizetti
March 21, 23, 25m, 1973
Beverly Sills (Marie), Beverly Evans (Countess of Berkenfeld), Marion Strickler (Duchess of Crackenthorp), Grayson Hirst (Tonio), Gerald Whitney (peasant), Spiro Malas (Sulpice), Don Watts (Hortensio), Thomas Simmons (corporal), Dmitri Bess (dancing master), Arthur Sousa (notary); Walter Herbert, conductor; Lotfi Mansouri, director; Beni Montresor, sets/costumes

---

1973-74

Mefistofele   Arrigo Boito
September 9, 12, 15m, 1973
Nancy Shade (Margherita/Elena), Kay Creed (Margherita's mother/Pantalis), Salvador Novoa (Faust), David Hall (Wagner/Nereus), Norman Treigle (Mefistofele); Werner Torkanovsky, conductor; Tito Capobianco, director; David Mitchell, sets; Hal George, costumes

Carmen   Georges Bizet
October 31, November 2, 4m, 1973
Esther Hinds (Micaëla), Jeanne Garson (Frasquita), Ann Howard (Carmen), Lila Stuart (Mercédès), William Dupre (Don José), Edgar Stone (Remendado), David Myrvold (Escamillo), Harold Enns (Zuniga), Charles Curtis (Morales), Howard Fried (Dancaïre); Walter Herbert, conductor; William Roesch, director; Terry Gates, sets; Howard Bay, costumes

The Marriage of Figaro   Wolfgang Amadeus Mozart
November 28, 30, December 2m, 1973
Johanna Meier (Countess), Joy Clements (Susanna), Katherine Hindrelet-Brydon (Barbarina), Susanne Marsee (Cherubino), Carol Weiss (Marcellina), Carolyn McDaniels, Barbara Park (country girls), James Atherton (Basilio/Curzio), John Darrenkamp (Count), Norman Treigle (Figaro) William Powers (Bartolo), Joseph Galiano (Antonio); Walter Herbert, conductor; James de Blasis, director; Henry Heymann, sets; Suzanne Mess, costumes

The Rhinegold   Richard Wagner
February 6, 8, 10m, 1974
Constance Haldeman (Freia), Patricia Smith (Woglinde), Katherine Hinderlet-Brydon (Wellgunde), Marvellee Cariaga (Fricka), Christine Krooskos (Erda/Flosshilde), Howard Fried (Mime), John Guarnieri (Froh), Ticho Parly (Loge), David Ward (Wotan), Alfred Anderson (Donner), Phillip Booth (Fasolt), Andrew Foldi (Alberich), Samuel Van Dusen (Fafner); Walter Herbert, conductor; George London, director; John Naccarato, sets/costumes

Tosca   Giacomo Puccini
March 27, 29, 31m, 1974
Marisa Galvany (Tosca), Eileen Moss (shepherd), Ermanno Mauro (Cavaradossi), Joseph Pinedo (Spoletta), Eugene Holmes (Scarpia), Michael Gallup (sacristan), Don Watts (Angelotti), Thomas Simmons (Sciarrone), Louis MacKay (jailer); Walter Herbert, conductor; Bliss Hebert, director; Allen Charles Klein, sets

The Daughter of the Regiment   Gaetano Donizetti
April 15, 22, 1974 (Phoenix only)
Beverly Sills (Marie), Beverly Evans (Countess of Berkenfeld), Peggy Castle (Duchess of Crackenthorp), Grayson Hirst (Tonio), Doug Burton (peasant), Spiro Malas (Sulpice), Don Watts (Hortensio), Thomas Simmons (corporal); Walter Herbert, conductor; William Roesch, director; Beni Montresor, sets/costumes

---

1974-75

Manon   Jules Massenet
October 30, November 1, 3m, 1974
Catherine Malfitano (Manon), Patricia Smith (Pousette), Teri Sinclair (Javotte), Diana Davidson (Rosette), Raymond Gibbs (des Grieux), Ken Remo (Guillot de Morfontaine), Douglas Lawrence (Lescaut), Michael Gallup (De Brétigny), Thomas Simmons (innkeeper), Harry Dworchak (Count des Grieux); Walter Herbert, conductor; Bliss Hebert, director; Allen Charles Klein, sets

Lucia di Lammermoor   Gaetano Donizetti
December 4, 6, 8m, 1974
Joan Sutherland (Lucia), Peggy Castle (Alisa), Franco Tagliavini

(Edgardo), Gordon Greer (Arturo), Richard Wagner (Normanno), John Darrenkamp (Enrico), Robert Hale (Raimondo); Richard Bonynge, conductor; Bliss Hebert, director; Henry Bardon, sets; Peter Hall, costumes

A Village Romeo and Juliet   Frederick Delius
January 15, 17, 19m, 1975
Patricia Wells (Vreli), Paula Copeland (pastry woman/slim girl), Martha Jane Howe (wheel of fortune woman/wild girl), Paula McDonnell (cheap jewelry woman), Carolee Thornburgh (woman), John Stewart (Sali), Cary Smith (Marti/fruit man/bargeman), Samuel Van Dusen (Manz/knick-knack man/hunchbacked bass fiddler/bargeman), David Holloway (dark fiddler), David Caylor (doll and puppet man), Frank Hallock (peasant), Jerry Whitney (indigent hornplayer), Jon Gruett (bargeman); Walter Herbert, conductor; Frank Corsaro, director; Theoni V. Aldredge, costumes

The Valkyrie   Richard Wagner
February 26, 28, March 2m, 1975
Johanna Meier (Sieglinde), Anna Green (Brünnhilde), Marvellee Cariaga (Fricka), Barbara Wilkinson (Helmwige), LaVerne Williams (Ortlinde), Marlene Delavan (Gerhilde), Adrienne Leonetti (Waltraute), Kathleen O'Brien (Siegrune), Barbara McAlister (Rossweisse), Emily Tracy (Grimgerde), Mara Baygulow (Schwertleite), Jon Andrew (Siegmund), Noel Tyl (Wotan), Samuel Van Dusen (Hunding); Walter Herbert, conductor; Ghita Hager, director; John Naccarato, sets/costumes

La Bohème   Giacomo Puccini
April 9, 11, 13m, 1975
Karan Armstrong (Mimì), Maria Di Giglio (Musetta), Raymond Gibbs (Rodolfo), John Gruett/David Caylor (Parpignol), John Darrenkamp (Marcello), David Myrvold (Schaunard), Harry Dworchak (Colline), Michael Gallup (Benoit/Alcindoro); Walter Herbert, conductor; Patrick Bakman, director; John Scheffler, sets; Suzanne Mess, costumes

---

1975-76

Recital: **An Operatic Evening**
September 23, 1975
Joan Sutherland, soprano; Huguette Tourangeau, mezzo-soprano; Richard Bonynge, piano

Il Trovatore   Giuseppe Verdi
October 4, 7, 10, 12, 1975
October 20, 22, 1975 (Phoenix)
Rachel Mathes (Leonora), Peggy Castle (Inez), Lili Chookasian (Azucena), Richard Kness (Manrico), Howard Fried (Ruiz), Eugene Holmes (di Luna), Harold Enns (Ferrando); Bruno Rigacci, conductor; William Roesch, director; Sally Jacobs, sets

Rusalka   Antonin Dvořák
December 3, 5, 7m, 9, 1975
United States Professional Premiere
Kathryn Bouleyn (Rusalka), Gwendolyn Killebrew (Ježibaba/Foreign Princess); Elaine Pavlick, Teri Sinclair, Melanie Sonnenberg (nymphs); William McDonald (Prince), Spiro Malas (Water Sprite); Theo Alcantara, conductor; Tito Capobianco, director; Santo Loquasto, sets/costumes

Siegfried   Richard Wagner
February 14, 17, 20, 22m, 1976
Marvellee Cariaga (Brünnhilde), Ashley Putnam (Forest Bird), Geraldine Dekker (Erda), Alberto Remedios (Siegfried), Paul Crook (Mime), Noel Tyl (Wotan), Derek Hammond-Stroud (Alberich), Thomas O'Leary (Fafner); Kenneth Schermerhorn, conductor; Ghita Hager, director; John Naccarato, sets/costumes

Der Rosenkavalier   Richard Strauss
March 27, 30, April 2, 3m, 1976
Johanna Meier (Feldmarschallin), Patricia Wise (Sophie), Lila Stuart, (Marianne), Sylvia Anderson (Octavian), Adrienne Leonetti (Annina); Dora Walker, Pat Goodwin, Nancy Tripp Smith (three noble orphans); Carolee Thornburgh (milliner), Aaron Bergell (singer), Howard Fried (Valzacchi), Gerald Whitney (animal vendor/innkeeper), Derek Hammond-Stroud (Faninal), Richard Van Allan (Baron Ochs), Thomas Simmons (major-domo), Michael Gallup (notary/commissary/major-domo); Paul Raabe, Dave Rush, John Hermann, David Garven (lackeys); Stefan Minde, conductor; Richard Abrams, director; Elizabeth Dalton, sets/costumes

Norma   Vincenzo Bellini
June 7, 10, 13m, 15, 1976
Beverly Sills (Norma), Tatiana Troyanos (Adalgisa), Adrienne Leonetti (Clotilde), John Alexander (Pollione), Robert Grayson (Flavio), Robert Hale (Oroveso); Charles Mackerras, conductor; Tito Capobianco, director; Carl Toms, sets; Jose Varona, costumes

---

Prior to this date, accurate information is not available for United States debuts.

1976-77

Otello   Giuseppe Verdi
October 9, 12, 15, 17m, 1976
Lynne Strow Piccolo* (Desdemona), Adrienne Leonetti (Emilia), Jon Andrew (Otello), Gary Fisher (Cassio), Robert Grayson (Roderigo), Thomas Tipton (Iago), Louis Lebherz (Lodovico), Vincent Russo (Montano), Ralph Bassett (herald); Bruno Rigacci, conductor; Patrick Bakman, director; Peter Wexler, sets/costumes

The Saint of Bleecker Street   Gian Carlo Menotti
December 1, 3, 5m, 7, 1976
Lorna Haywood (Annina), Lynn Cole-Adcock (Carmela), Beverly Wolff (Desideria), Jane Westbrook (Assunta), Joyce Jones (Maria Corona), Halle Kelly (Concettina), Lucille Mayer (old woman), Phillis Moody (young woman), Martha Hamilton (girl), Enrico Di Giuseppe (Michele), Aaron Bornstein (Corona's son), Richard Torigi (Don Marco), Andrew Taylor (Salvatore), Gerald Whitney (young man), Thomas Simmons (bartender/second guest), Gary Fisher (first guest), Jamison Gill (man's voice); Theo Alcantara/Monroe Kanouse (7), conductor; Tito Capobianco, director; Beeb Salzer, sets

Die Fledermaus   Johann Strauss, Jr.
January 23, 25, 28, 30m, 1977
Johanna Meier (Rosalinda), Gianna Rolandi (Adele), David Rae Smith (Orlofsky), Cornelis Opthof (Eisenstein), Ragnar Ulfung (Alfred), Thomas Simmons (Blind), Michael Terry (Frank), John Darrenkamp (Falke), Robert Schmorr (Frosch);

Judith Somogi/Monroe Kanouse (30), conductor; Lotfi Mansouri, director; Brian Jackson, sets

Götterdämmerung   Richard Wagner
February 19, 22, 25, 27m, 1977
Anna Green (Brünnhilde), Adrienne Leonetti (Gutrune), Marvellee Cariaga (Waltraute/second norn), Carolyne McDaniel (first norn), Joan Zajac (third norn), Pamela Lasalle (Woglinde), Shirley Harned (Wellgunde), Carolyn Maia (Flosshilde), Alberto Remedios (Siegfried), Adair McGowen (Gunther), Harold Enns (Alberich), William Wildermann/Thomas O'Leary (25, 27) (Hagen); Henry Holt, conductor; George London, director; John Naccarato, sets/costumes

La Traviata   Giuseppe Verdi
March 26, 29, April 1, 3m, 1977
April 9, 1977 (Palm Springs)
April 14, 16, 1977 (Pasadena)
Beverly Sills/Nancy Shade (9) (Violetta), Dora Walker (Annina), Adrienne Leonetti (Flora), William McDonald/Joseph Evans (9,14,16) (Alfredo), Gary Fisher (Gaston), Ryan Edwards (Germont), Ryan Allen (Douphol), Vincent Russo (Grenvil), Thomas Simmons (Marchese d'Obigny), Gerald Whitney (Giuseppe); Theo Alcantara, conductor; Tito Capobianco, director; Carl Toms, sets

---

1977-78

The Merry Widow   Franz Lehár
October 2, 4, 7, 9m, 1977
Beverly Sills (Hanna), Glenys Fowles (Valencienne), Mara Baygulova, (Sylviane/ Frou-Frou), Jane Westbrook (Olga/Margot), Melanie Sonnenberg (Praskowia/Dodo), Patricia Goodwin (Lolo), Cary Shipman (Jou-Jou), Lizanne Maxfield (Clo-Clo), Alan Titus (Danilo), Nolan Van Way (Camille), Andrew Foldi (Baron Zeta), Vincent Russo (Cascada), Ryan Allen (St. Brioche), William Mallory (Bogdanowitsch), Timothy Braden (Kromow), Thomas Simmons (Pritschitsch), David Rae Smith (Njegus); Theo Alcantara, conductor; Tito Capobianco, director; Carl Toms, sets/costumes

Don Giovanni   Wolfgang Amadeus Mozart
October 8, 11, 14, 16m, 1977
Anne Evans* (Anna), Ashley Putnam (Elvira), Janice Hall (Zerlina), Joseph Evans (Ottavio), Robert Hale (Giovanni), Carlos Chausson (Masetto), David Cornell (Commendatore), Richard Van Allen (Leporello); Theo Alcantara, conductor; Horacio Aragon, director; John Wright Stevens, sets

Carmen   Georges Bizet
October 18, 21, 23m, 25, 1977
Josella Ligi/Janice Hall (25) (Micaëla), Katherine Kennedy (Frasquita), Katherine Pring* (Carmen), Melanie Sonnenberg (Mercédès), Salvador Novoa (Don José), Howard Fried (Remendado), William Justus/Robert Hale (21, 23m, 25) (Escamillo), Carlos Chausson (Zuniga), Vincent Russo (Morales), Thomas Simmons (Dancaïre); Bruno Rigacci, conductor; Sarah Ventura, director; Terry Gates, sets; Howard Bay, costumes

Falstaff   Giuseppe Verdi
February 4, 7, 10, 12m, 1978
Nancy Shade (Alice Ford), Kathryn Bouleyn (Nanetta), Melanie Sonnenberg (Mistress Page), Muriel Costa-

Greenspon (Quickly), David Hall (Fenton), Joaquin Romaguera (Caius), Melvin Lowery (Bardolph), Spiro Malas (Falstaff), John Bröcheler* (Ford), David Cornell (Pistol); Bruno Rigacci, conductor; Tito Capobianco, director; Elemer Nagy, designer

Madama Butterfly
Giacomo Puccini

February 11, 14, 17, 19m, 1978
March 15, 1978 (Palm Springs)
Atsuko Azuma (Cio-Cio-San), Hilda Harris (Suzuki), Melanie Sonnenberg (Kate), Rico Serbo (Pinkerton), Howard Fried (Goro), John Bröcheler (Sharpless), John Del Carlo/Vincent Russo (15) (commissioner), Gary Fisher (Yamadori), Robert Roseberry (registrar), Michael Gallup (Bonze); Bruno Rigacci/Joseph De Rugeriis (15), conductor; Sarah Ventura, director; John Scheffler, designer

The Love for Three Oranges
Sergei Prokofiev

February 25, 28, March 3, 5m, 1978
West Coast Premiere
Diane Curry (Fata Morgana), Mara Baygulova (Linetta), Carolyne McDaniel (Nicoletta), Melanie Sonnenberg (Smeraldina), Muriel Costa-Greenspon (Princess Clarissa), Kathryn Bouleyn (Ninetta), Joseph Evans (The Prince), David Hall (Truffaldino), Leslie Harrington (Master of Ceremonies), John Del Carlo (Pantalone), Harold Enns (King of Clubs), Vincent Russo (Farfarello), William Dansby (herald/Tchelio), John Darrenkamp (Leandro), David Cornell (cook); Calvin Simmons, conductor; Tito Capobianco, director; Mario Vanarelli, sets/costumes

Aida
Giuseppe Verdi

August 4, 6m, 9, 1978
Verdi Festival
Martina Arroyo (Aida), Aprile Millo (high priestess), Carol Wyatt* (Amneris), Carlo Bini (Radames), Norman Mittelmann (Amonasro), Robert Hale (Ramfis), Phillip Booth (King), Gary Fisher (messenger); Antonio Tauriello, conductor; Tito Capobianco, director; Mario Cristini, sets

Concert: Requiem
Giuseppe Verdi

August 12, 1978
Verdi Festival
Martina Arroyo, Carol Wyatt, Carlo Bini, Robert Hale (soloists); San Diego Symphonic Chorale; Antonio Tauriello, conductor

---

1978-79

Hamlet
Ambroise Thomas

October 7, 9, 13, 15m, 1978
West Coast Premiere
Ashley Putnam (Ophelia), Isabel Veale* (Gertrude), Joseph Evans (Laertes), Sherrill Milnes (Hamlet), Robert Hale (Claudius), Joaquin Romaguera (Marcellus/gravedigger), David Dunlap (Horatio), Carlos Chausson (ghost of Hamlet's father), James Courtney (Polonius), Vincent Russo (gravedigger); Bruno Rigacci, conductor; Tito Capobianco, director; Carl Toms, sets

Rigoletto
Giuseppe Verdi

October 20, 22m, 26, 28, 1978
Janice Hall (Gilda), Nancy Jones (Countess Ceprano), Pamela Hicks (page), Joyce Jones (Giovanna), Adrienne Leonetti (Maddalena), Enrico di Giuseppe (the Duke), Gary Fisher (Borsa), Gary Nichols (herald), Louis Quilico (Rigoletto), Vincent Russo (Marullo), David Dunlap (Ceprano), James Courtney (Monterone), Carlos Chausson (Sparafucile);

Bruno Rigacci, conductor; Ronald Adler*, director; John Naccarato, sets; Carrie Robbins, costumes

Così fan tutte
Wolfgang Amadeus Mozart

October 27, 29m, 31, November 4, 1978
Sung-Sook Lee (Fiordiligi), Katherine Hindrelet-Brydon (Despina), Susanne Marsee (Dorabella), Joseph Evans (Ferrando), Lenus Carlson (Guglielmo), Andrew Foldi (Don Alfonso); Theo Alcantara, conductor; Jan Bouws*, director; John Naccarato, sets; John Naccarato/Edguard Johnson, costume designers

Manon Lescaut
Giacomo Puccini

May 12, 15, 18, 20m, 1979
Ilona Simon (Manon Lescaut), Marnie Clark (singer), Carlo Bini (des Grieux), Gary Fisher (Edmondo), Cary Archer Smith (Lescaut), Carlos Chausson (Geronte), Vincent Russo (innkeeper), Joseph Frank (dancing master/lamplighter), David Dunlap (sergeant), Gary Nichols (captain); John Mauceri, conductor; Tito Capobianco, director; Marsha Louis Eck, sets

Cavalleria Rusticana
Pietro Mascagni

May 19, 22, 25, 27m, 1979
Marvellee Cariaga (Santuzza), Melanie Sonnenberg (Lola), Jane Westbrook (Mamma Lucia), Harry Theyard (Turiddu), William Justus (Alfio); Joseph De Rugeriis, conductor; Fabrizio Melano, director; Allen Charles Klein, sets

Pagliacci
Ruggiero Leoncavallo

May 19, 22, 25, 27m, 1979
Diana Soviero (Nedda), Harry Theyard (Canio), David Hall (Beppe), William Justus (Tonio), John Del Carlo (Silvio); Robert Roseberry, Gerald Whitney (villagers); Joseph De Rugeriis, conductor; Fabrizio Melano, director; Allen Charles Klein, sets

La Loca
Gian Carlo Menotti

June 3, 5, 8, 10m, 1979
World Premiere
Beverly Sills (Juana), Susanne Marsee (Dona Manuela), Jane Westbrook (nurse); Marcia Cope, Martha Jane Howe (ladies-in-waiting); Joseph Evans (Miguel de Ferrera), John Bröcheler (Felipe/Fernando/Carlos V), Vincent Russo (chaplain), Robert Hale (Ximenes de Cisneros), Carlos Chausson (Marques de Denia), Wade Gregg (young boy), Nancy Coulson (Catalina); Calvin Simmons, conductor; Tito Capobianco, director; Mario Vanarelli, sets/costumes

I Lombardi
Giuseppe Verdi

June 22, 24m, 30, 1979
West Coast Premiere *Verdi Festival*
Cristina Deutekom (Giselda), Lynne Martindale-Schafer (Viclinda), Leslie Richards (Sofia), Rico Serbo (Arvino), Carlo Bergonzi (Oronte), Paul Plishka (Pagano), Carlos Chausson (Pirro), Michael Magiera (Prior), J. Patrick Raftery (Acciano); Maurizio Arena, conductor; Tito Capobianco, director; Mario Vanarelli, sets

La Traviata
Giuseppe Verdi

June 29, July 1m, 7, 1979
Verdi Festival
Diana Soviero (Violetta), Martha Jane Howe (Annina), Jane Westbrook (Flora), Vittorio Terranova (Alfredo), Michael Magiera (Gaston), John Bröcheler (Germont), J. Patrick Raftery (Douphol), David Dunlap (Grenvil), Vincent Russo (Marchese d'Obigny), James Flynn (Giuseppe), Jeffrey L. Shipman (messenger), Gary Nichols (servant); Hans Vonk*, conductor; Charles Nelson Reilly, director; Carl Toms, sets/costumes

Concert: Gala Verdi Concert

June 28, 1979 *Verdi Festival*
Cristina Deutekom, Leslie Richards, Carlo Bergonzi, Rico Serbo, John Bröcheler, Paul Plishka, J. Patrick Raftery (soloists); Saddleback Concert Chorale; John Balme/Michael Jackson Parker, accompanists; Don Walker, conductor

---

1979-80

Don Carlo
Giuseppe Verdi

October 6, 9, 12, 14m, 1979
Anne Evans (Elizabeth), Susan Lynn Dixon (celestial voice), Pamela Hicks (Tebaldo), Giuseppina Dalle Molle* (Princess Eboli), Grace Carlisle Magee (Countess of Arenberg), Luis Lima (Don Carlo), Neil Breeden (Count Lerma), Juan Pons (Rodrigo), Paul Plishka (Philip), Chester Ludgin (Grand Inquisitor), Carlos Chausson (friar), Gerald Whitney (herald); Bruno Rigacci, conductor; Bodo Igesz, director; Henry Bardon, sets; Suzanne Mess, costumes

The Abduction from the Seraglio
Wolfgang Amadeus Mozart

October 13, 16, 19, 21m, 1979
Benita Valente (Constanze), Gianna Rolandi (Blonde), Dale Smith (Belmonte), David Hall (Pedrillo), Spiro Malas (Osmin), Von Schauer (Pasha Selim); John Balme, conductor; Nathaniel Merrill, director; Toni Businger, sets

The Tales of Hoffmann
Jacques Offenbach

October 27, 30, November 2, 4m, 1979
Ashley Putnam (Olympia/Giulietta/Antonia), Hilda Harris (Nicklausse/voice of Antonia's mother), Barry McCauley (Hoffmann), David Hall (Andrés/Cochenille/Pittichinaccio/Frantz), Gerald Whitney (Nathanael), Michael Devlin (Lindorf/Coppélius/Dapertutto/Dr. Miracle), Steven Savino (Hermann), Carlos Chausson (Luther/Crespel/Schlemil), Melvin Lowery (Spalanzani); Joseph De Rugeriis, conductor; Tito Capobianco, director; Ming Cho Lee, sets; Jose Varona, costumes

Mefistofele
Arrigo Boito

May 9, 11m, 14, 17, 1980
Jeannine Altmeyer (Margherita/Elena), Beverly Evans (Pantalis/Marta), Enrico di Giuseppe (Faust), Melvin Lowery (Wagner/Nereus), Robert Hale (Mefistofele); Theo Alcantara, conductor; Gigi Denda, director; David Mitchell, sets; Hal George, costumes

Don Pasquale
Gaetano Donizetti

May 24, 27, 30, June 1m, 1980
Beverly Sills (Norina), Rico Serbo (Ernesto), Richard Fredricks (Malatesta), Melvin Lowery (Notary), Giorgio Tozzi (Don Pasquale); Theo Alcantara, conductor; Tito Capobianco, director; Robert O'Hearn, sets; Suzanne Mess, costumes

La Bohème
Giacomo Puccini

May 29, 31, June 3, 6, 8m, 1980
Diana Soviero/Madelyn Renee (8m) (Mimì), Inga Nielsen (Musetta), Luciano Pavarotti (Rodolfo), David Bates (Parpignol), Jan Derksen (Marcello), J. Patrick Raftery (Schaunard), Robert Hale (Colline), Steven Savino (Benoit), Melvin Lowery (Alcindoro), Robert Roseberry (customs guard), Gary Nichols (sergeant); Bruno Rigacci, conductor; Tito Capobianco, director; John Scheffler, sets; Suzanne Mess, costumes

Giovanna d'Arco Giuseppe Verdi
June 26, 28m, July 6, 1980
West Coast Premiere *Verdi Festival*
Adriana Maliponte (Giovanna), Luis Lima (Carlo VII), Melvin Lowery (Delil), Pablo Elvira (Giacomo), Carlos Chausson (Talbot); Edoardo Müller, conductor; Lotfi Mansouri, director; Wolfram Skalicki, sets

Il Trovatore Giuseppe Verdi
June 27, July 2, 5m, 1980 *Verdi Festival*
Martina Arroyo (Leonora), Juliane Gondek (Inez), Stella Silva (Azucena), Carlo Bini (Manrico), Melvin Lowery (Ruiz), Juan Pons (di Luna), Boris Martinovich (Ferrando), Steven Savino (old gypsy); Calvin Simmons, conductor; Tito Capobianco, director; Ming Cho Lee, sets

Concert: **Verdi Concert 1980**
July 1980 *Verdi Festival*
Martina Arroyo, Adriana Maliponte, Carlo Bini, Pablo Elvira, Juan Pons, Boris Martinovich (soloists); Saddleback Concert Chorale

---

1980-81

Elektra Richard Strauss
September 18, 21m, 24, 27, 1980
Pauline Tinsley (Elektra), Anne Evans (Chrysothemis), Kerstin Meyer (Klytemnestra), Aleicia Byrnes (overseer), Sallye Graves (trainbearer), Annette Winchell (confidante); Jane Westbrook, Nancy Jones, Sandra Dudek, Juliane Gondek, Pamela Hicks (maids); Mallory Walker (Aegisth), John Bröcheler (Orest), Stephen West (Tutor), David Bates (young servant), Steven Savino (old servant); Theo Alcantara, conductor; Regina Resnik, director; Lawrence Schafer, sets; Alfred Siercke, costumes

Die Fledermaus Johann Strauss, Jr.
October 5m, 8, 11, 16, 19m, 1980
Joan Sutherland (Rosalinda), Beverly Sills (Adele), Regina Resnik (Orlofsky), Alan Titus (Eisenstein), Giuseppe Campora (Alfred), Joseph Frank (Blind), Spiro Malas (Frank), Jake Gardner (Falke), Leonard Frey (Frosch); Richard Bonynge, conductor; Tito Capobianco, director; Zack Brown, sets; Oliver Smith, costumes

Werther Jules Massenet
October 24, 26m, 29, November 1, 1980
Pamela Hicks (Sophie), Katherine Ciesinski (Charlotte), John Brecknock (Werther), Robert Schmorr (Schmidt), J. Patrick Raftery (Albert), Stephen West (Le Bailli), Steven Savino (Johann); Antonio Tauriello, conductor; Jay Lesenger, director; John Conklin, sets/costumes

Tosca Giacomo Puccini
May 8, 11, 14, 17m, 1981
Martina Arroyo (Tosca), Marcia Cope (shepherd), Carlo Bini (Cavaradossi), Joseph Frank (Spoletta), Richard Fredricks (Scarpia), Steven Savino (sacristan), Carlos Chausson (Angelotti/jailer), Gary Nichols (Sciarrone); Bruno Rigacci, conductor; Tito Capobianco, director; Allen Charles Klein, sets; Suzanne Mess, costumes

Lucia di Lammermoor Gaetano Donizetti
May 16, 18, 22, 24m, 1981
Gianna Rolandi (Lucia), Sandra Dudek (Alisa), Barry

McCauley (Edgardo), David Hall (Arturo), Melvin Lowery (Normanno), John Bröcheler (Enrico), John Seabury (Raimondo); Joseph De Rugeriis, conductor; Patrick Bakman, director; Marsha Louis Eck, sets; Jose Varona, costumes

The Love for Three Oranges Sergei Prokofiev
May 30, June 1, 5, 7m, 1981
RoseMarie Freni (Fata Morgana), Sandra Dudek (Linetta), Susanna Lodato (Nicoletta), Kathleen Hegierski (Smeraldina), Melanie Sonnenberg (Princess Clarissa), Janice Hall (Ninetta), Joseph Evans (the Prince), David Hall (Truffaldino), Melvin Lowery (master of ceremonies), Harlan Foss (Pantalone), Richard McKee (King of Clubs), Vincent Russo (Farfarello), Ralph Bassett (herald/Tchelio), Carlos Chausson (Leandro), Louis Lebherz (cook); Calvin Simmons/Karen Keltner (7), conductor; Tito Capobianco, director; Mario Vanarelli, sets/costumes

Nabucco Giuseppe Verdi
June 19, 21m, 27, 1981 *Verdi Festival*
Cristina Deutekom (Abigaille), Aleicia Byrnes (Anna), Sandra Dudek (Fenena), John Sayers (Ismaele), Melvin Lowery (Abdallo), Kari Nurmela (Nabucco), Ezio Flagello (Zaccaria), Carlos Chausson (High Priest); Maurizio Arena, conductor; Ghita Hager, director; Nicola Benois, sets/costumes

Un Giorno Di Regno Giuseppe Verdi
June 20, 26, 28m, 1981 *Verdi Festival*
Arlene Saunders (Marchesa), Susanne Marsee (Giulietta), Bruce Reed (Edoardo), Melvin Lowery (Ivrea), J. Patrick Raftery (Belfiore), Harlan Foss (Kelbar), James Billings (Rocca), Steven Savino (Delmonte); Calvin Simmons, conductor; Tito Capobianco, director; Suzanne Mess, costumes

Concert: **Requiem** Giuseppe Verdi
June 25, 1981; *Verdi Festival*
On the Green at Rancho Bernardo
Cristina Deutekom, Susanne Marsee, Jon Fredric West, Ezio Flagello (soloists); San Diego Master Chorale; Theo Alcantara, conductor

---

1981-82

Andrea Chénier Umberto Giordano
September 11, 13m, 16, 19, 1981
Giovanna Cassolla* (Madeleine), Jane Shaulis (Countess), Susanna Lodato (Bersi), Nancy Carol Moore (Madelon), Carlo Bini (Andréa Chénier), Melvin Lowery (the Abbé), Joseph Frank (Incredibile), Gary Nichols (major-domo), William Justus (Charles Gerard), David Dunlap (Fléville), Edward Badrak (Dumas), Steven Savino (Fouquier-Tinville), Paul Cheak (Schmidt), Enrique Baquerizo (Roucher), Stephen West (Mathieu); Antonio Tauriello, conductor; Bliss Hebert, director; Robert O'Hearn, sets; Suzanne Mess, costumes

Susannah Carlisle Floyd
September 25, 27m, 30, October 3, 1981
Patricia Craig (Susannah), Virginia Sublett (Mrs. Gleaton), Marilyn Anderson (Mrs. Hayes), Jane Shaulis (Mrs. McClean), Grace Magee (Mrs. Ott), Richard Cassilly (Sam), Melvin Lowery (Little Bat), Samuel Ramey (Blitch), Stephen West (McClean), Neil Breeden (Hayes), Steven Savino (Ott), William Eichorn (Gleaton); Christopher Keene, conductor; Carlisle Floyd, director; Paul Shortt, sets; Patton Campbell, costumes

Faust Charles Gounod
October 9, 11m, 14, 17, 1981
October 1981 (Palm Springs)
Pamela Myers/Inga Nielsen [Palm Springs] (Marguerite), Susanna Lodato (Siébel), Nancy Carol Moore (Marthe), John Brecknock/Joseph Evans [Palm Springs] (Faust), J. Patrick Raftery/Joseph Shore [Palm Springs] (Valentin), David Dunlap (Wagner), Robert Hale (Méphistophélès); Joseph De Rugeriis, conductor; Charles Hamilton*/Robert Tannenbaum [Palm Springs], director; Wolfram Skalicki, sets/costumes

Concert: **Gala Benefit Concert**
to help the San Diego Symphony Orchestra Assocation
October 18, 1981
Dame Joan Sutherland, Teresa Berganza, Pamela Myers, Robert Hale, J. Patrick Raftery (soloists); Kurt Herbert Adler, Bruno Bartoletti, Richard Bonynge, Karen Keltner, Clay Pendergrass, Joseph De Rugeriis, conductors

Giulietta e Romeo Riccardo Zandonai
April 23, 25m, 28, May 1, 1982 *United States Premiere*
Giovanna Cassolla (Giulietta), Virginia Sublett (first lady), Sarah Pruetti (second lady), Joan Zajac (a woman), Sandra Dudek (Isabella), Carlo Bini (Romeo), Bruce Reed (singer), John Bröcheler (Tebaldo), Leonard Eagleson (Gregorio), Steven Savino (Sansone), Joaquin Romaguera (a Montague), Carlos Chausson (constable/Bernabo), Edward Badrak (servant); Michelangelo Veltri, conductor; Tito Capobianco, director; Carl Toms, sets/principal constumes

The Barber of Seville Gioachino Rossini
May 6, 8, 12, 16m, 1982
RoseMarie Freni (Rosina), Nancy Carol Moore (Berta), Bruce Reed (Almaviva), J. Patrick Raftery (Figaro), James Billings (Bartolo), Paul Plishka (Basilio), Steven Savino (Fiorello), Gary Prettyman (Ambrogio), Joaquin Romaguera (officer), Edward Badrak (notary); Joseph De Rugeriis, conductor; Robert Tannenbaum, director; Peter Hall, sets/costumes

Turandot Giacomo Puccini
May 21, 23m, 26, 29, 1982
Cristina Deutekom (Turandot), Pamela Myers (Liù), Carlo Bini (Calaf), Joaquin Romaguera (Altoum), David Hall (Pang), Joseph Frank (Pong), Harlan Foss (Ping), Carlos Chausson (Mandarin), Paul Plishka (Timur), Joseph Pechota (Prince of Persia); Theo Alcantara, conductor; Jay Lesenger, director; Robert Darling, sets; Suzanne Mess, costumes

Il Corsaro Giuseppe Verdi
June 18, 20m, 26, 1982 *Verdi Festival*
Rosalind Plowright (Medora), June Anderson (Gulnara), Alfonso Navarrete (Corrado), J. Patrick Raftery (Seid), Steven Savino (Giovanni), Joaquin Romaguera (Selim), Joseph Pechota (eunuch), Gary Nichols (slave); Edoardo Müller, conductor; Tito Capobianco, director; Bill Gorgensen, sets

Un Ballo in Maschera Giuseppe Verdi
June 19, 25, 27m, 1982 *Verdi Festival*
Josephine Barstow (Amelia), Janice Hall (Oscar), Gwynn Cornell (Ulrica), Adriaan van Limpt (Riccardo), Cornelis Opthof (Renato), Steven Savino (servant), Joaquin Romaguera (Judge), Carlos Chausson (Silvano), John Seabury (Sam), Kenneth Cox (Tom); Michelangelo Veltri, conductor; Michael Rennison, director; Zack Brown, sets/costumes

Verdi 1982 Jubilee V
June 24, 1982 *Verdi Festival*
Shirley Verrett, June Anderson, Rosalind Plowright, Gwynn

Cornell, Alfonso Navarrete, J. Patrick Raftery (soloists); Edoardo Müller/ Michelangelo Veltri/ Karen Keltner, conductors

---

1982-83

Gwendoline — Emmanuel Chabrier
October 2, 5, 8, 10m, 1982
United States Premiere
Rosalind Plowright (Gwendoline), J. Patrick Raftery (Arald), Jerold Norman (Armel), Melvin Lowery (Erik), Steven Savino (Aella), Edward Badrak (Dane); Antonio Tauriello, conductor; Tito Capobianco, director; Beni Montresor, sets/costumes

Madama Butterfly — Giacomo Puccini
October 9, 12, 15, 17m, 1982
Martina Arroyo (Cio-Cio-San), Mimi Lerner (Suzuki), Wendy Hillhouse (Kate), Joseph Evans (Pinkerton), Joaquin Romaguera (Goro), Frederick Burchinal (Sharpless), David Hamilton (commissioner), Melvin Lowery (Yamadori), Joseph Pechota (registrar), Stephen West (Bonze); Bruno Rigacci, conductor; Rhoda Levine, director; John Scheffler, sets; Suzanne Mess, costumes

La Périchole — Jacques Offenbach
October 23, 26, 29, 31m, 1982
Leigh Munro (la Périchole), Carol Kaszar (Estrella), Amy Burton (Guadalena), Sarah Pruetti (Virginella), Virginia Sublett (Ninetta), Dru McCain (Brambilla), Susan Lord (Manuelita), Diane Jennings (Frasquinella), William Workman (Paquillo), David Rae Smith (Don Andres), David Hall (Count of Panatellas), Harlan Foss (Don Pedro); Melvin Lowery, David Hamilton (notaries); Steven Savino (Marquis), Joaquin Romaguera (old prisoner), Richard LaBarge (turnkey); Andrew Litton/Karen Keltner (31), conductor; Jack Eddleman, director; John Scheffler, sets; Suzanne Mess, costumes

Henry VIII — Camille Saint-Saëns
February 12, 15, 18, 20m, 1983
United States Professional Premiere
Cristina Deutekom (Catherine of Aragon), Brenda Boozer (Anne Boleyn), Nancy Carol Moore (Lady Clarence), Jacque Trussel (Don Gomez), Sherrill Milnes (Henry VIII), Kenneth Cox (Cardinal Campeggio), Robert Schmorr (Earl of Surrey), Kevin Langan (Duke of Norfolk); Joseph Pechota, Robert Toschak, Steven Savino, Ronald Banks (courtiers); Neil Wilson-Nease (garter king-at-arms), Enrique Baquerizo (Cranmer), Edward Badrak (usher); Antonio Tauriello, conductor; Tito Capobianco, director; Thomas Munn/Bill Gorgensen, set designers

Aida — Giuseppe Verdi
February 25, 27m, March 2, 5, 1983
Gilda Cruz-Romo (Aida), Carol Kaszar (high priestess), Rachel Gettler*/Mariana Paunova (2, 5) (Amneris), Adriaan van Limpt (Radames), Joseph Shore (Amonasro), Dimitri Kavrakos (Ramfis), Thomas Paul (King), Neil Wilson-Nease (messenger); Theo Alcantara, conductor; Robert Tannenbaum, director; Mario Cristini/Bill Gorgensen, set designers; Suzanne Mess, costumes

Adriana Lecouvreur — Francesco Cilea
May 22, 26, 29m, June 1, 1983
206 Joan Sutherland (Adriana Lecouvreur), Amy Burton (Mlle. Jouvenot), Stella Silva (Princess de Bouillon), Jane Shaulis

(Mlle. Dangeville), Diane Jennings (maid), Vasile Moldoveanu (Maurizio), John Bröcheler (Michonnet), David Hall (Poisson), Ricardo Cassinelli* (the Abbé), Carlos Chausson (Quinault), Arnold Voketaitis (Prince of Bouillon), Steven Savino (major-domo); Richard Bonynge, conductor; Tito Capobianco, director; Robert O'Hearn, sets; Suzanne Mess, costumes

---

1983-84

Lohengrin — Richard Wagner
September 23, 25m, 28, October 1, 1983
Stephanie Sundine (Elsa), Pauline Tinsley (Ortrud), William Neill (Lohengrin), William Justus (Telramund), John Tomlinson* (Heinrich), Carlos Chausson (King's herald); Robert Schmorr, Neil Wilson, Steven Savino, Kenneth Cox (nobles of Brabant), Eric Redmond (Duke Gottfried von Brabant); Theo Alcantara, conductor; Jay Lesenger, director; Beni Montresor sets/costumes

Hamlet — Ambroise Thomas
October 7, 9m, 12, 15, 1983
Gianna Rolandi (Ophelia), RoseMarie Freni (Gertrude), Michael Cousins (Laertes), William Justus (Hamlet), Robert Hale (Claudius), Neil Wilson (Marcellus), Steven Savino (Horatio/gravedigger), Kenneth Cox (ghost of Hamlet's father), J. Raymond Fielder (Polonius), Joseph Pechota (gravedigger); Bruno Rigacci, conductor; Tito Capobianco, director; Carl Toms, sets

Cinderella — Gioachino Rossini
October 21, 23m, 26, 29, 1983
Amy Burton (Clorinda), Ann Murray (Cinderella), Jane Shaulis (Tisbe), John Aler (Don Ramiro), Alan Titus (Dandini), Richard McKee (Don Magnifico), Kenneth Cox (Alidoro); Karen Keltner, conductor; Robert Tannenbaum, director; Maurice Strike, sets

Anna Bolena — Gaetano Donizetti
February 10, 12m, 15, 18, 1984
Katia Ricciarelli (Anna Bolena), Susanne Marsee (Giovanna Seymour), Susan Quittmeyer (Smeton), Bruce Reed (Lord Riccardo Percy), Robert Hale (Henry VIII), Juan Pedro Garcia Marques (Lord Rochefort), Robert Schmorr (Hervey); Eve Queler, conductor; Jay Lesenger, director; Bill Gorgensen, sets

Don Giovanni — Wolfgang Amadeus Mozart
February 24, 26m, 29, March 3, 1984
Faye Robinson (Donna Anna), Marianna Christos (Donna Elvira), Melanie Sonnenberg (Zerlina), Stuart Burrows (Don Ottavio), Michael Devlin (Don Giovanni), Harlan Foss (Masetto), Kenneth Cox (Commendatore), Richard McKee (Leporello); Christopher Keene, conductor; Wolfgang Weber, director; Toni Businger, sets

Carmen — Georges Bizet
March 8, 11m, 14, 17, 1984
Pamela Myers (Micaëla), Amy Burton (Frasquita), Rachel Gettler (Carmen), Jane Shaulis (Mercédès), Jacque Trussel (Don José), David Hall (Remendado), Charles Long (Escamillo), Juan Pedro Garcia Marques (Zuniga), David Hamilton (Morales), Steven Savino (Dancaïre); Theo Alcantara, conductor; Anthony Besch, director; John Conklin, sets

I Masnadieri — Giuseppe Verdi
June 21, 24m, 30, 1984 *Verdi Festival*
Joan Sutherland (Amalia), Gordon Greer (Carlo), Kirk Redmann (Arminio), Antonio Salvadori (Francesco), Alfredo Zanazzo (Massimiliano), Kenneth Cox (Moser), Steven Savino (Rolla); Richard Bonynge, conductor; Tito Capobianco, director; Bill Gorgensen, sets

Simon Boccanegra — Giuseppe Verdi
June 23, 29, July 1m, 1984 *Verdi Festival*
Martina Arroyo (Amelia), Annette Winchell (maid), Adriaan van Limpt (Adorno), Sherrill Milnes (Boccanegra), Carlos Chausson (Paolo), Nicola Ghiuselev (Fiesco), Steven Savino (Pietro), Max R. Chodos (captain); Edoardo Müller, conductor; Nathaniel Merrill, director; Toni Businger, sets

---

1984-85

Peter Grimes — Benjamin Britten
September 28, 30m, October 3, 7, 1984
Patricia Craig (Ellen), Judith Christin (Auntie), Amy Burton, Candace Rogers (nieces), Luretta Bybee (Mrs. Sedley), Richard Cassilly (Peter Grimes), Michael Sylvester (Bob Boles), Joseph Frank (Rev. Adams), Peter Glossop (Balstrode), Harlan Foss (Ned Keene), Paul Hudson (Swallow), Kenneth Cox (Hobson), Robin Smith (Dr. Crabbe); James Lockhart, conductor; Richard Gregson, director; Carl Toms, sets/costumes

La Traviata — Giuseppe Verdi
October 12, 14m, 17, 20, 1984
Rosalind Plowright/Rosario Andrade (14) (Violetta), Candace Rogers (Annina), Jane Shaulis (Flora), Antonio Barasorda (Alfredo), Robert Schmorr (Gaston), J. Patrick Raftery (Germont), Harlan Foss (Douphol), Kenneth Cox (Grenvil), Robert Tota (Marchese d'Obigny), Gerald Whitney (Giuseppe), Gary Nichols (servant), Jeffrey Shipman (messenger); Thomas Fulton, conductor; David Walsh, director; Carl Toms, sets/costumes

Hansel and Gretel — Engelbert Humperdinck
October 26, 28m, 31, November 3, 1984
Betsy Norden (Gretel), Amy Burton (dew fairy), Rosanne Creffield (Hansel), RoseMarie Freni (Gertrude), Maureen Forrester (Witch), Robin Tabachnik (sandman), William Workman (Peter); Karen Keltner, conductor; Bruce Donnell, director; Harold Laxton, sets/costumes

The Merry Widow — Franz Lehár
February 3, 5, 8, 10m, 1985
Josephine Barstow (Hanna), Leigh Munro (Valencienne), Robin Tabachnik (Sylviane/Frou-Frou), Deidra Palmour (Olga/Margot), Luretta Bybee (Praskowia/Dodo), Carolyn Whyte (Lolo), Anita Colet (Jou-Jou), Phillis Williams (Clo-Clo), Jacque Trussel (Danilo), Jon Garrison (Camille), David Rae Smith (Baron Zeta), Harlan Foss (Cascada), Jon David Gruett (St. Brioche), Philip Larson (Bogdanowitsch), Robert Tota (Kromow), Richard Paul Fink (Pritschitsch), David Hall (Njegus); Scott Bergeson, conductor; Robert Helpmann, director; Carl Toms, sets/costumes

La Bohème — Giacomo Puccini
February 23, 26, March 1, 3m, 1985
Hei-Kyung Hong (Mimì), Leigh Munro (Musetta), Alexandru Ionitza (Rodolfo), Henry Fiske (Parpignol), Frederick

Burchinal (Marcello), Harlan Foss (Schaunard), Jeffrey Wells (Colline), David Hall (Benoit/Alcindoro), John Moir (customs guard), Ronald Banks (sergeant); Robin Stapleton, conductor; Rhoda Levine, director; John Scheffler, sets; Suzanne Mess, costumes

Oberto   Giuseppe Verdi
March 9, 12, 15, 17m, 1985
United States Professional Premiere
Rachel Gettler (Leonora), Susanne Marsee (Cuniza), Carol Kaszar (Imelda), Carlos Montané (Riccardo), Ferruccio Furlanetto (Oberto); Kees Bakels, conductor; Fabrizio Melano, director; Bill Gorgensen, sets; Charles Caine, costumes

Concert: **Luciano Pavarotti**, tenor
June 26, 1985; Sports Arena
Emerson Buckley, conductor

1985-86

The Tales of Hoffmann   Jacques Offenbach
September 28, October 1, 4, 6m, 1985
Nelly Miricioiu (Olympia/Antonia/Giulietta/Stella), Judith Forst (Muse/Nicklausse), Suzanna Guzman (voice of Antonia's mother), Luis Lima (Hoffmann), Leonard Eagleson (Andrés/Cochenille/Frantz/Pittichinaccio), Robert Schmorr (Nathanael/Spalanzani), James Morris (Lindorff/Coppélius/Dr. Miracle/Dappertutto), Carlos Chausson (Hermann/Schlemil), Richard Crist (Luther/Crespel); Theo Alcantara, conductor; Nathaniel Merrill, director; Günther Schneider-Siemssen, sets; Hill Reihs-Gromes, costumes

Eugene Onegin   Peter Ilyich Tchaikovsky
October 26, 29, November 1, 3m, 1985
Kathryn Bouleyn (Tatiana), Kathleen Hegierski (Olga), Lisa Turetsky (Larina), Fredda Rakusin (Filipievna), Richard Greager (Lenski), Bernard Fitch (Triquet), Michael Devlin (Onegin), Don Garrard (Gremin), Richard Paul Fink (captain/Zaretski); Stuart Challender*, conductor; John Copley, director; Robin Don, sets; Michael Stennett, costumes

The Marriage of Figaro   Wolfgang Amadeus Mozart
January 25, 28, 31, February 2m, 1986
Kathryn Bouleyn (Countess), Faith Esham (Susanna), Julia Holland (Barbarina), Susan Quittmeyer (Cherubino), Heather Begg (Marcellina); Carolyn Whyte, Anita Colet (country girls); Jeffrey Thomas (Basilio), David Hall (Curzio), Alan Titus (Count), J. Patrick Raftery (Figaro), Kevin Langan (Bartolo), Carlos Chausson (Antonio); Thomas Schuback, conductor; John Copley, director; Carl Toms, sets; Zack Brown, costumes

Otello   Giuseppe Verdi
February 8, 11, 14, 16m, 1986
Ilona Tokody (Desdemona), Suzanna Guzman (Emilia), Giuseppe Giacomini/Richard Cassilly (14) (Otello), Jon Garrison (Cassio), David Rudat (Roderigo), Silvano Carroli (Iago), Richard Vernon (Lodovico), James Patterson (Montano), Ronald Banks (herald); Michelangelo Veltri, conductor; Lotfi Mansouri, director; Wolfram Skalicki, sets/costumes

The Lighthouse   Peter Maxwell Davies
May 10, 14, 15, 17, 18m, 1986;
Old Globe Theatre
Michael Ballam (Sandy/Officer 1), Harlan Foss (Blazes/Officer 2), James Butler (Arthur/Officer 3/voice of the cards); Karen Keltner, conductor; Jack O'Brien, director; Kent Dorsey, sets; Sally Cleveland, costumes

Recital: **Renata Scotto**, soprano
May 16, 18, 1986; Old Globe Theatre
Robert de Ceunynck, piano

1986-87

Tosca   Giacomo Puccini
October 11, 14, 17, 19m, 1986
Marilyn Zschau (Tosca), Deidra Palmour (shepherd), Vladimir Popov (Cavaradossi), Richard Brunner (Spoletta), George Fortune (Scarpia), Richard McKee (sacristan), David Bernard (Angelotti), David Downing (Sciarrone), Iosif Buibas (jailer); Thomas Fulton, conductor; Sam Wanamaker, director; Allen Charles Klein/Sam Wanamaker, sets/costumes

Norma   Vincenzo Bellini
October 25, 28, 31, November 2m, 1986
Cristina Deutekom (Norma), Delores Ziegler (Adalgisa), Deidra Palmour (Clotilda), Antonio Barasorda (Pollione), Richard Brunner (Flavio), Nicola Ghiuselev (Oroveso); Edoardo Müller, conductor; Bernd Benthaak, director; Carl Toms, sets; Jose Varona, costumes

Recital: **Anna Russell**, raconteuse extraordinaire
November 7, 8, 9, 10, 1986; Old Globe Theatre
Robert Rosenberger, piano

Concert: **Dame Joan Sutherland**, soprano
January 23, 1987; Civic Theatre
Richard Bonynge, conductor

Recital: **Siegfried Jerusalem**, tenor
January 26, 1987; Old Globe Theatre
Siegfried Mauser, piano

The Flying Dutchman   Richard Wagner
February 7, 10, 13, 15m, 1987
Sabine Hass (Senta), Jane Shaulis (Mary), Siegfried Jerusalem (Erik), Michael Sylvester (Steersman), Roger Roloff (Dutchman), Kevin Langan (Daland); Matthias Kuntzsch, conductor; Bernd Benthaak, director; William Gorgensen, sets

The Barber of Seville   Gioachino Rossini
February 21, 24, 27, March 1m, 1987
Susanne Mentzer (Rosina), Jane Shaulis (Berta), Mark DuBois (Almaviva), Hermann Prey (Figaro), François Loup (Bartolo), Kevin Langan (Basilio), Rodney Gilfry (Fiorello), Stan Case (Ambrogio), Ronald Banks (officer); Karen Keltner, conductor; Wolfgang Weber, director; Alfred Siercke, sets/costumes

Recital: **Dame Kiri Te Kanawa**, soprano
February 28, 1987; Civic Theatre
Martin Katz, piano

Porgy and Bess   George Gershwin
March 5, 6, 7m, 7, 8m, 8, 1987
Carmen Balthrop/Henrietta Davis (6, 7, 8) (Bess), Priscilla Baskerville/Theresa Hamm (6, 7, 8) (Serena), Rita McKinley (Clara), Marjorie Wharton (Maria), Geraldine McMillian (Annie), Yvette Matthews (Lily), Denise Woods (strawberry woman), Larry Marshall/Kriss St. Hill (5, 7m, 8m) (Sportin' Life), Donnie Ray Albert/Michel Warren Bell (6, 7, 8) (Porgy), William Bradley-Johnson/Michael Edward-Stevens (6, 7, 8) (Crown), Jubilant Sykes (Jake), Russell St. John (Frazier), Ronn K. Smith (Mingo), Irwin Reese (Robbins), Mervin Wallace (Peter), Bryon Onque (Jim), Autris Paige (Undertaker), Robert McDaniel (Nelson), Cornelius White (crab man), Alfred J. Kiggins (detective), Ted Bouton (policeman), Richert Easley (coroner), Kiah Jackson (Scipio), Nelms McKelvain (Jasbo Brown); Roger Cantrell, conductor; Jack O'Brien, director; Douglas Schmidt, sets; Nancy Potts, costumes

The Telephone   Gian Carlo Menotti
May 9, 11, 13, 15, 17, 1987;
Old Globe Theatre
Amy Burton (Lucy), Wayne Turnage (Ben); Karen Keltner, conductor; Gian Carlo Menotti, director; Zack Brown, sets/costumes

The Medium   Gian Carlo Menotti
May 9, 11, 13, 15, 17, 1987;
Old Globe Theatre
Nadia Pelle (Monica), Beverly Evans (Madame Flora), Barbara Hocher (Mrs. Gobineau), Nancy Carol Moore (Mrs. Nolan), Francis Menotti (Toby), Harlan Foss (Mr. Gobineau); Karen Keltner, conductor; Gian Carlo Menotti, director; Zack Brown, sets/costumes

---

1987-88

Rigoletto   Giuseppe Verdi
October 10, 13, 16, 18m, 1987
Hei-Kyung Hong (Gilda), Kathleen O'Brien (Countess Ceprano), Deborah Clague (page), Martha Jane Weaver (Giovanna), Suzanna Guzman (Maddalena), Diego d'Auria (the Duke), Bernard Fitch (Borsa), John Rawnsley (Rigoletto), Harlan Foss (Marullo), David Downing (Ceprano), Stephen West (Monterone), Jeffrey Wells (Sparafucile); Edoardo Müller, conductor; Robert Tannenbaum, director; Lawrence Schafer, sets/costumes

The Elixir of Love   Gaetano Donizetti
October 31, November 3, 6, 8m, 1987
Glenys Fowles (Adina), Deborah Clague (Giannetta), Denes Gulyas (Nemorino), David Malis (Belcore), John Del Carlo (Dulcamara); Willie Anthony Waters, conductor; Lou Galterio, director; Robert Darling, sets/costumes

Recital: **Carol Vaness**, soprano
November 16, 1987; Sherwood Auditorium
Warren Jones, piano

Recital: **Tatiana Troyanos**, mezzo-soprano
January 25, 1988; Sherwood Auditorium
Warren Jones, piano

Recital: **Håkan Hagegård**, baritone
February 8, 1988; Sherwood Auditorium
Warren Jones, piano

Faust — Charles Gounod
February 13, 16, 19, 21m, 1988
Diana Soviero (Marguerite), Jane Bunnell (Siébel), Judith Christin (Marthe), Richard Leech (Faust), David Malis (Valentin), William Nolan (Wagner), Ferruccio Furlanetto (Méphistophélès); Karen Keltner, conductor; Francesca Zambello, director; Earl Staley, sets/costumes

Il Trovatore — Giuseppe Verdi
February 27, March 1, 4, 6m, 1988
Susan Dunn (Leonora), Dolora Zajick (Azucena), Jane Bunnell (Inez), Ruben Dominguez (Manrico), Bernard Fitch (Ruiz), Jonathan Summers (di Luna), Jeffrey Wells (Ferrando), Ronald Banks (old gypsy); Thomas Fulton, conductor; Richard Gregson, director; Ming Cho Lee, sets

Concert: **Requiem** — Giuseppe Verdi
March 9, 1988; Civic Theatre
Carol Neblett, Dolora Zajick, Dennis O'Neill, Jeffrey Wells, soloists; San Diego Opera Orchestra and Chorus, San Diego Master Chorale; Thomas Fulton, conductor

---

1988-89

Lucia di Lammermoor — Gaetano Donizetti
January 21, 24, 27, 29m, 1989
Gail Dobish (Lucia), Suzanna Guzman (Alisa), Richard Leech (Edgardo), Paul Austin Kelly (Arturo), Martin Chambers (Normanno), J. Patrick Raftery/Pablo Elvira (27, 29m) (Enrico), Kevin Langan (Raimondo); Edoardo Müller, conductor; Rhoda Levine, director; Neil Peter Jampolis, designer

The Peking Opera Company
January 25, 26, 28, 1989; Civic Theatre

Fidelio — Ludwig van Beethoven
February 11, 14, 17, 19m, 1989
Sabine Hass/Elizabeth Connell (14) (Leonora), Sunny Joy Langton (Marzelline), Graeme Matheson-Bruce (Florestan), Randall Outland (Jacquino), Tom Fox (Pizarro), Artur Korn (Rocco), Harry Dworchak (Fernando); Bruce Johnson, William Nolan (prisoners); Edward Downes, conductor; Robert Tannenbaum, director; Neil Peter Jampolis, sets/costumes

Recital: **Robert White**, tenor
February 20, 1989; Sherwood Auditorium
Russell Miller, piano

Don Pasquale — Gaetano Donizetti
March 4, 7, 10, 12m, 1989
Cheryl Parrish (Norina), Mark DuBois/Carroll Freeman (7, 10, 12m) (Ernesto), Victor Ledbetter (Malatesta), François Loup (Pasquale), Ronald Banks (notary); Karen Keltner, conductor; Wolfgang Weber, director; John Conklin, sets

Recital: **Marilyn Horne**, mezzo-soprano
April 8, 1989; Civic Theatre
Martin Katz, piano

Madama Butterfly — Giacomo Puccini
April 15, 18, 21, 23m, 26, 1989
Hiroko Nishida (Cio-Cio-San), Robynne Redmon (Suzuki),

Anne De Vries (Kate), Jonathan Welch (Pinkerton), Joseph Frank (Goro), Harlan Foss (Sharpless), Matthew Carey (commissioner), William Nolan (Yamadori), John Polhamus (registrar), Stephen West (Bonze); Kees Bakels, conductor; Adelaide Bishop, director; John Scheffler, sets; Zack Brown, costumes

---

1989-90

Boris Godunov — Modest Moussorgsky
October 21, 24, 27, 29m, 31, 1989
Soviet Arts Festival
Sylvia Wen (Xenia), Irina Bogacheva (Marina), Martha Jane Howe (innkeeper), Martha Jane Weaver (nurse), Julia Jamison (Feodor), Thomas Booth (Prince Shuisky), Teimuraz Gugushvili (simpleton), Allan Glassman (Grigory), Alexander Morozov (Boris Godunov), Robert Galbraith (Shchelkalov), Gia Asatiani (Pimen), Omar Khoperia (Varlaam), Philip Larson (Nikitich/Lavitsky), William Nolan (Mityukha/border guard/Chernikovsky), Bernard Fitch (Missail), Michael Darcy (a boyar/Krushchov), Stephen West (Rangoni); Jansoug Kakhidze, conductor; Nathaniel Merrill, director; Wolfram Skalicki, sets; Suzanne Mess, costumes

Recital: **Carol Neblett**, soprano
November 19, 1989; Sherwood Auditorium
Thomas Pasatieri, piano

La Bohème — Giacomo Puccini
January 20, 23, 26, 28m, 31, 1990
Ilona Tokody (Mimì), Irena Welhasch (Musetta), Dennis O'Neill (Rodolfo), Daniel S. Leal (Parpignol), Theodore Baerg (Marcello), Harlan Foss (Schaunard), Kevin Langan (Colline), Italo Tajo (Benoit/Alcindoro), John Polhamus (customs guard), Joseph Grienenberger (sergeant); Edoardo Müller, conductor; John Copley, director; John Conklin, sets; Vicki Feitscher, costumes

Dialogues of the Carmelites — Francis Poulenc
February 10, 13, 16, 18m, 1990
Nova Thomas (Blanche), Cheryl Parrish (Constance), Carol Neblett (Lidoine), Heather Begg (Marie), Maureen Forrester (Mme. de Croissy), Judith Christin (Jeanne), Martha Jane Howe (Mathilde), Kip Wilborn (Chevalier de la Force), Peter Van Derick (Marquis de la Force), Martin Chambers (Father), Michael Darcy (officer), Joseph Grienenberger (Thierry), Jeffrey Shipman (Javelinot), Michael Ballam (commissary), Harlan Foss (commissary/jailer); Richard Bonynge, conductor; Bliss Hebert, director; Günther Schneider-Siemssen, sets; Allen Charles Klein, costumes

The Daughter of the Regiment — Gaetano Donizetti
March 3, 6, 9, 11m, 1990
Nova Thomas (Marie), Heather Begg (Countess of Birkenfeld), Kit Goldman (Duchess of Crackenthorp), Paul Hartfield (Tonio), Daniel S. Leal (peasant), John Del Carlo (Sulpice), Harlan Foss (Hortensio), William Nolan (corporal); Richard Bonynge, conductor; Lou Galterio, director; Beni Montresor, sets/costumes

The Great Richard Wagner Concert
March 20, 1990; Civic Theatre
Johanna Meier, Gary Lakes, John Macurdy, soloists; Heinz Fricke, conductor

The Magic Flute — Wolfgang Amadeus Mozart
April 14, 17, 20, 22m, 25, 1990
Virginia Sublett (Queen of the Night), Hei-Kyung Hong (Pamina), Sylvia Wen (Papagena); Joan Gibbons, Gale Fuller, Deidra Palmour (three ladies); Denes Gulyas (Tamino), Anthony Laciura (Monostatos), David Malis (Papageno), Kenneth Cox (Sarastro), Herbert Eckhoff (speaker); Hong-Shen Li, J. Raymond Fielder (priests/armored men); Celeste Tavera, Diana Tash, Julia Jamison (three spirits); Karen Keltner, conductor; Wolfgang Weber, director; Maurice Sendak, sets/costumes

---

1990-91

Recital: **Hans Peter Blochwitz**, tenor
October 21, 1990; Sherwood Auditorium
Peter Grunberg, piano

Recital: **Dmitri Hvorostovsky**, baritone
October 28, 1990; Sherwood Auditorium
Mikhail Arkadiev, piano

Così fan tutte — Wolfgang Amadeus Mozart
January 19, 22, 25, 27m, 30, 1991
Carol Vaness (Fiordiligi), Barbara Bonney (Despina), Judith Forst (Dorabella), Keith Lewis (Ferrando), Håkan Hagegård (Guglielmo), Peter Strummer (Don Alfonso); Thomas Schuback, conductor; John Copley, director; Peter Cooke, sets; Michael Stennett, costumes

Albert Herring — Benjamin Britten
February 9, 12, 15, 17m, 1991
Christine Brewer (Lady Billows), Judith Lovat (Miss Wordsworth), Susan Graham (Nancy), Patricia Kern (Mrs. Herring), Martha Jane Howe (Florence), Barton Green (Albert Herring), Francis Egerton (Mayor), Harlan Foss (Vicar), Matthew Carey (Sid), James Scott Sikon (Supt. Budd); Mary Dombek (Emmie), Patricia Prunty (Cis), Christopher Johnson (Harry); Steuart Bedford, conductor; Colin Graham, director; Neil Peter Jampolis, sets; Debra Hanson, costumes

Die Fledermaus — Johann Strauss, Jr.
March 2, 5, 8, 10m, 13, 1991
Karen Huffstodt (Rosalinda), Cheryl Parrish (Adele), Suzanna Guzman (Orlofsky), Ronald Stevens (Eisenstein), Douglas Johnson (Alfred), Beau Palmer (Blind), Richard McKee (Frank), Victor Ledbetter (Falke), Zale Kessler (Frosch); Karen Keltner, conductor; Wolfgang Weber, director; Oliver Smith, sets; Ann Roth, costumes

The Passion of Jonathan Wade — Carlisle Floyd
April 13, 16, 19, 21m, 1991
West Coast Premiere
Sheryl Woods (Celia), Débria Brown (Nicey), Bridget Knott (girl), Erich Parce (Wade), Eric Perkins (Lt. Patrick), Harlan Foss (Riddle), Joseph Evans (Wardlaw), John Duykers (Pratt), Michel Warren Bell (Judge Bell), Julian Patrick (Townsend), William Nolan (wounded soldier/Branch), Daniel S. Leal (Union leaguer); Adam Russell, Joseph Grienenberger (soldiers); David Downing (Rector); Edward Badrak, Max Chodos (carpetbaggers); Michael Morgan (senator); Tom Touw (young boy); Shalonda French, Warren Nolan, Phillip Edwards, Scott Jones (youths); Kenneth Montgomery, conductor; Carlisle Floyd, director; Günther Schneider-Siemssen, sets; Allen Charles Klein, costumes

La Traviata Giuseppe Verdi
May 4, 7, 10, 11, 12m, 1991
Christine Weidinger/Frances Ginsberg (11) (Violetta), Patricia Minton Smith (Annina), Gale Fuller (Flora), Fernando de la Mora/Walter MacNeil (11) (Alfredo), Beau Palmer (Gaston), Richard Stilwell/Richard J. Clark (11) (Germont), Harlan Foss (Douphol), David Downing (Grenvil), Mark Anderson (Marchese d'Obigny), Daniel S. Leal (Giuseppe), Jeffery Shipman (servant), Joseph Grienenberger (messenger); Edoardo Müller, conductor; Wolfgang Weber, director; John Conklin, sets; David Walker, costumes

---

1991-92

Der Rosenkavalier Richard Strauss
January 18, 21, 24, 26m, 29, 1992
Ashley Putnam (Feldmarschallin), Barbara Kilduff (Sophie), Patricia Minton Smith (Marianne), Susanne Mentzer (Octavian), Suzanna Guzman (Annina); Dawn Veree Harrison, Angela Milia, Katherine Lundeen (three noble orphans); Betsy McLean (milliner), Jonathan Welch/Jorge Lopez-Yañez (29) (singer), Bernard Fitch (Valzacchi), Beau Palmer (animal vendor/major-domo/innkeeper), Georg Tichy* (Herr von Faninal), Artur Korn (Baron Ochs), Daniel S. Leal (major-domo), David Downing (notary); Matthew Alexander, James Banner, Joel Snyder, Gerald Whitney (lackeys); Kevin Bell (commissioner); Heinz Fricke, conductor; Wolfgang Weber, director; Allen Charles Klein, sets; Ray Diffen, costumes

The Marriage of Figaro Wolfgang Amadeus Mozart
February 8, 11, 14, 16m, 19, 1992
Rita Cullis* (Countess), Cheryl Parrish (Susanna), Sylvia Wen (Barbarina), Emily Manhart (Cherubino), Judith Christin/Martha Jane Howe (19) (Marcellina); Betsy McLean, Katherine Lundeen (country girls); Jerold Siena (Basilio), Beau Palmer (Curzio), David Malis (Count), John Pringle* (Figaro), François Loup (Bartolo), James Scott Sikon (Antonio); Edoardo Müller/Karen Keltner (19), conductors; John Copley, director; Zack Brown, sets/costumes

Recital: **Hermann Prey**, baritone
February 15, 1992; Sherwood Auditorium
Leonard Hokanson, piano

Recital: **Delores Ziegler**, mezzo-soprano
February 23, 1992; Sherwood Auditorium
Massimiliano Murrali, piano

The Rape of Lucretia Benjamin Britten
February 29, March 3, 6, 8m, 11, 1992
Rita Cullis (female chorus), Judith Lovat (Lucia), Melanie Sonnenberg (Lucretia), Martha Jane Howe (Bianca), Robert Tear (male chorus), Louis Otey (Tarquinius), Richard Zeller (Junius), Mark S. Doss (Collatinus); Christopher Keene, conductor; Jonathan Eaton, director; Neil Peter Jampolis, sets; Debra Hanson, costumes

The Merry Widow Franz Lehár
April 4, 7, 10, 12m, 15, 1992
Glenys Fowles (Hanna), Sunny Joy Langton (Valencienne), Catherine Stapleton (Sylviane/Frou-Frou), Melody Rossi (Olga/Margot), Anita Colet (Praskowia/Dodo), Betsy McLean (Lolo), Erica Rose (Jou-Jou), Dawn Veree Harrison (Clo-Clo), Theodore Baerg (Danilo), Gregory Kunde (Camille), John Del Carlo (Baron Zeta), Richard Byrne (Cascada), Dennis McNeil (St. Brioche), David Downing (Bogdanowitsch), Jeffrey Calof

(Kromow), William Nolan (Pritschitsch), Beau Palmer (Njegus); Karen Keltner, conductor; Lou Galterio, director; Carl Toms, sets/costumes

Carmen Georges Bizet
April 25, 28, May 1, 3m, 6, 1992
Ai-Lan Zhu (Micaëla), Jeralyn Refeld (Frasquita), Adria Firestone (Carmen), Gale Fuller (Mercédès), Arthur Davies (Don José), Dennis McNeil (Remendado), Richard Paul Fink (Escamillo), Mark S. Doss (Zuniga), Richard Byrne (Morales), Matthew Carey (Dancaïre); Kees Bakels, conductor; Rosalind Elias, director; John Conklin, sets; Peter J. Hall, costumes

---

1992-93

Concert: **Luciano Pavarotti**, tenor
October 22, 1992; Sports Arena
Leone Magiera, conductor

The Barber of Seville Gioachino Rossini
January 23, 26, 29, 31m, February 3, 1993
Delores Ziegler (Rosina), Ellen Rabiner (Berta), Don Bernardini (Almaviva), Jeffrey Black/David Malis (29) (Figaro), François Loup (Bartolo), Kevin Langan (Don Basilio), Roberto Gomez (Fiorello), Barry Dennen/Christopher Harlan (31) (Ambrogio), Edward Badrak (officer); Edoardo Müller, conductor; John Copley, director; John Conklin, sets; Michael Stennett, costumes

Madama Butterfly Giacomo Puccini
February 13, 16, 19, 21m, 24, 1993
Elizabeth Hynes (Cio-Cio-San), Yun Deng (Suzuki), Sarah Blaze (Kate), César Hernández (Pinkerton), Douglas Perry (Goro), Richard Stilwell (Sharpless), Scott Raines (commissioner), Roberto Gomez (Yamadori), Joseph Grienenberger (registrar), Michel Warren Bell (Bonze); Edoardo Müller, conductor; Adelaide Bishop, director; John Scheffler, sets; Zack Brown, costumes

Don Giovanni Wolfgang Amadeus Mozart
March 6, 9, 12, 14m, 17, 1993
Rita Cullis (Donna Anna), Patricia Schuman (Donna Elvira), Emily Manhart (Zerlina), Hans Peter Blochwitz (Don Ottavio), Ferruccio Furlanetto (Don Giovanni), Victor Ledbetter (Masetto), John Macurdy (Commendatore), Dean Peterson (Leporello); Edoardo Müller, conductor; Wolfgang Weber, director; Carl-Friedrich Oberle, sets/costumes

The Pearl Fishers Georges Bizet
March 27, 30, April 2, 4m, 7, 1993
Jan Grissom (Leila), Patrick Power (Nadir), Michael Lewis* (Zurga), Mark S. Doss (Nourabad); Karen Keltner, conductor; Johnathon Pape, director; Darren Scott Maynard, sets; Marjorie McCown, costumes

Werther Jules Massenet
April 17, 20, 23, 25m, 28, 1993
Jeanine Thames (Sophie), Jean Rigby* (Charlotte), Anita Colet (Käthchen), Richard Leech (Werther), Beau Palmer (Schmidt), Vernon Hartman (Albert), Herbert Eckhoff (bailiff), James Scott Sikon (Johann), Mark Andrew Richards (Brühlmann); Richard Bonynge, conductor; Bliss Hebert, director; Allen Charles Klein, sets/costumes

---

1993-94

Recital: **José Carreras,** tenor
July 5, 1993; Civic Theatre
Enrique Ricci, piano

Eugene Onegin Peter Ilyich Tchaikovsky
January 22, 25, 28, 30m, February 2, 1994
Renée Fleming (Tatiana), Kathleen Hegierski (Olga), Martha Jane Howe (Larina), Débria Brown (Filipievna), Hans Peter Blochwitz (Lensky), Douglas Perry (Triquet), Jeffrey Black (Onegin), Stefan Szkafarowsky (Gremin), David Downing (captain/Zaretsky); Kenneth Montgomery, conductor; John Copley, director; Robin Don, sets; Michael Stennett, costumes

Rigoletto Giuseppe Verdi
February 12, 15, 18, 20m, 23, 1994
Sheryl Woods (Gilda), Sarah Blaze (Countess Ceprano/page), Martha Jane Weaver (Giovanna), Suzanna Guzman (Maddalena), Fernando de la Mora (the Duke), Beau Palmer (Borsa), Haijing Fu (Rigoletto), David Downing (Marullo), Michael L. Morgan (Ceprano), James Scott Sikon (Monterone), Valentin Peytchinov (Sparafucile); Elio Boncompagni, conductor; Wolfgang Weber, director; Zack Brown, sets/costumes

Rappaccini's Daughter Daniel Catán
March 5, 8, 11, 13m, 16, 1994
United States Premiere
North American Voices Project
Encarnación Vázquez (Beatriz), Ellen Rabiner (Isabela); Patricia Minton, Andrea Mays, Diane Winterton (off-stage voices); Fernando de la Mora (Giovanni), Ignacio Clapés (Dr. Baglioni), Oscar Sámano (Dr. Rappaccini); Eduardo Diazmuñoz, conductor; Johnathon Pape, director; John Conklin, sets; Barbara Bush, costumes

La Sonnambula Vincenzo Bellini
April 9, 12, 15, 17m, 20, 1994
Deborah Riedel* (Amina), Patricia McAfee (Teresa), Sylvia Wen (Lisa), Ramón Vargas (Elvino), Julien Robbins (Rodolfo), James Wood (Alessio), Adam Russell (notary); Richard Bonynge, conductor; Leon Major, director; Zack Brown, sets/costumes

The Tales of Hoffmann Jacques Offenbach
April 30, May 3, 6, 8m, 11, 1994
Nova Thomas (Olympia/Giulietta/Antonia/Stella), Jean Rigby (Nicklausse/muse), Patricia McAfee (voice of Antonia's mother), Jerry Hadley (Hoffmann), Graeme Ewer* (Andrés/Cochenille/Pittichinaccio/Frantz), César Ulloa (Nathanael/Spalanzani), James Wood (Hermann/Schlémil), Louis Otey (Lindorf/Coppélius/Dapertutto/Dr. Miracle), Herbert Eckhoff (Luther/Crespel); Richard Bonynge, conductor; Wolfgang Weber, director; Günther Schneider-Siemssen, sets; Hill Reihs-Gromes, costumes

---

1994-95

Rusalka Antonin Dvořák
January 21, 24, 27, 29m, February 1, 1995
Renée Fleming (Rusalka), Adrienne Dugger (foreign princess), Carter Scott (Ježibaba), Judith Lovat, Manhua Zhan, Annette Daniels (nymphs); Neil Rosenshein (Prince), Mark S. Doss (Water Sprite), Roberto Gomez (hunter); Albert Rosen, conductor; Wolfgang Weber, director; Günther Schneider-Siemssen, sets; Deitmar Solt, costumes

Lucia di Lammermoor
Gaetano Donizetti

February 11, 14, 17, 19m, 22, 1995

Martile Rowland (Lucia), Sarah Blaze (Alisa), Ramón Vargas (Edgardo), Joseph Hu (Arturo), Beau Palmer (Normanno), Haijing Fu (Enrico), Richard Vernon (Raimondo); Willie Anthony Waters, conductor; Johnathon Pape, director; Neil Peter Jampolis, sets; Peter J. Hall, costumes

Porgy and Bess
George Gershwin

March 8, 9, 10, 11m, 11, 12, 1995

North American Voices Project

Marquita Lister/Charlae Olaker (9, 11m, 12) (Bess), Luvenia Garner/Angela R. Simpson (9, 11m, 12) (Serena), Kimberly Jones (Clara), Ann Duquesnay (Maria), Sabrina Carten (Annie), Lou Ann Pickett (Lily), Hope Briggs (strawberry woman), Larry Marshall (Sportin' Life), Alvy Powell/Terry Cook (9, 11m, 12) (Porgy), Stacey Robinson/Lester Lynch (8, 10, 11)/Jeffrey La Var (12) (Crown), Elex Lee Vann (Jake), Keith Crawford (Frazier), Barron Coleman (Mingo), Richard Taylor (Robbins), Stanley Jackson (Peter), Mathew J. Minor (Jim), Henry Jones (Undertaker), John Lesane (Nelson), David Lee Brewer (crab man), Charles Sanders (detective), Russell Johnson (coroner), Richard Taylor (African drummer); John DeMain/Douglas Fisher (12), conductor; Hope Clarke, director; Kenneth Foy, sets; Judy Dearing, costumes

---

Recital: **Jerry Hadley**, tenor; **Thomas Hampson**, baritone

March 18, 1995; Civic Theatre

Craig Rutenberg, piano

Macbeth
Giuseppe Verdi

March 25, 28, 31, April 2m, 5, 1995

Rosalind Plowright (Lady Macbeth), Patricia McAfee (nurse); E.J. Mout, Erick Rarick (apparitions); Antonio Barasorda (Macduff), Roman Tsymbala (Malcolm), Michael Stevens (servant/herald), Timothy Noble (Macbeth), Ronald Banks (assassin/apparition), Kenneth Cox (Banquo), Philip Larson (Doctor); Edoardo Müller, conductor; Wolfgang Weber, director; Davis West, sets; Suzanne Mess, costumes

La Bohème
Giacomo Puccini

April 22, 25, 28, 30m, May 3, 1995

Patricia Racette (Mimì), Rosemary Musoleno (Musetta), Richard Leech (Rodolfo), Daniel S. Leal (Parpignol), Mark Oswald (Marcello), Jeff Mattsey (Schaunard), Yanni Yannissis (Colline), James Scott Sikon (Benoit/Alcindoro), David Shaffer (customs guard), Ronald Banks (sergeant); Edoardo Müller, conductor; Lesley Koenig, director; John Conklin, sets; Martin Pakledinaz, costumes

---

1995-96

Recital: **Cecilia Bartoli**, mezzo-soprano

September 17, 1995; Civic Theatre

Steven Blier, piano

Tosca
Giacomo Puccini

January 20, 23, 26, 28m, 31, 1996

Nelly Miricioiu (Tosca), Casey McKinley (shepherd), César Hernández (Cavaradossi), Alan Fischer (Spoletta), James Morris (Scarpia), Roberto Gomez (sacristan), David Downing (Angelotti/Sciarrone), Philip Larson (jailer); Edoardo Müller, conductor; Bliss Hebert, director; Jean-Pierre Ponnelle, sets; Suzanne Mess, costumes

The Elixir of Love
Gaetano Donizetti

February 10, 13, 16, 18m, 21, 1996

Deborah Riedel (Adina), Sylvia Wen (Giannetta), Patrick Power (Nemorino), David Malis (Belcore), Andrew Shore* (Dulcamara); Karen Keltner, conductor; John Cox, director; Roger Butlin, sets; Stephen Brimson-Lewis, costumes

The Passion of Jonathan Wade
Carlisle Floyd

March 2, 5, 8, 10m, 1996

North American Voices Project

Sheryl Woods (Celia), Débria Brown (Nicey), Deanna Barraza (girl), Erich Parce (Wade), Beau Palmer (Lt. Patrick), David Downing (Riddle/Rector), Joseph Evans (Wardlaw), John Duykers (Pratt), Michel Warren Bell (Judge Bell), Julian Patrick (Townsend), William Nolan (wounded soldier/Branch), Daniel S. Leal (Union leaguer); Ryan Lowe, Joseph Grienenberger (soldiers); Joseph Sundstrom, Walter Du Melle (carpetbaggers); Arthur Wheatfall (senator); Kaira Cooper, Remy Abraham, Epherium Morgan, Warren Nolan (youths); Kenneth Montgomery, conductor; Carlisle Floyd, director; Günther Schneider-Siemssen, sets; Allen Charles Klein, costumes

Cinderella
Gioachino Rossini

April 6, 9, 12, 14m, 1996

Evelyn de la Rosa (Clorinda), Margaret Lattimore (Cinderella), Carter Scott (Tisbe), Bradley Williams (Don Ramiro), Erich Parce (Dandini), François Loup (Don Magnifico), Kevin Langan (Alidoro); Karen Keltner, conductor; Linda Brovsky, director; Claude Girard/ Bernard Uzan, sets/costumes

Aida
Giuseppe Verdi

April 27, 30, May 3, 5m, 8, 1996

Michèle Crider* (Aida), Sherri Dukes Williams (high priestess), Stefania Kaluza* (Amneris), Lando Bartolini (Radames), Mark Rucker (Amonasro), Hao Jiang Tian (Ramfis), Andrew Wentzel (King), Matthew Bitetti (messenger); Michelangelo Veltri, conductor; Dejan Miladinovic, director; Michael Yeargan, sets; Peter J. Hall, costumes

---

1996-97

Carmen
Georges Bizet

January 18, 21, 24, 26m, 29, 1997

Cynthia Clayton (Micaëla), Sylvia Wen (Frasquita), Adria Firestone (Carmen), Sarah Blaze (Mercédès), Richard Leech (Don José), Beau Palmer (Remendado), Louis Otey (Escamillo), James Butler (Zuniga), Roberto Gomez (Morales), Stephen Powell (Dancaïre); Richard Bonynge, conductor; James de Blasis, director; John Conklin, sets; Peter J. Hall, costumes

The Italian Girl in Algiers
Gioachino Rossini

February 8, 11, 14, 16m, 1997

Anita De Simone (Elvira), Vivica Genaux (Isabella), Ava Baker Liss (Zulma), Bruce Fowler (Lindoro), Reinhard Dorn* (Taddeo), James Butler (Haly), John del Carlo (Mustafà); Karen Keltner, conductor; Leon Major, director; Zack Brown, sets/costumes

The Conquistador
Myron Fink

March 1, 4, 7, 9m, 1997

North American Voices Project

World Premiere

Kerry O'Brien (Ghost of Doña Leonora), Elizabeth Hynes (Doña Elena), Adria Firestone (Doña Francisca), Vivica Genaux (Isabel), Jerry Hadley (Don Luis de Carvajal), Beau Palmer (Alvaro), John Duykers (Dr. Guerrero), Louis Otey (Don Alvaro de Zuniga), David Downing (Gaspar), Duane McDevitt (Dr. Ribera), Stephen Powell (Felipe Núñez), Kenneth Cox (Sahagún), James Scott Sikon (Baltasar), Philip Larson (Machado), Diane Winterton, Richelle Marie Triglia, Lee Jessica Froelich, Chelsea Basler, Casey McKinley, Scot Fagerland, Mark Loewen (Doña Francisca's family), Gerry Whitney (Juan Talalpa), John Slivon (an officer), Walter Du Melle (a merchant), David Shaffer (a landowner); Karen Keltner, conductor; Sharon Ott, director; Kent Dorsey, sets; Deborah Dryden, costumes

La Traviata
Giuseppe Verdi

April 5, 8, 11, 13m, 16, 1996

Deborah Riedel (Violetta), Patricia McAfee (Annina), Carter Scott (Flora), Jorge Lopez-Yañez (Alfredo), Joseph Hu (Gaston), Richard Zeller (Germont), Duane McDevitt (Douphol), David Downing (Grenvil), James Scott Sikon (Marquis d'Obigny), John Slivon (Giuseppe), Walter Du Melle (messenger), Jeffrey Shipman (servant); Richard Bonynge, conductor; Wolfgang Weber, director; John Conklin, sets; David Walker, costumes

---

Concert: **Plácido Domingo**, tenor

with Ainhoa Arteta, soprano

April 10, 1997; Civic Theatre

Edoardo Müller, Conductor

Turandot
Giacomo Puccini

April 26, 29, May 2, 4m, 7, 1997

Jane Eaglen (Turandot), Ai-Lan Zhu (Liù), Richard Margison (Calaf), Beau Palmer (Pang), Joseph Hu (Pong), Alan Fischer (Altoum), Kevin Langan (Timur), Stephen Powell (Ping), Roberto Gomez (Mandarin); Edoardo Müller, conductor; Lotfi Mansouri, director; David Hockney, sets; Ian Falconer, costumes

---

The Abduction from the Seraglio [*Mozart*] 79-80
Adriana Lecouvreur [*Cilea*] 82-83
Aida [*Verdi*] 66-67, 72-73, 77-78, 82-83, 95-96
Albert Herring [*Britten*] 90-91
Andrea Chénier [*Giordano*] 81-82
Anna Bolena [*Donizetti*] 83-84
Un Ballo in Maschera [*Verdi*] 81-82
The Barber of Seville [*Rossini*] 65-66, 71-72, 81-82, 86-87, 92-93
La Bohème [*Puccini*] 65-66, 68-69, 74-75, 79-80, 84-85, 89-90, 94-95
Boris Godunov [*Moussorgsky*] 71-72, 89-90
Carmen [*Bizet*] 67-68, 73-74, 77-78, 83-84, 91-92, 96-97
Cavalleria Rusticana [*Mascagni*] 78-79
Cinderella [*Rossini*] 83-84, 95-96
The Conquistador [*Fink*] 96-97
Il Corsaro [*Verdi*] 81-82
Così fan tutte [*Mozart*] 78-79, 90-91
The Daughter of the Regiment [*Donizetti*] 72-73, 73-74, 89-90,
Dialogues of the Carmelites [*Poulenc*] 89-90
Don Carlo [*Verdi*] 79-80
Don Giovanni [*Mozart*] 77-78, 83-84, 92-93
Don Pasquale [*Donizetti*] 79-80, 87-88
Don Quixote [*Massenet*] 68-69
Elektra [*R. Strauss*] 80-81
The Elixir of Love [*Donizetti*] 86-87, 95-96
Eugene Onegin [*Tchaikovsky*] 85-86, 93-94
Falstaff [*Verdi*] 77-78
Faust [*Gounod*] 65-66, 69-70, 81-82, 86-87
Fidelio [*Beethoven*] 87-88
Die Fledermaus [*J. Strauss Jr.*] 76-77, 80-81, 90-91
The Flying Dutchman [*Wagner*] 86-87
Gianni Schicchi [*Puccini*] 71-72
Giovanna d'Arco [*Verdi*] 79-80
Giulietta e Romeo [*Zandonai*] 81-82
Götterdämmerung [*Wagner*] 76-77
Gwendoline [*Chabrier*] 82-83
Hamlet [*Thomas*] 78-79, 83-84
Hansel and Gretel [*Humperdinck*] 84-85
Help, Help the Globolinks! [*Menotti*] 71-72
Henry VIII [*Saint-Saëns*] 82-83
The Italian Girl in Algiers [*Rossini*] 96-97
The Lighthouse [*Davies*] 85-86
La Loca [*Menotti*] 78-79
Lohengrin [*Wagner*] 83-84
I Lombardi [*Verdi*] 78-79
The Love for Three Oranges [*Prokofiev*] 77-78, 80-81
Lucia di Lammermoor [*Donizetti*] 74-75, 80-81, 87-88, 94-95
Macbeth [*Verdi*] 94-95

Madama Butterfly [*Puccini*] 70-71, 77-78, 82-83, 87-88, 92-93
The Magic Flute [*Mozart*] 67-68, 89-90
Manon [*Massenet*] 74-75
Manon Lescaut [*Puccini*] 78-79
The Marriage of Figaro [*Mozart*] 73-74, 85-86, 91-92
I Masnadieri [*Verdi*] 83-84
Medea [*Henderson*] 72-73
The Medium [*Menotti*] 86-87
Mefistofele [*Boito*] 73-74, 79-80
The Merry Widow [*Lehár*] 77-78, 84-85, 91-92
The Moon [*Orff*] 69-70
Nabucco [*Verdi*] 80-81
Norma [*Bellini*] 75-76, 86-87
Oberto [*Verdi*] 84-85
Otello [*Verdi*] 76-77, 85-86
Pagliacci [*Leoncavallo*] 69-70, 78-79
The Passion of Jonathan Wade [*Floyd*] 90-91, 95-96
The Pearl Fishers [*Bizet*] 92-93
La Périchole [*Offenbach*] 82-83
Peter Grimes [*Britten*] 84-85
Porgy and Bess [*Gershwin*] 86-87, 94-95
The Rape of Lucretia [*Britten*] 91-92
Rappaccini's Daughter [*Catán*] 93-94
Requiem [*Verdi*] 77-78, 80-81, 86-87
The Rhinegold [*Wagner*] 73-74
Rigoletto [*Verdi*] 68-69, 78-79, 86-87, 93-94
Romeo and Juliet [*Gounod*] 72-73
Der Rosenkavalier [*R. Strauss*] 75-76, 91-92
Rusalka [*Dvořák*] 75-76, 94-95
The Saint of Bleecker Street [*Menotti*] 76-77
Salome [*R. Strauss*] 67-68
Siegfried [*Wagner*] 75-76
Simon Boccanegra [*Verdi*] 83-84
La Sonnambula [*Bellini*] 93-94
Susannah [*Floyd*] 81-82
The Tales of Hoffmann [*Offenbach*] 69-70, 79-80, 85-86, 93-94
Tannhäuser [*Wagner*] 69-70
The Telephone [*Menotti*] 86-87
Tosca [*Puccini*] 66-67, 73-74, 80-81, 86-87, 95-96
La Traviata [*Verdi*] 70-71, 76-77, 78-79, 84-85, 90-91, 96-97
Il Trovatore [*Verdi*] 75-76, 79-80, 86-87
Turandot [*Puccini*] 71-72, 81-82, 96-97
The Valkyrie [*Wagner*] 74-75
A Village Romeo and Juliet [*Delius*] 74-75
Werther [*Massenet*] 80-81, 92-93
The Young Lord [*Henze*] 66-67

San Diego Opera Chronology
1965 - 1997
COMPOSERS

Ludwig van Beethoven
Fidelio — 87-88

Vincenzo Bellini
La Sonnambula — 93-94
Norma — 75-76, 86-87

Georges Bizet
Carmen — 67-68, 73-74, 77-78, 83-84, 91-92, 96-97
The Pearl Fishers — 92-93

Arrigo Boito
Mefistofele — 73-74, 79-80

Benjamin Britten
Albert Herring — 90-91
Peter Grimes — 84-85
The Rape of Lucretia — 91-92

Daniel Catán
Rappaccini's Daughter — 93-94

Emmanuel Chabrier
Gwendoline — 82-83

Francesco Cilea
Adriana Lecouvreur — 82-83

Peter Maxwell Davies
The Lighthouse — 85-86

Frederick Delius
A Village Romeo and Juliet — 74-75

Gaetano Donizetti
Anna Bolena — 83-84
Don Pasquale — 79-80, 87-88
Lucia di Lammermoor — 74-75, 80-81, 87-88, 94-95
The Daughter of the Regiment — 72-73, 73-74, 89-90
The Elixir of Love — 86-87, 95-96

Antonin Dvořák
Rusalka — 75-76, 94-95

Myron Fink
The Conquistador — 96-97

Carlisle Floyd
Susannah — 81-82
The Passion of Jonathan Wade — 90-91, 95-96

George Gershwin
Porgy and Bess — 86-87, 94-95

Umberto Giordano
Andrea Chénier — 81-82

Charles Gounod
Faust — 65-66, 69-70, 81-82, 86-87
Romeo and Juliet — 72-73

Alva Henderson
Medea — 72-73

Hans Werner Henze
The Young Lord — 66-67

Engelbert Humperdinck
Hansel and Gretel — 84-85

Franz Lehár
The Merry Widow — 77-78, 84-85, 91-92

Ruggiero Leoncavallo
Pagliacci — 69-70, 78-79

Pietro Mascagni
Cavalleria Rusticana — 78-79

Jules Massenet
Don Quixote — 68-69
Manon — 74-75
Werther — 80-81, 92-93

Gian Carlo Menotti
Help, Help the Globolinks! — 71-72
La Loca — 78-79
The Medium — 86-87
The Saint of Bleecker Street — 76-77
The Telephone — 86-87

Modest Moussorgsky
Boris Godunov — 71-72, 89-90

Wolfgang Amadeus Mozart
Così fan tutte — 78-79, 90-91
Don Giovanni — 77-78, 83-84, 92-93
The Abduction from the Seraglio — 79-80
The Magic Flute — 67-68, 89-90
The Marriage of Figaro — 73-74, 85-86, 91-92

Jacques Offenbach
La Périchole — 82-83
The Tales of Hoffmann — 69-70, 79-80, 85-86, 93-94

Carl Orff
The Moon — 69-70

Francis Poulenc
Dialogues of the Carmelites — 89-90

Sergei Prokofiev
The Love for Three Oranges — 77-78, 80-81

Giacomo Puccini
Gianni Schicchi — 71-72
La Bohème — 65-66, 68-69, 74-75, 79-80, 84-85, 89-90, 94-95
Madama Butterfly — 70-71, 77-78, 82-83, 87-88, 92-93
Manon Lescaut — 78-79
Tosca — 66-67, 73-74, 80-81, 86-87, 95-96
Turandot — 71-72, 81-82, 96-97

Gioachino Rossini
Cinderella — 83-84, 95-96
The Barber of Seville — 65-66, 71-72, 81-82, 86-87, 92-93
The Italian Girl in Algiers — 96-97

Camille Saint-Saëns
Henry VIII — 82-83

Johann Strauss Jr.
Die Fledermaus — 76-77, 80-81, 90-91

Richard Strauss
Der Rosenkavalier — 75-76, 91-92
Elektra — 80-81
Salome — 67-68

Peter Ilyich Tchaikovsky
Eugene Onegin — 85-86, 93-94

Ambroise Thomas
Hamlet — 78-79, 83-84

Giuseppe Verdi
Aida — 66-67, 72-73, 77-78, 82-83, 95-96
Don Carlo — 79-80
Falstaff — 77-78
Giovanna d'Arco — 79-80
I Lombardi — 78-79
I Masnadieri — 83-84
Il Corsaro — 81-82
Il Trovatore — 75-76, 79-80, 86-87
La Traviata — 70-71, 76-77, 78-79, 84-85, 90-91, 96-97
Macbeth — 94-95
Nabucco — 80-81
Oberto — 84-85
Otello — 76-77, 85-86
Requiem — 77-78, 80-81, 86-87
Rigoletto — 68-69, 78-79, 86-87, 93-94
Simon Boccanegra — 83-84
Un Ballo in Maschera — 81-82

Richard Wagner
The Flying Dutchman — 86-87
Götterdämmerung — 76-77
Lohengrin — 83-84
Siegfried — 75-76
Tannhäuser — 69-70
The Rhinegold — 73-74
The Valkyrie — 74-75

Riccardo Zandonai
Giulietta e Romeo — 81-82

- A -

Abraham, Remy, 95-96
Abrams, Richard, 75-76
Adams, William, 65-66, 66-67, 67-68, 68-69, 69-70, 70-71, 71-72
Adler, Kurt Herbert, 81-82
Adler, Ronald*, 78-79
Aguirre, Francisco, 68-69
Albert, Donnie Ray, 86-87
Alcantara, Theo, 75-76, 76-77, 77-78, 78-79, 79-80, 80-81, 81-82, 82-83, 83-84, 85-86
Aldredge, Theoni V., 74-75
Alexander, John, 75-76
Alexander, Matthew, 91-92
Allen, Ross, 72-73
Allen, Ryan, 76-77, 77-78
Altmeyer, Jeannine, 79-80
Amara, Lucine, 66-67
Anderson, Alfred, 73-74
Anderson, June, 81-82
Anderson, Marilyn, 81-82
Anderson, Mark, 90-91
Anderson, Sylvia, 75-76
Andrade, Rosario, 84-85
Andrew, Jon, 72-73, 74-75, 76-77
Aragon, Horacio, 77-78
Arena, Maurizio, 78-79, 80-81
Arkadiev, Mikhail, 90-91
Armstrong, Karan, 74-75
Arroyo, Martina, 77-78, 79-80, 80-81, 82-83, 83-84
Arteta, Ainhoa, 96-97
Asatiani, Gia, 89-90
Atack, Sharon, 70-71
Atherton, James, 73-74
Austin, Robert, 69-70
Avendano, Tony, 69-70
Azuma, Atsuko, 77-78

- B -

Badrak, Edward, 81-82, 82-83, 90-91, 92-93
Baerg, Theodore, 89-90, 91-92
Bahrt, William, 67-68
Baird, Edward, 66-67
Bakels, Kees, 84-85, 88-89, 91-92
Bakman, Patrick, 74-75, 76-77, 80-81
Ballam, Michael, 85-86, 89-90
Balme, John, 78-79, 79-80
Balthrop, Carmen, 86-87
Banks, Ronald, 82-83, 84-85, 85-86, 86-87, 87-88, 88-89, 94-95
Banner, James, 91-92
Baquerizo, Enrique, 81-82, 82-83
Barasorda, Antonio, 84-85, 86-87, 94-95
Barbe, William, 67-68
Bardon, Henry, 74-75, 79-80
Baris, Sam, 67-68
Barlow, Klara, 69-70, 71-72

Barraza, Deanna, 95-96
Barstow, Josephine, 81-82, 84-85
Bartoletti, Bruno, 81-82
Bartoli, Cecilia, 95-96
Bartolini, Lando, 95-96
Baskerville, Priscilla, 86-87
Basler, Chelsea, 96-97
Bassett, Ralph, 76-77, 80-81
Bates, David, 79-80, 80-81
Bay, Howard, 73-74, 77-78
Baygulova, Mara, 74-75, 77-78
Beck, William, 65-66
Bedford, Steuart, 90-91
Begg, Heather, 85-86, 89-90
Bell, Kevin, 91-92
Bell, Michel Warren, 86-87, 90-91, 92-93, 95-96
Beni, Gimi, 66-67, 68-69
Benois, Nicola, 80-81
Benthaak, Bernd, 86-87
Berganza, Teresa, 81-82
Bergell, Aaron, 75-76
Bergeson, Scott, 84-85
Bergonzi, Carlo, 78-79
Bernard, David, 86-87
Bernardini, Don, 92-93
Besch, Anthony, 83-84
Bess, Dmitri, 72-73
Billings, James, 80-81, 81-82
Bini, Carlo, 77-78, 78-79, 79-80, 80-81, 81-82
Bishop, Adelaide, 88-89, 92-93
Bitetti, Matthew, 95-96
Black, Jeffrey, 92-93, 93-94
Blankenship, William, 67-68, 70-71
Blaze, Sarah, 92-93, 93-94, 94-95, 96-97
Blier, Steven, 95-96
Blochwitz, Hans Peter, 90-91, 92-93, 93-94
Blum, Margot, 66-67
Bogacheva, Irina, 89-90
Bolger, Bruce, 67-68
Boncompagni, Elio, 93-94
Bonini, Peggy, 68-69
Bonney, Barbara, 90-91
Bonynge, Richard, 74-75, 75-76, 80-81, 81-82, 82-83, 83-84, 86-87, 89-90, 92-93, 93-94, 96-97
Booth, Phillip, 73-74, 77-78
Booth, Thomas, 89-90
Boozer, Brenda, 82-83
Bornstein, Aaron, 76-77
Bouleyn, Kathryn, 75-76, 77-78, 85-86
Bouton, Ted, 86-87
Bouws, Jan*, 78-79
Braden, Timothy, 77-78
Bradley-Johnson, William, 86-87
Brecknock, John, 80-81, 81-82
Breeden, Neil, 79-80, 81-82
Brewer, Christine, 90-91
Brewer, David Lee, 94-95
Briggs, Hope, 94-95
Brimson-Lewis, Stephen, 95-96
Bröcheler, John*, 77-78, 78-79, 80-81, 81-82, 82-83

Brovsky, Linda, 95-96
Brown, Débria, 90-91, 93-94, 95-96
Brown, Melvin, 65-66
Brown, Zack, 80-81, 81-82, 85-86, 86-87, 88-89, 91-92, 92-93, 93-94, 96-97
Brundage, Eugene, 66-67, 69-70
Brunner, Richard, 86-87
Buckley, Emerson, 84-85
Buibas, Iosif, 86-87
Bullard, Gene, 65-66, 68-69, 71-72
Bunnell, Jane, 87-88
Burchinal, Frederick, 82-83, 84-85
Burrows, Stuart, 83-84
Burton, Amy, 82-83, 83-84, 84-85, 86-87
Burton, Doug, 73-74
Bush, Barbara, 93-94
Businger, Toni, 79-80, 83-84
Butler, James, 85-86, 96-97
Butlin, Roger, 95-96
Bybee, Luretta, 84-85
Byrne, Richard, 91-92
Byrnes, Aleicia, 80-81

- C -

Caine, Charles, 84-85
Calof, Jeffrey, 91-92
Campbell, Patton, 81-82
Campora, Giuseppe, 80-81
Cantrell, Roger, 86-87
Capobianco, Tito, 73-74, 75-76, 76-77, 77-78, 78-79, 79-80, 80-81, 81-82, 82-83, 83-84
Carey, Matthew, 88-89, 90-91, 91-92
Cariaga, Marvelee, 69-70, 71-72, 72-73, 73-74, 74-75, 75-76, 76-77, 78-79
Carlson, Lenus, 78-79
Carreras, José, 93-94
Carroli, Silvano, 85-86
Carten, Sabrina, 94-95
Caruso, Robert, 69-70
Case, Stan, 86-87
Casei, Nedda, 68-69, 71-72
Cassilly, Richard 71-72, 81-82, 84-85, 85-86
Cassinelli, Ricardo*, 82-83
Cassolla, Giovanna*, 81-82
Castel, Nico, 69-70, 71-72
Castle, Peggy, 73-74, 74-75, 75-76,
Caylor, David, 72-73, 74-75
Challender, Stuart*, 85-86
Chambers, Martin, 88-89, 89-90
Chastain, Paula, 66-67
Chausson, Carlos, 77-78, 78-79, 79-80, 80-81, 81-82, 82-83, 83-84, 85-86
Cheak, Paul, 81-82
Cherico, Roxana, 68-69
Chodos, Max R., 83-84, 90-91
Chookasian, Lili, 75-76
Christin, Judith, 84-85, 87-88, 89-90, 91-92
Christos, Marianna, 83-84

Ciesinski, Katherine, 80-81
Clague, Deborah, 87-88
Clapés, Ignacio, 93-94
Clark, Marnie, 78-79
Clark, Richard J., 90-91
Clarke, Hope, 94-95
Clayton, Cynthia, 96-97
Clements, Joy, 71-72, 73-74
Cleveland, Sally, 85-86
Cole, Glenn, 66-67
Cole-Adcock, Lynn, 76-77
Coleman, Barron, 94-95
Colet, Anita, 84-85, 85-86, 91-92, 92-93
Collymore, Ray, 66-67
Conklin, John, 80-81, 83-84, 88-89, 89-90, 90-91, 91-92, 92-93, 93-94, 94-95, 96-97
Connell, Elizabeth, 88-89
Cook, Terry, 94-95
Cooke, Peter, 90-91
Cooper, Kaira, 95-96
Cope, Marcia, 78-79, 80-81
Copeland, Paula, 74-75
Copley, John, 85-86, 89-90, 90-91, 91-92, 92-93, 93-94
Cornell, David, 77-78
Cornell, Gwynn, 81-82
Corsaro, Frank, 74-75
Cossa, Dominic, 65-66
Costa-Greenspon, Muriel, 77-78
Coulson, Nancy, 78-79
Courtney, James, 78-79
Cousins, Michael, 83-84
Cox, Jean, 69-70
Cox, John, 95-96
Cox, Kenneth, 81-82, 82-83, 83-84, 84-85, 89-90, 94-95, 96-97
Cozzens, Leslie, 67-68
Craig, Jack, 68-69, 69-70
Craig, John , 65-66
Craig, Patricia, 81-82, 84-85
Crawford, Keith, 94-95
Creed, Kay, 73-74
Creffield, Rosanne, 84-85
Crider, Michèle*, 95-96
Crisci, Morris, 67-68
Crist, Richard, 85-86
Cristini, Mario, 66-67, 72-73, 77-78, 82-83
Crook, Paul, 75-76
Cruz-Romo, Gilda, 70-71, 82-83
Cullis, Rita*, 91-92, 92-93
Curatilo, Gwen, 66-67
Curry, Diane, 77-78
Curtis, Charles, 72-73, 73-74

- D-

d'Auria, Diego, 87-88
Dalis, Irene, 72-73
Dallas, Dorothy, 67-68, 68-69, 70-71

213

Dalle Molle, Giuseppina*, 79-80
Dalton, Elizabeth, 75-76
Daniels, Annette, 94-95
Dansby, William, 77-78
Darcy, Michael, 89-90
Darling, Robert, 69-70, 72-73, 81-82, 87-88
Darrenkamp, John, 73-74, 74-75, 76-77, 77-78
Davidson, Diana, 74-75
Davies, Arthur, 91-92
Davis, Henrietta, 86-87
Davis, Sylvia, 67-68
de Blasis, James, 72-73, 73-74, 96-97
de Ceunynck, Robert, 85-86
de la Mora, Fernando, 90-91, 93-94
de la Rosa, Evelyn, 95-96
de Paul, Judith, 69-70
De Rugeriis, Joseph, 77-78, 78-79, 79-80, 80-81, 81-82
De Simone, Anita, 96-97
De Vries, Anne, 88-89
Dearing, Judy, 94-95
Deis, Lila, 68-69
Dekker, Geraldine, 75-76
Del Carlo, John, 77-78, 78-79, 87-88, 89-90, 91-92, 96-97
Delavan, Marlene, 74-75
DeMain, John, 94-95
Denda, Gigi, 79-80
Deng, Yun, 92-93
Dennen, Barry, 92-93
Dennis, Alfred, 71-72
Derick, Peter Van, 89-90
Derksen, Jan, 79-80
Deutekom, Cristina, 78-79, 80-81, 81-82, 82-83, 86-87
Devlin, Michael, 68-69, 71-72, 72-73, 79-80, 83-84, 85-86
Di Giglio, Maria, 74-75
Di Giuseppe, Enrico, 76-77, 78-79, 79-80
Di Virgilio, Nicholas, 65-66
Diazmuñoz, Eduardo, 93-94
Diffen, Ray, 91-92
Dimitri, Bess, 71-72
Dixon, Susan Lynn, 79-80
Dobish, Gail, 88-89
Dombek, Mary, 90-91
Domingo, Plácido, 65-66, 66-67, 96-97
Dominguez, Ruben, 87-88
Don, Robin, 85-86, 93-94
Donnell, Bruce, 84-85
Dorn, Reinhard*, 96-97
Dorsey, Kent, 85-86, 96-97
Doss, Mark S., 91-92, 92-93, 94-95
Downes, Edward, 88-89
Downing, David, 86-87, 87-88, 90-91, 91-92, 93-94, 95-96, 96-97
Dryden, Deborah, 96-97
Du Melle, Walter, 95-96, 96-97
DuBois, Mark, 86-87, 88-89
Dudek, Sandra, 80-81, 81-82
Dugger, Adrienne, 94-95
Dunlap, David, 78-79, 81-82
Dunlop, John Robert, 70-71
Dunn, Susan, 87-88
Dupre, William, 73-74
Duquesnay, Ann, 94-95
Duykers, John, 90-91, 95-96, 96-97
Dworchak, Harry, 74-75, 88-89

- E -

Eaglen, Jane, 96-97
Eagleson, Leonard, 81-82, 85-86
Easley, Richert, 86-87
Eaton, Jonathan, 91-92
Eck, Marsha Louis, 78-79, 80-81
Eckhoff, Herbert, 89-90, 92-93, 93-94
Eddleman, Jack, 82-83
Edward-Stevens, Michael, 86-87
Edwards, Phillip, 90-91
Edwards, Ryan, 76-77
Egerton, Francis, 90-91
Eichorn, William, 81-82
Elgar, Anne, 65-66, 68-69
Elias, Rosalind, 91-92
Ellsworth, John, 66-67
Elvira, Pablo, 79-80, 88-89
Endsley, George, 65-66
Enns, Harold, 65-66, 67-68, 68-69, 69-70, 73-74, 75-76, 76-77, 77-78
Esham, Faith, 85-86
Evans, Anne, 77-78, 79-80, 80-81
Evans, Beverly, 72-73, 73-74, 79-80, 86-87
Evans, Joseph, 76-77, 77-78, 78-79, 80-81, 81-82, 82-83, 90-91, 95-96
Ewer, Graeme*, 93-94

- F -

Fagerland, Scot, 96-97
Falconer, Ian, 96-97
Feitscher, Vicki, 89-90
Fielder, J. Raymond, 83-84, 89-90
Fink, Richard Paul, 84-85, 85-86, 91-92
Fiorito, John, 71-72, 72-73
Firestone , Adria, 91-92, 96-97
Fischer, Alan, 95-96, 96-97
Fisher, Douglas, 94-95
Fisher, Gary, 76-77, 77-78, 78-79
Fiske, Henry, 84-85
Fitch, Bernard, 85-86, 87-88, 89-90, 91-92
Flagello, Ezio, 80-81
Fleming, Renée, 93-94, 94-95
Fleming, Sarah, 71-72
Floyd, Alpha, 72-73
Floyd, Carlisle, 81-82, 90-91, 95-96
Flynn, James, 78-79
Foldi, Andrew, 68-69, 71-72, 73-74, 77-78, 78-79
Ford, John A., 65-66
Forrester, Maureen, 84-85, 89-90
Forst, Judith, 85-86, 90-91
Fortune, George, 86-87
Foss, Harlan, 80-81, 81-82, 82-83, 83-84, 84-85, 85-86, 86-87, 87-88, 88-89, 89-90, 90-91
Fowler, Bruce, 96-97
Fowles, Glenys, 77-78, 87-88, 91-92
Fox, Tom, 88-89
Foy, Kenneth, 94-95
Frank, Joseph, 78-79, 80-81, 81-82, 84-85, 88-89
Fredricks, Richard, 65-66, 66-67, 68-69, 79-80, 80-81
Freeman, Carroll, 88-89
French, Shalonda, 90-91
Freni, RoseMarie, 80-81, 81-82, 84-85
Frey, Leonard, 80-81
Fricke, Heinz, 89-90, 91-92

Fried, Howard, 66-67, 67-68, 69-70, 70-71, 71-72, 72-73, 73-74, 75-76, 77-78
Froelich, Lee Jessica, 96-97
Fu, Haijing, 93-94, 94-95
Fuller, Gale, 89-90, 90-91, 91-92
Fulton, Thomas, 84-85, 86-87, 87-88
Furlanetto, Ferruccio, 84-85, 87-88, 92-93

- G -

Gagan, Raymond, 67-68
Galbraith, Robert, 89-90
Galiano, Joseph, 73-74
Gallup, Michael, 70-71, 71-72, 73-74, 74-75, 75-76, 77-78
Galterio, Lou, 87-88, 89-90, 91-92
Galvany, Marisa, 73-74
Ganz, Forrest, 68-69
Garabedian, Edna, 71-72
Garcia, Yvonne, 68-69
Garcia Marques, Juan Pedro, 83-84
Gardner, Jake, 80-81
Garner, Luvenia, 94-95
Garrard, Don, 85-86
Garrison, Jon, 84-85, 85-86
Garson, Jeanne, 71-72, 73-74
Garven, David, 75-76
Gates, Terry, 73-74, 77-78
Genaux, Vivica, 96-97
George, Hal, 73-74, 79-80
Gettler, Rachel*, 82-83, 83-84, 84-85
Ghiglia, Lorenzo, 68-69
Ghiuselev, Nicola, 83-84, 86-87
Giacomini, Giuseppe, 85-86
Gibbons, Joan, 89-90,
Gibbs, Raymond, 65-66, 68-69, 69-70, 72-73, 74-75
Gibin, Giovanni, 66-67
Gilbert, Alan, 68-69
Gilfry, Rodney, 86-87
Gill, Jamison, 68-69, 72-73, 76-77
Ginsberg, Frances, 90-91
Girard, Claude, 95-96
Glassman, Allan, 89-90
Glattly, Ellison, 71-72
Glossop, Peter, 68-69, 84-85
Glover, Robert, 67-68
Goldman, Kit, 89-90
Gomez, Roberto 92-93, 94-95, 95-96, 96-97
Gondek, Juliane, 79-80, 80-81
Gonzales, Charles, 65-66
Goodwin, Patricia, 75-76, 77-78
Gorgensen, Bill, 81-82, 82-83, 83-84, 84-85, 86-87
Graham, Colin, 90-91
Graham, Susan, 90-91
Graves, Sallye, 80-81
Grayson, Robert, 75-76, 76-77
Greager, Richard, 85-86
Green, Anna, 74-75, 76-77
Green, Barton, 90-91
Greer, Gordon, 74-75, 83-84
Gregg, Wade, 78-79
Gregson, Richard, 84-85, 87-88
Grienenberger, Joseph, 89-90, 90-91, 92-93, 95-96
Grissom, Jan, 92-93
Gruett, Jon David, 74-75, 84-85
Grunberg, Peter, 90-91

Guarnieri, John, 73-74
Gugushvili, Teimuraz, 89-90
Gulyas, Denes, 87-88, 89-90
Guzman, Suzanna, 85-86, 87-88, 88-89, 90-91, 91-92, 93-94

- H -

Hadley, Jerry, 93-94, 94-95, 96-97
Hagegård, Håkan, 87-88, 90-91
Hager, Ghita, 72-73, 74-75, 75-76, 80-81
Haldeman, Constance, 71-72, 73-74
Hale, Robert, 74-75, 75-76, 77-78, 78-79, 79-80, 81-82, 83-84
Hall, David, 73-74, 77-78, 78-79, 79-80, 80-81, 81-82, 82-83, 83-84, 84-85, 85-86
Hall, Janice, 77-78, 78-79, 80-81, 81-82
Hall, Peter J., 74-75, 81-82, 91-92, 94-95, 95-96, 96-97
Hallock, Frank, 74-75
Hamilton, Charles*, 81-82
Hamilton, David, 82-83, 83-84
Hamilton, Martha, 76-77
Hamm, Theresa, 86-87
Hammond-Stroud, Derek, 75-76
Hampson, Thomas, 94-95
Hand, Catherine, 71-72
Hanna, Lloyd, 66-67
Hanson, Debra, 90-91, 91-92
Harlan, Christopher, 92-93
Harned, Shirley, 76-77
Harrington, Leslie, 77-78
Harris, Hilda, 77-78, 79-80
Harrison, Dawn Veree, 91-92
Harrower, Rexford, 68-69
Hartfield, Paul, 89-90
Hartman, Vernon, 92-93
Hass, Sabine, 86-87, 88-89
Haywood, Lorna, 76-77
Hebert, Bliss, 69-70, 71-72, 73-74, 74-75, 81-82, 89-90, 92-93, 95-96
Hecht, Joshua, 66-67, 67-68
Hegierski, Kathleen, 80-81, 85-86, 93-94
Helpmann, Robert, 84-85
Herbert, Walter, 65-66, 66-67, 67-68, 68-69, 69-70, 70-71, 71-72, 72-73, 73-74, 74-75
Hermann, John, 68-69, 75-76
Hernández, César, 92-93, 95-96
Heymann, Henry, 72-73, 73-74
Hicks, Pamela, 78-79, 79-80, 80-81
Hillhouse, Wendy, 82-83
Hindrelet-Brydon, Katherine, 73-74, 78-79
Hinds, Esther, 71-72, 73-74
Hirst, Grayson, 72-73, 73-74
Hocher, Barbara, 86-87
Hockney, David, 96-97
Hokanson, Leonard, 91-92
Holland, Julia, 85-86
Holloway, David, 74-75
Holmes, Eugene, 72-73, 73-74, 75-76
Holse, Glen, 68-69
Holt, Henry, 76-77
Hong, Hei-Kyung, 84-85, 87-88, 89-90
Horne, Marilyn, 88-89
Howard, Ann, 73-74
Howe, Martha Jane, 74-75, 78-79, 89-90, 90-91, 91-92, 93-94

Hu, Joseph, 94-95, 96-97
Hudson, Paul, 84-85
Huffstodt, Karen, 90-91
Hvorostovsky, Dmitri, 90-91
Hynes, Elizabeth, 92-93, 96-97

- I -

Igesz, Bodo, 79-80
Immerman, Margaret, 71-72
Ionitza, Alexandru, 84-85

- J -

Jackson, Brian, 76-77
Jackson, Kiah, 86-87
Jackson, Stanley, 94-95
Jacobs, Sally, 75-76
Jamison, Julia, 89-90
Jampolis, Neil Peter, 88-89, 90-91, 91-92, 94-95
Jennings, Diane, 82-83
Jerusalem, Siegfried, 86-87
Johnson, Bruce, 88-89
Johnson, Christopher, 90-91
Johnson, Douglas, 90-91
Johnson, Edguard, 78-79
Johnson, Leonard, 66-67
Johnson, Russell, 94-95
Jones, Gwen, 70-71
Jones, Henry, 94-95
Jones, Joyce, 72-73, 76-77, 78-79
Jones, Kimberly, 94-95
Jones, Nancy, 78-79, 80-81
Jones, Scott, 90-91
Jones, Warren, 87-88
Jordan, Andree, 67-68
Justus, William, 77-78, 78-79, 81-82, 83-84

- K -

Kakhidze, Jansoug, 89-90
Kaluza, Stefania*, 95-96
Kane, Larry, 65-66
Kanouse, Monroe, 76-77
Kaszar, Carol, 82-83, 84-85
Katz, Martin, 86-87, 88-89
Kaufmann, Jacobo, 71-72
Kavrakos, Dimitri, 82-83
Keene, Christopher, 81-82, 83-84, 91-92
Kellner, Peggy, 65-66, 66-67, 67-68, 68-69, 71-72
Kelly, Halle, 76-77
Kelly, Paul Austin, 88-89
Keltner, Karen, 80-81, 81-82, 82-83, 84-85, 85-86, 86-87, 87-88, 88-89, 89-90, 90-91, 91-92, 92-93, 95-96, 96-97
Kennedy, Katherine, 77-78
Kern, Patricia, 90-91
Kessler, Zale , 90-91
Khoperia, Omar, 89-90
Kiggins, Alfred J., 86-87
Kilduff, Barbara, 91-92
Killebrew, Gwendolyn, 75-76
Klein, Allen Charles, 66-67, 69-70, 73-74, 74-75, 78-79, 80-81, 86-87, 89-90, 90-91, 91-92, 92-93, 95-96

Kleinman, Marlena, 70-71
Kness, Richard, 75-76
Knight, Kathleen, 69-70
Knott, Bridget, 90-91
Koenig, Lesley, 94-95
Korn, Artur, 88-89, 91-92
Kramarich, Irene, 66-67
Krebil, Dorothy, 67-68
Krooskos, Christina, 69-70, 73-74
Kunde, Gregory, 91-92
Kuntzsch, Matthias, 86-87

- L -

La Var, Jeffrey, 94-95
LaBarge, Richard, 82-83
Lachonas, Chris, 67-68, 70-71
Laciura, Anthony, 89-90
Lakes, Gary, 89-90
Lane, Morgan, 65-66, 66-67, 67-68, 71-72
Langan, Kevin, 82-83, 85-86, 86-87, 88-89, 89-90, 92-93, 95-96, 96-97
Langton, Sunny Joy, 88-89, 91-92
Larson, Philip, 84-85, 89-90, 94-95, 95-96, 96-97
Lasalle, Pamela, 76-77
Lattimore, Margaret, 95-96
Lawrence, Douglas, 74-75
Laxton, Harold, 84-85
Leal, Daniel S., 89-90, 90-91, 91-92, 94-95, 95-96
Lebherz, Louis, 76-77, 80-81
Ledbetter, Victor, 88-89, 90-91, 92-93
Lee, Ming Cho, 70-71, 71-72, 79-80, 87-88
Lee, Sung-Sook, 78-79
Leech, Richard, 87-88, 88-89, 92-93, 94-95, 96-97
Leonetti, Adrienne, 74-75, 75-76, 76-77, 78-79
Lerner, Mimi, 86-87
Lesane, John, 94-95
Lesenger, Jay, 80-81, 81-82, 83-84
Levine, Rhoda, 82-83, 84-85, 88-89
Lewis, Carolyn, 71-72
Lewis, Keith, 90-91
Lewis, Michael, 92-93
Li, Hong-Shen, 89-90
Ligi, Josella, 77-78
Lima, Luis, 79-80, 85-86
Lind, Tony, 67-68
Liss, Ava Baker, 96-97
Lister, Marquita, 94-95
Litton, Andrew, 82-83
Lockhart, James, 84-85
Lodato, Susanna, 80-81, 81-82
Loewen, Mark, 96-97
London, George, 73-74, 76-77
Long, Charles, 83-84
Lopez-Yañez, Jorge, 91-92, 96-97
Loquasto, Santo, 75-76
Lord, Susan, 82-83
Loup, François, 86-87, 88-89, 91-92, 92-93, 95-96
Lovat, Judith, 90-91, 91-92, 94-95
Lowe, Ryan, 95-96
Lowery, Melvin, 77-78, 79-80, 80-81, 81-82, 82-83
Ludgin, Chester, 66-67, 79-80
Lundeen, Katherine, 91-92
Lynch, Lester, 94-95
Lynch, Robert, 67-68
Lynn, Norma, 66-67

- M -

MacKay, Louis, 66-67, 67-68, 69-70, 70-71, 73-74
Mackay, Margery, 65-66
MacKenzie, Mary, 65-66
Mackerras, Charles, 75-76
MacNeil, Walter, 90-91
Macurdy, John, 89-90, 92-93
Magee, Grace, 79-80, 81-82
Magiera, Leone, 92-93
Magiera, Michael, 78-79
Maia, Carolyn, 76-77
Major, Leon, 93-94, 96-97
Malas, Spiro, 72-73, 73-74, 75-76, 77-78, 79-80, 80-81
Malfitano, Catherine, 74-75
Maliponte, Adriana, 79-80
Malis, David, 87-88, 89-90, 91-92, 92-93, 95-96
Mallory, William, 77-78
Manhart, Emily, 91-92, 92-93
Mansouri, Lotfi, 72-73, 76-77, 79-80, 85-86, 96-97
Manton, Raymond, 67-68
Margison, Richard, 96-97
Marsee, Susanne, 73-74, 78-79, 80-81, 84-85
Marshall, Larry, 86-87, 94-95
Martell, Richard, 69-70
Martin, Janis, 69-70
Martindale-Schafer, Lynne, 78-79
Martinovich, Boris, 79-80
Masuko, Tom, 70-71
Mathes, Rachel, 75-76
Matheson-Bruce, Graeme, 88-89
Matthews, Yvette, 86-87
Mattsey, Jeff, 94-95
Mauceri, John, 78-79
Mauro, Ermanno, 73-74
Mauser, Siegfried, 84-85
Maxfield, Lizanne, 77-78
Mayer, Lucille, 76-77
Maynard, Darren Scott, 92-93
Mays, Andrea, 93-94
McAfee, Patricia, 93-94, 94-95, 96-97
McAlister, Barbara, 74-75
McCain, Dru, 82-83
McCauley, Barry, 79-80, 80-81
McClellan , John, 71-72
McCown, Marjorie, 92-93
McCullach, William, 71-72
McCullagh, Jack, 65-66, 69-70
McDaniel, Carolyne, 76-77, 77-78
McDaniel, Robert, 86-87
McDaniels, Carolyn, 73-74
McDevitt, Duane, 96-97
McDonald, William, 75-76, 76-77
McDonnell, Paula, 74-75
McGowen, Adair, 76-77
McKay, Louis, 70-71
McKee, Richard, 80-81, 83-84, 86-87, 90-91
McKelvain, Nelms, 86-87
McKinley, Casey, 95-96, 96-97
McKinley, Rita, 86-87
McKinney, Thomas, 71-72, 72-73
McLean, Betsy, 91-92
McMillian, Geraldine, 86-87
McNeil, Dennis, 91-92
Meier, Johanna, 73-74, 74-75, 75-76, 76-77, 89-90
Melano, Fabrizio, 78-79, 84-85
Menotti, Francis, 86-87

Menotti, Gian Carlo, 86-87
Mentzer, Susanne, 86-87, 91-92
Merrill, Nathaniel 79-80, 83-84, 85-86, 89-90
Mess, Suzanne, 72-73, 73-74, 74-75, 79-80, 80-81, 81-82, 82-83, 84-85, 89-90, 94-95, 95-96
Meyer, Kerstin, 80-81
Michalski, Raymond, 71-72
Miladinovic, Dejan, 95-96
Milia, Angela, 91-92
Miller, Russel, 88-89
Millo, Aprile, 77-78
Milnes, Sherrill, 78-79, 82-83, 83-84
Minde, Stefan, 75-76
Minor, Mathew J., 94-95
Minton, Patricia, 93-94
Miricioiu, Nelly, 85-86, 95-96
Mitchell, David, 73-74, 79-80
Mittelmann, Norman, 77-78
Moir, John, 84-85
Moldoveanu, Vasile, 82-83
Montané, Carlos, 84-85
Montgomery, Jack, 66-67
Montgomery, Kenneth, 90-91, 93-94, 95-96
Montresor, Beni, 72-73, 73-74, 82-83, 83-84, 89-90
Moody, Phillis, 76-77
Moore, Nancy Carol, 81-82, 82-83, 86-87
Morgan, Epherium, 95-96
Morgan, Michael L., 90-91, 93-94
Morozov, Alexander, 89-90
Morris, James, 85-86, 95-96
Moss, Eileen, 73-74
Mout, E.J., 94-95
Müller, Edoardo, 79-80, 81-82, 83-84, 86-87, 87-88, 88-89, 89-90, 90-91, 91-92, 92-93, 94-95, 95-96, 96-97
Munn, Thomas, 82-83
Munro, Leigh, 82-83, 84-85
Murrali, Massimiliano, 91-92
Musoleno, Rosemary, 94-95
Myers, Pamela, 81-82, 83-84
Myrvold, David, 73-74, 74-75

- N -

Naccarato, John, 69-70, 73-74, 74-75, 75-76, 76-77, 78-79
Nagy, Elemer, 77-78
Nagy, Robert, 69-70
Navarrete, Alfonso, 81-82
Neblett, Carol, 87-88, 89-90
Neill, William, 83-84
Nelem, Ron, 69-70
Nelson, Tom, 71-72
Nichols, Gary, 78-79, 79-80, 80-81, 81-82, 84-85
Nielsen, Inga, 79-80, 81-82
Nishida, Hiroko, 88-89
Niska, Maralin, 65-66, 67-68
Noble, Timothy, 94-95
Nolan, Warren, 90-91, 95-96
Nolan, William, 87-88, 88-89, 89-90, 91-92, 95-96
Norden, Betsy, 84-85
Norman, Jerold, 82-83
Novoa, Salvador, 73-74, 77-78
Nurmela, Kari, 80-81

- O -

Oberle, Carl-Friedrich, 92-93
O'Brien, Jack, 85-86, 86-87
O'Brien, Kathleen, 74-75, 87-88
O'Brien, Kerry, 96-97
Oehl, Neil Gilbert, 65-66
O'Hearn, Robert, 79-80, 81-82, 82-83
Olaker, Charlae, 94-95
O'Leary, Thomas, 67-68, 75-76, 76-77
Olvis, William, 67-68
O'Neill, Dennis, 87-88, 89-90
Onque, Bryon, 86-87
Opthof, Cornelis, 76-77, 81-82
Oswald, Mark, 94-95
Otey, Louis, 91-92, 93-94, 96-97
Ott, Sharon, 96-97
Outland, Randall, 88-89
Owens, Judith, 67-68
Owens, R. Lee, 65-66, 66-67, 68-69

- P -

Paige, Autris, 86-87
Pakledinaz, Martin, 94-95
Palmer, Beau, 90-91, 91-92, 92-93, 93-94, 94-95, 95-96, 96-97
Palmer, Thomas, 67-68, 71-72
Palmour, Deidra, 84-85, 86-87, 89-90
Pape, Johnathon, 92-93, 93-94, 94-95
Parce, Erich, 90-91, 95-96
Park, Barbara, 72-73, 73-74
Parker, Louise, 66-67
Parker, Michael Jackson, 78-79
Parly, Ticho, 73-74
Parrish, Cheryl, 88-89, 89-90, 90-91, 91-92
Pasatieri, Thomas, 89-90
Patrick, Julian, 69-70, 90-91, 95-96
Patterson, James, 85-86
Patton, Barbara, 67-68
Paul, Thomas, 82-83
Paunova, Mariana, 82-83
Pavarotti, Luciano, 79-80, 84-85, 92-93
Pavek, Janet, 67-68
Pavlick, Elaine, 75-76
Pechota, Joseph, 81-82, 82-83
Pelle, Nadia, 86-87
Pendergrass, Clay, 81-82
Perkins, Eric, 90-91
Perry, Douglas, 92-93, 93-94
Peterson, Dean, 92-93
Peterson, Donna, 67-68
Peterson, Glade, 72-73
Peytchinov, Valentin, 93-94
Piccolo, Lynne Strow*, 76-77
Pickett, Lou Ann, 94-95
Pinedo, Joseph, 73-74
Pitt, Alan, 67-68, 66-67, 68-69, 69-70
Plishka, Paul, 78-79, 79-80, 81-82
Plowright, Rosalind, 81-82, 82-83, 84-85, 94-95
Polhamus, John, 88-89, 89-90
Ponnelle, Jean-Pierre, 95-96
Pons, Juan, 79-80
Popov, Vladimir, 86-87
Powell, Alvy, 94-95
Powell, John, 65-66

Powell, Stephen, 96-97
Power, Patrick, 92-93, 95-96
Powers, William, 73-74
Prettyman, Gary, 81-82
Prey, Hermann, 86-87, 91-92
Price, Perry, 69-70, 71-72
Pring, Katherine*, 77-78
Pringle, John*, 91-92
Pruetti, Sarah, 81-82, 82-83
Prunty, Patricia, 90-91
Putnam, Ashley, 75-76, 77-78, 78-79, 79-80, 91-92

- Q -

Queler, Eve, 83-84
Quilico, Louis, 78-79
Quittmeyer, Susan, 85-86

- R -

Raabe, Paul, 75-76
Rabiner, Ellen, 92-93, 93-94
Racette, Patricia, 94-95
Raftery, J. Patrick, 78-79, 79-80, 80-81, 81-82, 82-83, 84-85, 85-86, 88-89
Raines, Scott, 92-93
Rakusin, Fredda, 85-86
Ramey, Samuel, 81-82
Rarick, Erick, 94-95
Rawnsley, John, 87-88
Rayson, Benjamin, 65-66
Reardon, John, 69-70
Redmann, Kirk, 83-84
Redmon, Robynne, 88-89
Redmond, Eric, 83-84
Reed, Bruce, 80-81, 81-82, 83-84
Reese, Irwin, 86-87
Refeld, Jeralyn, 91-92
Reihs-Gromes, Hill, 85-86, 93-94
Reilly, Charles Nelson, 78-79
Remedios, Alberto, 75-76, 76-77
Remo, Ken, 66-67, 67-68, 68-69, 69-70, 74-75
Renee, Madelyn, 79-80
Rennison, Michael, 81-82
Resnik, Regina, 80-81
Ricci, Enrique, 93-94
Richards, Leslie, 78-79
Richards, Mark Andrew, 92-93
Riedel, Deborah*, 93-94, 95-96, 96-97
Riegel, Kenneth, 66-67
Rigacci, Bruno, 75-76, 76-77, 77-78, 78-79, 79-80, 80-81, 82-83, 83-84
Rigby, Fred, 68-69
Rigby, Jean*, 92-93, 93-94
Robbins, Carrie, 78-79
Robinson, Faye, 83-84
Robinson, Stacey, 94-95
Roesch, William, 70-71, 73-74, 75-76
Rogers, Candace, 84-85
Rolandi, Gianna, 76-77, 79-80, 80-81, 83-84
Roloff, Roger, 86-87
Romaguera, Joaquin, 77-78, 78-79, 81-82, 82-83
Rose, Erica, 91-92
Roseberry, Robert, 77-78, 78-79, 79-80
Rosecrans, Charles, 72-73

Rosen, Albert, 94-95
Rosenberger, Robert, 86-87
Rosenshein, Neil, 94-95
Rossi, Melody, 91-92
Roth, Ann, 90-91
Rowland, Martile, 94-95
Royal, William, 71-72
Rucker, Mark, 95-96
Rudat, David, 85-86
Rush, Dave, 75-76
Russell, Adam, 90-91
Russell, Anna, 86-87
Russo, Vincent, 76-77, 77-78, 78-79, 80-81
Rutenberg, Craig, 94-95

- S -

Salvadori, Antonio, 83-84
Salzer, Beeb, 76-77
Sámano, Oscar, 93-94
Sanders, Charles, 94-95
Saunders, Arlene, 80-81
Savino, Steven, 79-80, 80-81, 81-82, 82-83, 83-84
Sayers, John, 80-81
Schafer, Lawrence, 80-81, 87-88
Schauer, Von, 79-80
Schauler, Eileen, 66-67
Scheffler, John, 74-75, 77-78, 79-80, 82-83, 84-85, 88-89, 92-93
Schermerhorn, Kenneth, 75-76
Schmidt, Douglas, 86-87
Schmorr, Robert, 76-77, 80-81, 82-83, 83-84, 84-85, 85-86
Schneider-Siemssen, Günther, 85-86, 89-90, 90-91, 93-94, 94-95, 95-96
Schuback, Thomas, 85-86, 90-91
Schuman, Patricia, 92-93
Schwartzman, Seymour, 70-71
Scott, Carter, 94-95, 95-96, 96-97
Scotto, Renata, 85-86
Seabury, John, 80-81, 81-82
Sendak, Maurice, 89-90
Serbo, Rico, 77-78, 78-79, 79-80
Sergi, Arturo, 67-68
Shade, Nancy, 73-74, 76-77, 77-78
Shaffer, David, 94-95, 96-97
Shane, Rita, 67-68
Shaulis, Jane, 81-82, 82-83, 83-84, 84-85, 86-87
Shelle, Eilene, 72-73
Shelley, Julia, 72-73
Shipman, Cary, 77-78
Shipman, Jeffrey L., 78-79, 84-85, 89-90, 90-91, 96-97
Shore, Andrew*, 95-96
Shore, Joseph, 81-82, 82-83
Shortt, Paul, 81-82
Siena, Jerold, 91-92
Siercke, Alfred, 80-81, 86-87
Sikon, James Scott, 90-91, 91-92, 92-93, 93-94, 94-95, 96-97
Sills, Beverly, 69-70, 72-73, 73-74, 75-76, 76-77, 77-78, 78-79, 79-80, 80-81
Silva, Stella, 79-80, 82-83
Simmons, Calvin, 77-78, 78-79, 79-80, 80-81
Simmons, Thomas, 71-72, 72-73, 73-74, 74-75, 75-76, 76-77, 77-78

Simon, Ilona, 78-79
Simpson, Angela R., 94-95
Sinclair, Teri, 74-75, 75-76
Skalicki, Wolfram, 79-80, 81-82, 85-86, 89-90
Slivon, John, 96-97
Sloan, Gilbert, 68-69
Smith, Cary Archer, 74-75, 78-79
Smith, Dale, 79-80
Smith, David Rae, 76-77, 77-78, 82-83, 84-85
Smith, Nancy Tripp, 75-76
Smith, Oliver, 80-81, 90-91
Smith, Patricia Minton, 73-74, 74-75, 90-91, 91-92
Smith, Robin, 84-85
Smith, Ronn K., 86-87
Snyder, Joel, 91-92
Solt, Deitmar, 94-95
Somogi, Judith, 76-77
Sonnenberg, Melanie, 75-76, 77-78, 78-79, 80-81, 83-84, 91-92
Sousa, Arthur, 72-73
Soviero, Diana, 78-79, 79-80, 87-88
St. Hill, Kriss, 86-87
St. John, Russell, 86-87
Staley, Earl, 87-88
Stapleton, Catherine, 91-92
Stapleton, Robin, 84-85
Stennett, Michael, 85-86, 90-91, 92-93, 93-94
Stevens, John Wright, 77-78
Stevens, Michael, 94-95
Stevens, Ron, 70-71
Stevens, Ronald, 90-91
Stewart, John, 71-72, 74-75, 68-69
Stilwell, Richard, 90-91, 92-93
Stone, Edgar, 71-72, 73-74
Stone, Jean, 66-67
Strickler, Marion, 72-73
Strummer, Peter, 90-91
Stuart, Lila, 71-72, 73-74, 75-76
Stuart, Val, 69-70
Sublett, Virginia, 81-82, 82-83, 89-90
Summers, Jonathan, 87-88
Sundine, Stephanie, 83-84
Sundstrom, Joseph, 95-96
Sutherland, Joan, 74-75, 75-76, 80-81, 81-82, 82-83, 83-84, 86-87
Sykes, Jubilant, 86-87
Sylvester, Michael, 84-85, 86-87
Szkafarowsky, Stefan, 93-94

- T -

Tabachnik, Robin, 84-85
Tagliavini, Franco, 74-75
Tajo, Italo, 89-90
Tannenbaum, Robert, 81-82, 82-83, 87-88, 88-89
Tash, Diana, 89-90
Tauriello, Antonio, 77-78, 80-81, 81-82, 82-83
Tavera, Celeste, 89-90
Taylor, Andrew, 76-77
Taylor, Richard, 94-95
Te Kanawa, Kiri, 86-87
Tear, Robert, 91-92
Terranova, Vittorio, 78-79
Terry, Michael, 76-77
Thames, Jeanine, 92-93
Theyard, Harry, 78-79

Thomas, Jeffrey, 85-86
Thomas, Nova, 89-90, 93-94
Thomson, Heather, 67-68, 69-70
Thornburgh, Carolee, 74-75, 75-76
Tian, Hao Jiang, 95-96
Tichy, Georg*, 91-92
Tinsley, Pauline, 80-81, 83-84
Tipton, Thomas, 76-77
Titus, Alan, 77-78, 80-81, 83-84, 85-86
Todd, Carol, 65-66
Tokody, Ilona, 85-86, 89-90
Tomlinson, John*, 83-84
Toms, Carl, 75-76, 76-77, 77-78, 78-79, 81-82, 83-84, 84-85, 85-86, 86-87, 91-92
Torigi, Richard, 76-77
Torkanovsky, Werner, 73-74
Toscano, Carol, 66-67
Toschak, Robert, 82-83
Tota, Robert, 84-85
Tourangeau, Huguette, 75-76
Touw, Tom, 90-91
Tozzi, Giorgio, 79-80
Tracy, Emily, 74-75
Treigle, Norman, 65-66, 67-68, 69-70, 71-72, 73-74
Triglia, Richelle Marie, 96-97
Trimbel, Michael, 68-69
Troyanos, Tatiana, 75-76, 87-88
Trussel, Jacque, 82-83, 83-84, 84-85
Tsymbala, Roman, 94-95
Turetsky, Lisa, 85-86
Turgeon, Bernard, 69-70
Turnage, Wayne, 86-87
Turner, Claramae, 66-67, 67-68
Tyl, Noel, 74-75, 75-76

- U -

Ulfung, Ragnar, 76-77
Ulloa, César, 93-94
Uzan, Bernard, 95-96

- V -

Valente, Benita, 79-80
Vann, Elex Lee, 94-95
Van Allan, Richard, 75-76, 77-78
Van Dusen, Samuel, 71-72, 72-73, 73-74, 74-75
van Limpt, Adriaan, 81-82, 82-83, 83-84
Van Way, Nolan, 77-78
Vanarelli, Mario, 77-78, 78-79, 80-81
Vaness, Carol, 87-88, 90-91
Vargas, Ramón, 94-95
Varona, Jose, 75-76, 79-80, 80-81, 86-87
Vázquez, Encarnación, 93-94
Vaughan, Desmond, 70-71
Veale, Isabel*, 78-79
Velsir, Patricia, 65-66
Veltri, Michelangelo, 81-82, 85-86, 95-96
Venora, Lee, 68-69
Ventura, Sarah, 77-78
Vernon, Richard, 85-86, 94-95
Verrett, Shirley, 81-82
Voketaitis, Arnold, 82-83
Vonk, Hans*, 78-79

- W -

Wagner, Richard, 74-75
Walker, David, 90-91, 96-97
Walker, Don, 78-79
Walker, Dora, 75-76, 76-77
Walker, John, 69-70
Walker, Mallory, 80-81
Wallace, Mervin, 86-87
Walsh, David, 84-85
Wanamaker, Sam, 86-87
Ward, David, 73-74
Warfield, Sandra, 72-73
Waters, Willie Anthony, 87-88, 94-95
Watts, Don, 71-72, 72-73, 73-74
Weathers, Felicia, 67-68, 70-71, 72-73
Weaver, Martha Jane, 87-88, 89-90, 93-94
Webb, Chris, 70-71
Weber, Wolfgang, 86-87, 88-89, 89-90, 90-91, 91-92, 92-93, 93-94, 94-95, 96-97
Weidinge, Christine, 90-91
Weiss, Carol, 73-74
Welch, Jonathan, 88-89, 91-92
Welhasch, Irena, 89-90
Wells, Jeffrey, 84-85, 87-88
Wells, Patricia, 74-75
Wen, Sylvia, 89-90, 91-92, 93-94, 95-96, 96-97
Wentworth, Richard, 65-66
Wentzel, Andrew, 95-96
West, Davis, 70-71, 71-72, 94-95
West, Jon Fredric, 80-81
West, Stephen, 80-81, 81-82, 82-83, 87-88, 88-89, 89-90
Westbrook, Jane, 76-77, 77-78, 78-79, 80-81
Wexler, Peter, 76-77
Wharton, Marjorie, 86-87
Wheatfall, Arthur, 95-96
White, Cornelius, 86-87
White, Orville, 66-67, 69-70
White, Robert, 88-89
Whitney, Gerald, 72-73, 74-75, 75-76, 76-77, 78-79, 79-80, 84-85, 91-92
Whitney, Gerry, 96-97
Whyte, Carolyn, 84-85, 85-86
Wilborn, Kip, 89-90
Wildermann, William, 76-77
Wilkinson, Barbara, 74-75
Williams, Bradley, 95-96
Williams, LaVerne, 74-75
Williams, Nancy, 69-70
Williams, Phillis, 84-85
Williams, Sherri Dukes, 95-96
Wilson, Lizanne, 66-67
Wilson-Nease, Neil, 82-83
Winchell, Annette, 80-81, 83-84
Winell, Roger, 70-71
Winterton, Diane, 93-94, 96-97
Wise, Patricia, 75-76
Wolff, Beverly, 76-77
Wood, James, 93-94
Woods, Denise, 86-87
Woods, Sheryl, 90-91, 93-94, 95-96
Workman, William, 82-83, 84-85
Wyatt, Carol*, 77-78

- Y -

Yannissis, Yanni, 94-95
Yeargan, Michael, 95-96

- Z -

Zajac, Joan, 76-77, 81-82
Zajick, Dolora, 87-88
Zambello, Francesca, 87-88
Zanazzo, Alfredo, 83-84
Zeffirelli, Franco, 70-71
Zeller, Richard, 91-92, 96-97
Zhan, Manhua, 94-95
Zhu, Ai-Lan, 91-92, 96-97
Ziegler, Delores, 86-87, 91-92, 92-93
Zschau, Marilyn, 86-87

San Diego Opera
The Company
1995-96 & 1996-97

Romaine, Bill
Shumaker, Portia
Skimina, Barbara
Smith, Sylvia
Wright, Mary

MUSIC:
Bruck, Douglas
Fink, Myron
Floyd, Carlisle
Gilley, Laurann
Keltner, Karen
Parker, Michael
Randall, Dorothy
Roach, Kristin
Stamper, Robin
Wright, Martin

GUEST CONDUCTORS:
Bonynge, Richard
Montgomery, Kenneth
Müller, Edoardo
Veltri, Michelangelo

PRODUCTION:
Allen, Ronald G.
Bruce, Garnett
Eagan, Jason Scott
Fields, Scott
Foster, Joan
Jones, Christine A.
Krumrey, Ned
La Motte, Jane
Lott, Robert
Mahan, Chris
Mittleman, Pamela
Moreland, Donald
Murphy, Jan E.
Peters, Mary Yankee
Smit, Knighten
Smith, Kathleen
Tucker, Leslie Anne
Vodicka, Ron
West, Missy
Wetherell, Kimberly

GUEST DIRECTORS/CHOREOGRAPHERS:
Brovsky, Linda
Cox, John
de Blasis, James
Floyd, Carlisle
Hebert, Bliss
Mahon, Maxine
Major, Leon
Malashock, John
Mansouri, Lotfi
Miladinovic, Dejan
Newcomb, Jamie
Ott, Sharon
Weber, Wolfgang

DESIGNERS:
Barrett, Marie
Brimson-Lewis, Stephen
Butlin, Roger
Conklin, John
Dorsey, Kent
Dryden, Deborah

Falconer, Ian
Girard, Claude
Hall, Peter J.
Hirsch, Gregory Allen
Klein, Allen Charles
Hockney, David
Mess, Suzanne
Ponnelle, Jean-Pierre
Ross, Stephen
Schuler, Duane
Schneider-Siemssen, Günther
Smith, Kendall
Solger, Christine A.
Uzan, Bernard
Vodicka, Ron
Walker, David
Yeargan, Michael

SCENIC STUDIO:
Adams, Greg
Alexander, Dean
Brittingham, Craig
Bucon, Calvin
Bunker, Barry
Carroccia, Al
Kaye-Jolgren, Debrah
Link, Gary
Lowe, Leticia
Petrovich, Victoria
Resenbeck, Douglas
Reynolds, Michael L.
Steele, Valerie
Torzeski, Wes
Walchuk, John
Wallace, Timothy

TECHNICAL:
Adams, Ellen
Adams, Rick
Adams, Tony
Alexander, Michael
Alvarez, Bill
Armatis, Anne
Baliel, Terry
Bateson, Kent
Berhow, Magda
Beverley, R. Scott
Bobbett, Victoria
Brittingham, Merry
Burgess, Dale
Burke, Gregory A.
Carroll, George
Christopher, Emily
Clifton, Don
Couchman, Donna
Davis, Sandra
Day, Lawrence E.
Doomey, Barbara
Dougherty, Robert
Easterling, David
Espinoza, Manny
Evans, Larry
Fenwick, Steven
Franklin, William
Galvin, Michael P.
Gonzalez, William
Harris, Mary
Hendrickson, Joel
Hodges, Linda
Indermill, Marilyn
Judson, Steve
Keel, J. Eric

King, Milton
King, Sharon
Krewsun, Tina
Lopez, Evaristo
Lucus, Tara
Lutz, Heather
Manuel, Dennis
Martinez, John
McCambridge, Jeff
McClure, Carole
McClure, Ginny
McCoy, Bruce
McKenzie, Sally
Medhurst, Pam
Miriello, Anne
Moad, Chris
Monreal, Joe
Mosher, Mike
Nace, Frederick
Nash, Peggy
Noll, Sue
Ocegueda, Margreet
Pater, Mary
Peasley, Mike
Pecoraro, Nunzia
Peters, John David
Rae, Stacy
Rathmell, Bob
Regna, Michael
Rosensteel, Michael
Salyer, Jon R.
Scott, Bill
Seppanen, Annette
Sharp, Robert
Sheposh, Christopher
Slater, John
Stompoly, Pam
Sutton, Grace
Szydelko, Mark C.
Taggart, Jack
Vaughan, Mary
Watson, Judy
Winston, Michael E.
Yount, Christel

Stage crew personnel are members of
IATSE Local 122

Wardrobe personnel are members of
IATSE Local 905

Wig and Makeup personnel are members
of IATSE Local 706

PRINCIPAL SINGERS:
Abraham, Remy
Arteta, Ainhoa
Barraza, Deanna
Bartoli , Cecilia
Bartolini, Lando
Basler, Chelsea
Bell, Michel Warren
Berlinghieri, Chad
Bitetti, Matthew
Blaze, Sarah
Brown, Débria
Butler, James
Clayton, Cynthia
Cooper, Kaira

Cox, Kenneth
Crider, Michèle
De Simone, Anita
de la Rosa, Evelyn
Del Carlo, John
Domingo, Plácido
Dorn, Reinhard
Downing, David
Du Melle, Walter
Duykers, John
Eaglen, Jane
Evans, Joseph
Fagerland, Scot
Firestone, Adria
Fischer, Alan
Fowler, Bruce
Froelich, Lee Jessica
Genaux, Vivica
Gomez, Roberto
Grienenberger, Joseph
Hadley, Jerry
Hernández, César
Hu, Joseph
Hynes, Elizabeth
Kaluza, Stefania
Langan, Kevin
Larson, Philip
Lattimore, Margaret
Leal, Daniel S.
Leech, Richard
Liss, Ava Baker
Loewen, Mark
Lopez-Yañez, Jorge
Loup, François
Lowe, Ryan
Malis, David
Margison, Richard
McAfee, Patricia
McDevitt, Duane
McKinley, Casey
Mendoza, Mauricio
Miricioiu, Nelly
Morgan, Epherium
Morris, James
Nolan, Warren
Nolan, William
O'Brien, Kerry
Otey, Louis
Palmer, Beau
Parce, Erich
Patrick, Julian
Powell, Stephen
Power, Patrick
Rarick, Eric
Riedel, Deborah
Rucker, Mark
Rynne, David
Scott, Carter
Shaffer, David
Shipman, Jeffrey
Shore, Andrew
Sikon, James Scott
Slivon, John
Sundstrom, Joseph
Tian, Hao Jiang
Triglia, Richelle Marie
Voss, Ealynn
Wen, Sylvia
Wentzel, Andrew
Wheatfall, Arthur
Whitney, Gerry
Williams, Bradley

Williams, Sherry Dukes
Winterton, Diane
Woods, Sheryl
Zeller, Richard
Zhu, Ai-Lan

ORCHESTRA:
American Federation of Musicians, Local
325

STRINGS:
Belgique, Joel
Berg, Robert
Berton, Gregory
Bookstein, Marcia
Brinton, Randall
Campbell, Glen
Campbell, Rebekah
Clendenning, Sarah
Constantino, Hernan
Deatherage, Michael
Dirks, Karen
Engley, Alicia
Feld, Lynn
Feld, Otto
Goodkind, Alice
Green, Jonathan
Hermanns, Donald
Hill, Joni
Hill, Nancy
Holland-Moritz, Karla
Homnick, Angela
Johnston, Margaret
Kammerdiner, Selma
Law, Wanda
Levine, Richard
Lochner, Nancy
Moore, John
Nilsen, Martha
Palamidis, Alex
Pandurski, Igor
Rickmeier, Allan
Robboy, Ronald
Robboy, Susan Hintz
Rue, Marilyn
Sasaki, Shigeko
Stein, Edmund
Stubbs, John
Swanson, Anthony
Szanto, Mary Oda
Thomas, Marilyn
Thrane, Jean
Wais, Michael
Womack, Stan
Young, Jean
Zeavin, Dorothy
Zelickman, Joan

WINDS, BRASS, PERCUSSION:
Ashmead, Elizabeth
Barranger, Mary
Bedell, Mark
Buckley, Beth
Bursill-Hall, Damian
Cable, George
Coady, Jill
Ellis-MacLeod, Charles
Fast, Arlen
Fellinger, Michael

219

Garbutt, Matthew
Gordon, Richard
Grant, Alan
Green, Elizabeth
Green, Sidney
Gref, Warren
Hall, Doug
Hebert, Britt
Hoffman, James
Johnston, George
Lorge, John
Michel, Dennis
Michel, Peggy
Plank, James
Popejoy, Keith
Price, Calvin
Randall, Dorothy
Sasaki, Tatsuo
Savage, David
Spear, Elizabeth
Sterling, Sheila
Swanson, Peter
Szanto, John
Tunnicliff, Teresa
Vaughn, Donna
Walk, Michael
White, Danette
Wilds, John

BANDA:
Brandt, Timothy
Bretsnyder, Cheryl
Buchman, Heather
Dillard, George
Dyke, William (Joe)
Emrich, Emory
Foster, Steve
Ingber, Jonathan
McBane, Lachlan
Parker, Michael
Perkins, Barry
Price, Calvin
Sundfor, Paul
Szanto, Jon
Titlow, Louise

LIBRARIANS:
Fisch, Nancy
Wilds, John
Wagner, Joseph

PERSONNEL MANAGER:
Cable, George

CHORUS:
American Guild of Musical Artists
(AGMA)

SOPRANOS:
Agler, Sarah
Barraza, Deanna
Bishop, Jane
Boland, Susan
Chertkow-Levy, Judith
Dooley, April
Graves, Sallye
Gross, Gwendolen
Ireland, Catherine
Mays, Andrea
McAfee, Patricia

McLaren, Debra
McLean, Betsy
Milia, Angela
Minton, Patricia
Palmer, Lori
Phelps, Christine
Rose, Erica
Rose, Tina
Sublett, Virginia
Torresen, Lesley
Triglia, Richelle Marie
Watson, Nona
Weston, Megan
Whittier, Marcia
Winterton, Diane
Zugger, Teresa

ALTOS:
Adams, Nicky K.
Ali, Susan
Camarena, Sandra
Cartwright, Rita Cantos
Colet, Anita
Field, Sue
Friedrichs, Lisa
Froelich, Lee Jessica
Gandhi, Priti
Goggins, Janet Anne
Greene, Wendy
Hawkins, Penelope
Liss, Ava Baker
Lord, Susan
Lundeen, Katherine
McAfee, Patricia
McCann, Gina
McOmber, Erin
Renner, Martha
Sinegal, Goldie F.
Smith, Melody K.
Srygley, Jane
Whatley, Martha

TENORS:
Alexander, Matthew
Ancheta, Al Ferdinand R.
Anderson, Garrett
Arteaga, Juan
Berlinghieri, Chad
Boydston, Jim
Castaneda, Jorge
Cline, Edward
Cottone, John
Fisher, Rankin
Flynn, James
Frees, Michael
Head, Corey
Johnson, Ralph
Leal, Daniel S.
Long, Gregory
Lowe, Ryan
McDuffie, Thomas
McKee, Dennis
Millan, Rene
Nettles, John
Phipps, Terry
Ramsey, Charles
Roberts, James
Rubin, Jay
Schmidt, David
Slivon, John
Stephens, Jr., J. Spence
Sumner, Timothy Allen

Sundstrom, Joseph H.
Travers, Dennis
Whitney, Gerald

BASSES:
Ballard, Anthony
Banks, Ronald
Cline, Edward
Cross, Terry
Darcy, Michael
Du Melle, Walter
Ensberg, Philip
Fagerland, Scot
Grienenberger, Joseph
Hollingsworth, Edward
Johnson, Ralph
Labertew, Kenneth
LaFetra, Richard
Lasater, Kent J.
Loewen, Mark
Martin, Vincent
McDevitt, Duane
Naglich, Daniel
Padilla, Salvador
Park, Ray
Pechota, Joe
Roseberry, Robert
Rubin, Jay
Russell, Patrick
Shaffer, David
Shipman, Jeffrey
Simmons, Kevin
Sones, Charles
Thompson, Erskine
Wanamaker, Warren
Wheatfall, Arthur
White, John
Zilvinskis, Joe H.

AUXILIARY CHORUS:
Abraham, Remy
Bloom, Martin
Bolden, Shirley
Busch, Sarah
Canales, Ericka
Child, Ginger
Collier, Barbara
Cooper, Kaira
DeWitt-Haynes, Francine
Eccles, Darby
Fitting, Fran
Flournoy, Shelton
Gandhi, Priti
Gilbert, Glen
Gregory, Rita
Hampton, Tonia
Harris, Raymond
Hogan-Bean, Kerry
Iocolano, John
Jackson, Yvette
Jambeau, Lisa
Johnson, Jr., Larry
Lang, Willie
Lentulo, Elisabeth Hartig
Matthews, Ardele
Morgan, Epherium L.
Nolan, Warren
Oliver, Dwan
Pipkins, Geraldine
Shaw, Monique
Simmons, Deandre
Simmons, Kevin

Skiles, Jennifer
Teply, Miriana
Travers, Dennis
White, Morris
Zugger, Teresa

CHILDREN'S CHORUS:
Ambasing, Rachel
Basler, Chelsea
Cobb, Philip
Cory, Nicholas
Curavic, Danica
Drake, Andrew
Hackim, Christina
Hernandez, Margret
Johnson, Beau
Johnson, Chelsea
Johnson, Lane
Johnson, Libby
McClure, Heather
McClure, Meghan
McKinley, Brady
McKinley, Casey
Michel, Hans
Morrison, Richard
Newbegin, Dawn
Ozawa, Matthew
Peeling, Bethany
Peeling, Sarah
Pipkin, Aaron
Popescu, Alina
Popescu, Roxanna
Puig, Maria
Rarick, Erick
Sanford, Stuart
Schneider, Kathryn
Song, Michael
Stone, Brian
Stromberg, Ingrid
Stromberg, Kirsten
Sykes, Geoffrey
Tarkow, Soshi
Vargas, Monroe
Vincelett, Sarah
Wanetick, Hart
Whitney, Gerry
Witek, Michelle

DANCERS:
Aguilar, Chris
Alcántara, Manuel
Cutri, Alison
Dabrowski, Denise
Dunsizer, Tammy
Engle, Kevin
Hoss, Natalie
Kalivas, Peter
Maigue, Theresa
Manzo, Andrew
Martin, Veronica
Montilius, Yvonne
Morgan, Chris
Poolos, Sylvia
Pourazar, Kayvon
Ritchie, Gwen
Swallow, Buffy
Xander, Maj

ACROBATS:
Fern Street Circus:
Caneftrelli, Ottavio

Jackson, Leticia
Lindley, Sheryl
Lindsey, Corky
Nixon, Annette
Patterson, Joanna

SUPERNUMERARIES:
Acord, Elizabeth
Allen, Priscilla
Bandy, David
Bell, Greg
Berg, John
Blaze, Morris
Borntrager, Bob
Bourqui, Joseph
Braga, Chris
Bryant, Ken
Bunting, Jeffery
Burgess, David
Burke, Terence
Buzzell, Florence
Buzzelli, George
Caesar, Kenneth
Caldwell, Ted
Campbell, Benjamin
Carrillo, Christopher
Castanon, Sandra
Chavarria, Marcus
Christy, George
Ciccone, Anthony
Clark, Doug
Clark, Greg
Clark, Kelly
Coble, David
Cochran, John
Compton, Alexandra
Connelly, Casey
Conole, Karen
Cornosky, Tom
Custer, Thomas
Crowder, Dean
Davis, Alice
Davis, Donald R.
Decker, Shanna
Denhart, Hallie
Di Lullo, Anthony
Dizon, Dennis
Doering, Mark
Doering, Michael
Dorsey, Dana
Doyle, William
Drehner Jr., John
Duckworthy, Nathan
Dumas, Hinaka
Dunlap, Bruce
Fares, Patricia
Fay, Patty
Flaster, Michael
Flint, George
Fore, Jason
Francella, Richard
Fraser, Betty
Freeman, David B.
Fusaro, Chalaina
Fusaro, Ryan
Gaucher, Marie-France
Gauthier, Michael
Gaybis, Annie
Goldbarg, Lisa
Goldstrom, Steve
Gomez, Miguel
Goode-Wanamaker, Katie

Gordon, Sean
Gorton, Lora
Gosink, Barbara B.
Gross, Todd
Grosvenor, Craig
Grucza, Jack
Hall, Betsy
Hall, Shirley
Hall, William
Hamilton, Ray
Hansen, John
Harris, Alan
Hawkins, Cynthia
Hersch, Jeremy
Hershey, Joel
Highsmith, Jim
Hollingsworth, Blair
Hollingsworth, Trevor
Hostomska, Klara
Howarth, Rob
Hubert, Steve
Hudson, Sharon
Ikenberg, Daniel
Jenner, Joylinda
Jensen, Steven
Johnson, Rànald
Jones, Melissa
Jones, R.J.
Kane, Timothy
Kapa, Don
Karr, Jim
Kaye, Bob
Kempf, Charles
Kempf, Pilar
Kightlinger, Peter
Kortum, Karl A.
Kuamoo, Gaylord Lee
Lasbury, Sue
Lawrence, A.J.
Leach, Daniel
Ledermann, Ruth
Legerrette, Linda
Leon, Julissa
LeSane, Anthony
Leventhal, Stacy
Lilley, Rodney
Littlejohn, Jerrod
Livingston, Clifton
Lore, Priscilla
Lorenz, Joe
Marguiles, Robert
Maule, Steven
McCord, Carly
McGill, Shawn
Merten, Katherine
Middendorff, John
Montano, Grover
Morehead, Patrick
Muller, Ridgely
Muyco, Sharon
Myers, Percy
Navarra, Ninfa
Nelson, Lollie
Nelson, Patricia R.
Newton, David
Nichols, Robert
Nobilette, Kenneth
Novak, Edward
O'Donovan, Danny
O'Donovan, Suzette
O'Rourke, Melrose
Oliphant, Michael

Oliver, Katie
Olson, Alexandra
Olson, Bob
Ordway, Brion
Ortiz, Christina
Palm, Donna
Patacca, Catherine A.
Peck, William
Pecoraro, George
Pecoraro, Joe
Perrin, Ed
Polesetsky, Harold
Price, Mark
Price, Wendell
Puente, Michael
Purchase, Gordon
Putigano, David
Quirk, Anthony T.
Ramos, Edward
Ramos, Justino
Randle, Ben
Razo, Mary
Reynolds, Michael
Rhoades, Linda
Ricketts, Doug
Ritacco, Joe
Roberts, Chris
Roseberry, Amber
Roseberry, Rebecca
Runholt, Rusty
Russell, Peggy Irene
Russo, Meredith
Ryan, Mark
Rynne, David
Rynne, Melanie
Safford, David
Salea, Salah
Santford, Kim
Sapienza, Jennifer
Scalco, Richard
Schaffer, James
Schiff, Arthur
Schmidt, Bryan
Schwald, Andrea
Scott, Ernest
Sheppard, Tracy Lee
Sherr, Jessica
Sleeper, Meghan
Sleeper, Michael
Smith, Lisa
Smith, Peter
Stai, Chris
Stanley, Paul
Steele, Phillip
Swanstrom, Jessie
Swenson, Eric
Tanner, Dale
Themen, Tony
Tillotson, Maura
Tolstad, Marie
Tower, Christine
Travaglini, Joseph
Ureña, Ernest
Ureña, Erin
Verbano, William
Wagner, Viqi
Waller, Nick
Warnken, John
Wasserman, David
Waugh, Patti
Wheatfall, Daniel
Wheatfall, Natalie

White, Aaron
Wier, Kelly
Williams, Duncan
Williams, Jef
Wilson, Ray
Wright, Rick
Young, Jonathan
Zeglin, John
Ziga, Martin

Additional Production Credits for the 1995-96 & 1996-97 Seasons:

Scenery for *Tosca* is owned and was constructed in the San Francisco Opera shops and is owned by the San Francisco Opera Association. Costumes supplied by Malabar Ltd., Toronto.

The production of *The Elixir of Love* is owned by The Dallas Opera.

Scenery for *The Passion of Jonathan Wade* was constructed by the San Diego Opera Scenic Studio.

Scenery and costumes for *Cinderella* were created for L'Opéra de Montréal.

Aida is a co-production with Dallas Opera.
Scenery for *Aida* was constructed by San Diego Opera Scenic Studio. Costumes for this production were built and are owned by Dallas Opera.

Scenery for *Carmen* was originally created for Houston Grand Opera and is owned by San Diego Opera.
Costumes for *Carmen* were designed for The Dallas Opera

The sets and costumes for *The Italian Girl in Algiers* were originally designed for, and are owned by, The Washington Opera.

Scenery and properties for *The Conquistador* were built by San Diego Opera Scenic Studio.
The composer and librettist would like to express their appreciation to Pearl Arenson, Cheryl Brown and Joe Columbo for their help in bringing this work to the stage.

Scenery for *La Traviata* was constructed in the San Francisco Opera Shops and is owned by the San Francisco Opera Association.

Scenery for *Turandot* was constructed in the San Francisco Opera Shops and is co-owned by the San Francisco Opera Association and the Lyric Opera of Chicago.

Traditionally, the Colophon is a place to identify the paper and typesetting styles in a book... but I prefer to use it to talk about the people who helped give it shape and form.

Putting together a book, I've discovered, is almost as complex as creating a world-premiere opera... and almost as many people are involved. But it starts with one person at a time. I've said before that artists are interconnected – one connection from my online photography group is Robert Godwin. As with everything else about this project, things happened when needed... this was one of them. We talked about self-publishing, he ended up pitching the idea of printing the book to his colleagues at the national imaging firm of Applied Graphics Technologies (AGT) in Los Angeles; they were interested; the Opera was interested; I was happy, and the consultation process began to gather speed.

All pre-press work was handled by AGT in Foster City, California, with the printing taking place at AGT in Los Angeles. Technicians and department heads from both facilities worked together on each phase of the book: images, text, proofing, printing, binding. They ensured that my images were perfectly translated from the silver and chemistry of photographic prints – to digital files – to ink on paper. This is a "brave new world" for me, and all my questions were patiently answered as they worked with me through the complex printing process.

I worked with everyone from designers and scanners to producers, support staff, and pressmen – we often had seven or eight experts in the viewing room at once – all under the coordination of Robert Godwin. And yes, seeing my pages come off the press was more than exciting! This book is the beneficiary of AGT's world-class experience and astonishing technical wizardry.

At AGT, our book was hardly their biggest project, but it always received their most extraordinary attention, in every detail. As everywhere, it's people who make the difference... and everyone adopted *The Art of Making Opera* as their own. This was a team effort in every sense, but teams are made up of individuals: in Los Angeles, key players are Robert Godwin, Ariel Minguez, Mary Suarez, Brandon Bessey, Oscar Ruiz, Alex Kloby, Tom DiGenova, Zarius Durant, and the pressmen. The Foster City crew: Theresa Savage, Sally Heit, Kim Lathan, Kevin Montgomery, Joanne Ayoub, Steve Brune and others... I am very grateful for the way you turned the dream into reality.

Another part of the equation was the photographic prints of the 350+ images in the book. These were made by The Photo Factory in San Diego, a black & white specialty lab. I expected they would be able to provide what was needed for the printers; the friendly advice and everyday encouragement for my project is what distinguishes them from just any commercial lab. From the front counter to the darkroom to the owner of the adjunct gallery, I was always warmly welcomed – and it didn't seem to matter how many negatives I was bringing in or how fast I needed the prints back. My images were presented to their best advantage (and often improved on) by the skill and dedication of The Photo Factory staff. I would particularly like to thank Elsa Flores, my primary printer who seemed to intuitively understand what my images needed; Dennis Klepin in Production; Adrian Velasquez, who helped keep me sane; and Dorothy Metcalfe and Richard Cavin.

It's been an extraordinary journey, the creation of this book of ours... how we got here is every bit as satisfying as the finished product. Thank you all.

– ML Hart

"I just feel so strongly that we are here for such a short time – it's painful to be criticized, it's disappointing if things are failures, but the doing of it is what is the important thing, it really is.
Now I've put my heart and soul into directing [this film], I hope it's a great success. But in the two years that I've worked on it, it's given me far more than I've given it, and we've had a fantastic time – up and down, extremes of emotion, sometimes depressing, sometimes tough, sometimes ecstatically happy, but it's been fantastic."

— Kenneth Branagh
director & actor